To Mom,
Merry Christmas!
I haven't read
this book. I hope
you enjoy it! Thanks
for all your support
over the years!
Love,
Donna

IF WISHES WERE HORSES

The Education of a
Veterinarian

LORETTA GAGE, D.V.M.
and Nancy Gage

ST. MARTIN'S PAPERBACKS

IF WISHES WERE HORSES

Copyright © 1992 by Loretta Gage, D.V.M. and Nancy Gage.

Cover photograph by Joyce Fay.

All rights reserved. No part of this book may be used or reproduced in any manner whatsoever without written permission except in the case of brief quotations embodied in critical articles or reviews. For information address St. Martin's Press, 175 Fifth Avenue, New York, N.Y. 10010.

Library of Congress Catalog Card Number: 92-27468

ISBN: 0-312-92877-7

Printed in the United States of America

St. Martin's Press hardcover edition/January 1993
St. Martin's Paperbacks edition/January 1994

St. Martin's Paperbacks are published by St. Martin's Press, 175 Fifth Avenue, New York, N.Y. 10010.

10 9 8 7 6 5 4 3 2 1

This book is dedicated to our mother, Anna R. Gage, and to the memory of our father, Charles A. Gage.

CONTENTS

ACKNOWLEDGMENTS

WE want to thank our agent, Gail Hochman, for her faith and guidance, her assistant, Marianne Merola, and our editor, Barbara Anderson, for her enthusiasm and her excellent suggestions for improving the manuscript.

We are also grateful for the love and support of our mother, and for the help of Kent Wiechert, Dave Riley, Cyndi Gurulé, and our cousins, Shirley and Ernie Rowe.

There are a number of writers whose work was an inspiration and model; we owe them thanks, as well: Charles LeBaron, Scott Turow, Perri Klass, Maxine Kumin, and James Herriot.

Loretta also wants to thank her classmates, with a special thanks to Linda Chittum, Ethel Connelly, Mary Cooper, Jeff Fay, and Brad Frye; friends and mentors Sue Ann Lesser, Sharon Holland, Steve Derwelis, Delia Harman, David Tumlinson, and Randy Levins; the faculty and staff of the College of Veterinary Medicine of Colorado State University, in particular, Mike Smith, Sherry McConnell, Colin Dunlop, Walter Bruyninckx, Steve Wheeler, and La Rue Johnson; dear friends Cher Wise, Jim Boardman, Walt Taylor, Dwight Hooton, Bill McGlothing, Jay Koch, Lori Straba, Emmitt Mundy, Colonel and Eddie Sands and their wonderful family, with a special thanks to Billy; the many animals that provided so much of her education; and thanks to God for all His blessings.

Nancy owes deep thanks to many people for their support, both over the long years of apprenticeship and in the shorter course of work on this book—to her daughter and son, Amber and Dean Staley; to her friends and teachers, David Richard Jones, Susan Jones, Tony Hillerman, Rudolfo Anaya, Michael Dixon, Valerie Smith, Candy Klaschus, Susan Lewis-Duran, Jeanette Boyer, Layne Torkelson, Wendy Jones, Vera John-Steiner, David King Dunaway, Sara Tucker, Susan Schmidt, David Howard, Mary Dougherty, Mark A. R. Facknitz, Grubb Graebner, Judith Walker, Nancy Beverly, Patricia Clark Smith, Tom Mayer, and Bob Hartung; and to her husband, Jay Koch, without whom none of it would have happened.

A NOTE ABOUT MEMORY, AUTOBIOGRAPHY, AND TRUTH

I knew as I was living these experiences that I was going to write about them, and so I took copious notes to support my memory. Still, while I tape-recorded class lectures quite often, I did not record conversations with classmates and professors. Therefore, the conversations that pepper the book are reconstructed and reported to the best of my memory. In no instance did I intentionally distort the facts or misrepresent the experience. Yet the book is a subjective account.

In conveying something of the subject matter and medical procedures, I have striven to be clear and comprehensible to a lay reader rather than comprehensive and exhaustive in my explanations. Therefore, this material is somewhat oversimplified, and in some cases I have omitted exhaustive medical detail.

Finally, all of the names have been changed to protect the privacy of my friends, teachers, and colleagues, except for those of my family. The names of some of the animals have been changed, as well.

"If wishes were horses, beggars might ride."
—JOHN RAY

PROLOGUE

THE dark red mare was lying in a bed of wood chips and she
didn't move when I opened the stall door. For a horrible moment, I thought she was dead, but then I saw her ears swivel
just the tiniest bit as she took note of my presence. I clipped
the lead rope to her halter and pulled up her head.

"Come on, Mama!"

The mare lowered her head to the wood-chip bedding. I
tugged again on the rope. The big animal resisted. I tugged
again, rocking my weight against hers. She set her thousand
pounds against me. I crouched beside her, stroked her neck.
"You gotta do it, old girl." Her fine red coat was stiff with dried
sweat. "Come on, Mama!" I stood up and pulled again. She
didn't move. I swung the braided cotton rope and brought it
down hard across her haunches. Once, twice, and at last the
sick horse struggled to her feet.

She was desperately ill with colic that she had been fighting
for almost two full days. Midmorning the day before, her
owner, a cattle rancher, had called for advice from the eastern
New Mexico town of Tucumcari, three hours away. I had told
him the signs to monitor—pulse rate, gum color, gut
sounds—and what treatment he could do himself. Most important, I'd urged him to find a vet close at hand; he'd said
there was none. It was up to him, then, to judge the severity

of the colic and weigh that against the stress and expense of the trip to Albuquerque and the veterinary clinic where I'd been working since I had graduated from vet school four months before. It wasn't a decision I could make for him. Phone diagnoses were difficult to impossible, and into the equation he would have to factor the horse's monetary value, her emotional value, if any, the money and effort he was willing to spend, and his willingness to gamble.

He'd called again that evening; the mare was no better. He'd still hedged on bringing her in. At 2:00 A.M. Sunday, he'd called for the third time. He was going to load the horse and leave immediately. He wanted me and my boss, Dr. Tom Tromboldt, an equine surgeon, to meet him and the horse at the clinic.

At 3:30 A.M. I'd left the house to prepare for colic surgery. Day was just breaking when the truck and trailer pulled through the gate and the mare was unloaded and led through the double doors of the clinic.

Colic is a mysterious affliction. Some colics pass untreated, just mild bellyaches. Some respond to medical treatment—usually a gallon of mineral oil pumped through a nasal tube into the horse's stomach and the injection of painkilling and antispasmotic drugs. Some require, and are cured by, surgery—if there is a foreign body in the gut or if an intestine has twisted. And some are fatal in spite of everything we know to do.

Surgery is useless to a horse that colics because of anterior enteritis—an inflammation of the small intestine—but it isn't always possible to tell beforehand. This, unfortunately, was the case with the red mare, Rough Elegance.

Radiographs are of no use in detecting a twisted gut; they cannot penetrate the density of the equine abdomen. Even if we could get a picture of the more than eighty feet of looping bowel, a torsion would be nearly impossible to read. Surgery, therefore, is not an easy call to make. When medical therapy has failed, it's the last hope and option, however.

We worked quickly on Rough Elegance. We injected her with a painkiller, then prepared her for abdominocentesis—a belly tap. We clipped her belly, scrubbed it with antiseptic, numbed the area with a local anesthetic, and shoved a cannula through the hide, muscle, and membrane to draw a sample of her abdominal fluid. The volume and character of the fluid would give us more information to factor into the equation. A high protein value with normal white blood cell count could indicate a devitalized intestine. An abnormal number of white blood cells could indicate infection. It is certainly possible to draw normal fluid from critically ill horses and abnormal fluid from nonsurgical cases, however.

Through her rectal wall, Tom palpated what he could reach of her gut; he could feel nothing out of place. We passed a stomach tube through her nostril to check for an accumulation of liquid in her stomach, which could indicate a blocked bowel. I sucked on the free end of the tube to begin the flow, then held it down into the bucket. A couple of gallons rushed out. More evidence that she may need surgery, but also inconclusive, because an enteritis, or inflammation, could also account for the shutdown of the gut and the buildup of fluid.

Nothing we did gave us the total assurance that the mare had a blockage or a twist, but as Tom weighed our findings—relentless pain, no response to medications, the absense of gut sounds, and deteriorating vital signs—he felt he had no choice but to recommend surgery.

When the rancher made the hard decision to bring the horse to Albuquerque, he committed to sparing no expense, to going to the limit of our ability and knowledge. And so we installed an intravenous catheter and began running fluids and antibiotics into the mare in preparation for surgery.

I called Jackie Overman, another vet in the practice, to come in and assist, for it takes at least three people to manipulate a horse onto our operating table. Jackie arrived just as we were ready to induce the mare. We put her under with an injectable drug and then inserted the endotracheal tube, which would deliver a steady flow of halothane and oxygen to keep her anesthetized during the surgery. We strapped her two front legs together, then her two hind legs, and hooked them to the overhead hydraulic hoist, which lifted the unconscious mare onto the surgery table. The table was fitted with a heated water bed, which distributed her weight and helped prevent the accidental pinching of a major blood vessel or nerve, either of which could cause permanent damage.

Tom's surgical experience told him to expect to find the gut displaced or twisted, and he "ran," or manually examined, the sixty-five feet of freely movable bowel, straightening it, feeling its texture, looking for pathology that could explain the mare's pain. The first part of the small intestine was angry and inflamed, but there was nothing we could simply *fix*. There was nothing to do but close her up. The surgery, of course, only added to her problem, her stress, pain, and fatigue. We were quiet as Tom closed her belly, frustrated and angry at this condition that eluded our diagnosis.

Rough Elegance was slow to recover from the anesthetic—down until almost noon—one indication of how tired she was from the two days of pain and the early-morning trip to Albuquerque. We monitored her closely in the padded recovery stall. Jackie and I manned a tail rope and a head rope until she was up and steady on her feet. It's a scary and dangerous time, for even with this precaution, a horse groggy from anesthetic can panic and fatally injure itself as it thrashes around.

Once the mare was secure in her footing, Jackie offered to stay with her for a while so I could go home and catch a nap and a shower.

I went back to the clinic in the late afternoon, just before closing. As the staff headed home, I was left alone to watch over the sick mare and continue her treatment: injections of antibiotics, Torbugesic and xylazine for pain, and an antiendotoxin; monitoring of vital signs; measurement of serum electrolytes; running intravenous fluid replacement, for the mare was dehydrated from diarrhea; insertion of a stomach tube to draw off secretions, for the inflamed bowel hadn't yet begun to work effectively. All this to be done as quickly as possible, because she also needed to rest.

Shortly after midnight, my sister, Nancy, stopped in to bring me a sandwich, but I was beyond hunger, in that strange state where fatigue itself seems to fuel the body. She stayed awhile, curious about the horse and the treatment. She had followed me out to the barn to get my patient.

The tractable and well-schooled horse did not resist once I got her to her feet, and I led her across the dark lot, in through the double rear doors of the clinic, and across the green rubber floor. It could have been any time of day or night. There were no windows in this large room, and the overhead lights were bright and even, so there were no shadows. All was uniformly light—the enameled paint, the wooden cabinets, the metal doors, the green floor.

The horse looked awful.

She was a well-made quarter horse, with a finely chiseled head and the heavily muscled shoulders and high, powerful hindquarters of that breed. However, her coat was dull and flecked with wood chips and the white residue of her fever-induced sweat. Pain made visible, she held her head low and shifted her weight from side to side, lifting first the right hind leg, then the left, just the smallest bit, a frantic and monotonous tap dance, quieted and cushioned by the rubber floor. Her lips worked constantly, flapping loosely, feverishly. Around her neck, just behind her ears, a large bandage of white gauze and bright blue wrap held her IV catheter in place.

I opened the cupboard for supplies, and as I turned back to my patient, I caught my reflection in the polished chrome of the paper-towel dispenser. I, too, looked awful.

I had combed and braided my hair in the predawn hours of the day now ending, but strands had worked loose in the long hours of work and worry. They stuck out around my ears and forehead, a ragged aura. The skin under my eyes was dark and puffy, my brow drawn and tight. The whites of my eyes were shot through with red, and the lines in my forehead seemed to have grown deeper.

"Is she going to die?" Nancy asked.

This was not a question I wanted to answer. "The prognosis isn't good," I said with all the professional distance I could muster.

"But if you knew for absolute certain that she wasn't going

to make it . . ." Nancy stopped. She wanted me to tell her that everything was going to be all right. She wanted me to deny the grim realities of my profession and help her escape this room and this night, with hope intact. It made me angry, but I was too tired and too busy to fight. I said nothing.

"I mean," Nancy tried again, "if you were sure she wouldn't make it, you wouldn't let her suffer like this, would you?"

"I suppose it's possible she'll make it." I paused. "Besides, her owner has just paid over two thousand dollars for surgery, and we don't give up until he gives up."

Nancy looked stricken.

"If we thought there was absolutely no chance whatsoever, of course we'd advise him to end it," I said finally. It wasn't much encouragement, but it was more than I truly felt.

I turned back to my work, and my hands and body moved as though of their own accord, as if they had taken the controls from my too-tired brain: muscle memory, the product of the endless repetitions of these same tasks I had performed again and again in school.

I injected 10 mg. of Torbugesic into the IV line to combat pain, checked and double-checked the drip rate, for too fast a feed of the calcium-spiked fluid could precipitate a cardiac arrhythmia. I looped a bit of mane around the IV line to hold it in place, then clamped it back on itself, like a beautician securing a woman's hair. I stepped down along the mare's right flank and held the diaphragm of my stethoscope to her belly, listening for gut sounds, the gurgles and churnings that would tell me that the bowel was working. It was pretty quiet in there. I moved the stethoscope to another spot and listened again—still quiet, too quiet. There was not enough going on.

I inserted a thermometer in her rectum, held it while the animal continued to rock rhythmically in pain. In a few minutes, I read it, wiped it, and put it in the pocket of my lab coat. I moved up the left flank now, stopped again and listened for rumblings in her guts. I was suddenly aware of the steady drone of the ventilation system. I crossed the room and turned it off. The room that had seemed so still was suddenly even quieter, deathly still, except for the small, steady sound of hooves on rubber.

I listened again, trying hard to hear the faintest hope-giving increase in her bowel activity. I listened to the too-loud pounding of her heart, checked her pulse rate against my watch, looked up once more to check the drip rate into the IV catheter.

I'd made a circuit of the rocking mare, who seemed oblivious to everything I did. I turned away and jotted down on her chart all the vital signs I had collected. I turned back, face-to-face with the mare, and smoothed aside the dark red forelock. I was so powerless against her suffering.

Like a mother testing a child for fever, I pressed my lips to her broad forehead. I stroked her huge round jaws. I kissed her again. "God loves you, Mama," I said, more to comfort myself than the mare. "You're okay, Mama. God loves you."

For a moment, the mare stopped rocking. Her lips were still. Her ears flicked forward. She listened. It was as if her pain had stopped, as if she was going to be fine now, as if she was healed.

And then it all began again.

I kissed her once more and moved on with my work. I got a bucket and a long, soft rubber tube, which I moistened and threaded into the mare's nostril, talking softly all the while, assuring her, encouraging her. The mare resisted only slightly, and I sucked on the free end of the tube, trying to siphon fluid from her stomach. I held the tube down into the bucket. Nothing came out. Again. Again, nothing. Again, and again. Finally some thin foam issued from the nostril, moved slowly down the tube, stopped. I sucked again. The foam slid farther down the tube, but there was no rush of liquid, no emptying into the bucket. I pulled the stomach tube free, leaned against the wall, and looked at my patient.

Her pulse was 70. Normal is 28 to 44. Her temperature was 102. Normal is 98.6 to 100.

"Can *you* hear anything in her gut?" I asked Nancy, and handed her the stethoscope. She held it to the mare's side, listened, and shrugged.

"Maybe something," she said hopefully. "What do you do now?"

"When this bag's empty," I said, indicating the IV drip, "I'll take her back out to the stall and let her rest. Then I'll do it all again in about an hour and a half." I stroked the tired, hurting animal and thought for a moment. "Unless she's sleeping. Then I guess I'll let her get some rest."

Nancy soon went home, and the night passed in just this way. In the morning, however, when the sun had just risen above the Sandia Mountains to the east, about an hour before the rest of the clinic staff would arrive, I went out to the stable, and Rough Elegance was on her feet. She turned and put her head over the half door of her stall and looked at me. I had feared I would find her dead.

Her pulse had slowed and her temperature had dropped a bit. She was still. She seemed comfortable; there was no evidence of pain.

When Tom arrived, he asked me for an update, and, cautious in my optimism, I said that she seemed somewhat better.

He looked at me strangely, as if I'd made an inappropriate joke. "She's dead, right?"

"No, really, she's better."

He looked at me as if I'd been up way too long, as if I'd gone round the bend. His expression seemed to ask, What did I know, fresh out of school, the greenhorn? His look said, Of course she's not better. What kind of an idiot are you?

We walked out together, and at the sound of our voices, Rough Elegance put her huge head over the stall door and watched us with her soft brown eyes.

"I'll be damned," said Tom. The rookie was right.

I was too tired to shout and dance when I got home and told Nancy, but I couldn't quit grinning. She sounded almost awestruck when she said, "You healed her."

I laughed at that and shook my head, though I was pleased to think it might be so. "It was Tom's treatment plan. I just carried it out."

"When you kissed her, I mean." Just the nutty, sentimental stuff I should have expected from my sister.

"No," I said. I hadn't gone to school for all those years to work some kind of magic with kisses and sweet nothings. Nancy looked at me strangely.

"She seemed to turn around right then, don't you think?"

"No, she didn't."

"But she did."

I shook my head. I was exhausted.

"Then what was it that saved her? You thought she was going to die."

What was it that had saved her? For a moment, I stopped and thought, as if I really could answer that innocent question. I wiped my face with both hands. "Couldn't tell you. I'm too tired to think right now, anyway."

Nancy nodded. "Go to bed."

"Okay." I got up and stumbled toward my room.

I heard Nancy's voice calling behind me. "It was the kiss!"

I opened my door and called back to her. "No, it most certainly was not. Now good night!" I pulled off my clothes, lay down, pulled the sheet over me, closed my eyes. The images of the long night came back to me as I sank toward sleep. My thoughts roamed.

The turnaround of the fine red mare had been remarkable. She'd been very near the end when she'd arrived at the clinic. It was extraordinary, really. She'd been very sick for many, many hours. The three-hour trip had taxed her energy. Surgery had stressed her weakened system. Her vital signs had been very definitely not the signs of an animal on the mend. Yet she was alive this morning and getting better.

Maybe this particular horse simply had a distinctly strong will for life—whatever that was—or maybe the treatment had been just right, or maybe whatever had inflamed her gut had simply run its course. Maybe it just wasn't a good day to die.

Or maybe it *had* been the kiss and the laying on of hands.

But the odds were that she'd been cured by the action of some scientific principle that we did not yet fully understand, that our supportive care had kept her alive while she healed herself. I'd learned so much those four long years of vet school, and there was still so much that we as a profession did not know—and so much, too, that I as a novice practitioner had to learn.

The odds were that it had been no miracle. My education was just beginning, but I was pretty sure that I hadn't cured a colic with a kiss.

I thought, though, as I fell toward my dreams, that I would probably keep kissing my patients, whatever their afflictions, just to be on the safe side. And then, at last, I slept.

PART 1

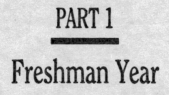

Freshman Year

CHAPTER 1

———————

Legal Alien

IT was the first day of school, and I had a fat wad of papers to prove that I belonged here at Colorado State University's College of Veterinary Medicine—a schedule of classes, a campus map, my letter of acceptance, and guaranteed student loan papers. I carried them all with me, my visa to this foreign land, to prove my immigrant status. My papers were in order. I had my green card. I wasn't a native, but I was a *legal* alien.

The truth is, I carried them to prove to *myself* that I belonged here. Magic documents to ward off evil spirits and self-doubt.

I had awakened at 1:40, again at 2:25, again at 4:43. Though my alarm was set for 6:00 A.M., I checked those red numerals all night long, afraid I would oversleep. I was checking reality, waking to be sure I wasn't just dreaming, to orient myself here in Fort Collins, in the ramshackle farmhouse on Douglas Road.

From across the hall, I could hear the deep, steady breathing of Lloyd Worthen, my new roommate and landlord. Through my open window, I could hear the faraway bawling of a cat. I could almost hear my own eager heart.

At 5:30, I had given up on sleep and risen to the day that had been so long coming, the day I would start vet school.

Lloyd was still asleep, and so was Jennifer Myers, who lived upstairs in a self-contained apartment but was more a roommate than a neighbor. They were both juniors, and their year would not start for several days yet.

I went barefoot to the kitchen, stealthy as a burglar, and filled the coffeepot with cold water, a slow, quiet trickle from the tap. We would in time become something of a family, but we were still strangers in that late summer of 1985. I had met Lloyd just the month before in Albuquerque and agreed almost immediately to move in with him and Jennifer. He seemed easygoing enough. And the price was right. I had met Jennifer only two days earlier, when I arrived. They had helped me unload my boxes from the back of my truck. I had folded away my jeans and sweaters, made the bed with my Indian-print blanket, and hung the picture collage of my family and friends and the eight-by-ten of the beagle I had left behind with my ex-boyfriend. But it wasn't home, not yet.

The coffee began to perk and its aroma drifted through the house. I heard Lloyd stumble to the bathroom and then down the hall to the kitchen door, where he stared at me as though through a blur. Skinny, balding, six four, and wearing only his undershorts, he looked something like a giant plucked stork—and something like an escaped lunatic.

"Good morning," I said as softly as you would say to either.

He nodded, took a mug from the dish rack, filled it with coffee, and drank before he spoke. "This was your last chance to sleep in for a long, long time," he said.

"I couldn't sleep."

He nodded again. "I know."

He grinned at me then, and I saw that he did know. We might be strangers, but the most important thing in my life was also the most important thing in his. What we knew about each other mattered more than what we didn't.

The parking lot was full of shine and polish: all BMWs and Volvos and new four-by-fours, or so it seemed to me, cruising for a space in old Blue, my dilapidated twenty-year-old GMC pickup. I stopped and double-checked my campus map to make sure I wasn't in a faculty lot, and then I saw the custom license plate that read VET-2-B. Okay, right place. I left old Blue parked between late-model sedans and crossed the field to the anatomy building.

At 8:00 A.M., we assembled in 108, the lecture hall that was to be our second home for the whole of freshman year. I chose a seat near the back of the room, between what I immediately thought of as two late-model students. Shine and polish. At thirty-four, I was a decade older than the average freshman, and the oldest woman in the class.

The orientation faculty filed onto the proscenium stage, and the buzz of voices quieted. Dr. Helena Matthews, who had interviewed me months before, stepped forward to welcome us.

"Look at one another," she said. "You are the crème de la crème."

My 124 classmates looked like the cream, all right. I was struck by the whiteness of their complexions. Later, I would find out that in our class there were 2 Hispanics, 1 Native American, 3 Asians, and 119 generic whites. It wasn't just the fairness of their skin that made them look like the elect, however. They were well scrubbed and nicely dressed, with the confident air of cheerleaders, rodeo queens, football players, and class presidents. Indeed, they looked more like high school students than college graduates. They seemed predominantly blond, very healthy, very hearty—like skiers. Different from me, the other.

"These are your colleagues," Dr. Matthews continued. "You will know one another for the rest of your lives. You must now set aside your competitive feelings and learn to cooperate. From now on, you must be willing to help each other every step of the way."

It seemed strange to me that these young blond people were to become my friends and colleagues, that I would come to know them and be one of them. Even the word *colleague* sounded strange to my ear—male and grown-up. I wondered whether the concept was as foreign to the younger women. We smiled at one another, looking around the room, adjusting to the notion that we were all now, somehow, a community.

Dr. Elmer Howard spoke next. He, too, said that we were special. Dr. Leon Joseph continued heaping praise upon us: We

5

were smart, we were accomplished, we were valued, and we were loved. It was like rain on thirsty ground. I drank it in.

Dr. Brian Tennant looked at us solemnly before he began. "Not all of you will make it," he said. "Some of you will fail."

Perhaps my 124 new colleagues turned again and looked at one another. I don't know. I stared down at my new notebook at the words I had just written: *Some will fail.*

Some of the cream was going to sink.

I put down my new felt-tip pen. I had also written in clean blue ink: "Dr. Matthews: Cooperate, don't compete, colleagues now. Dr. Howard: We're here to help, just ask. Dr. Joseph: Great class, good luck." These were doodles, not notes. I had caught myself in a silly attempt to remember every word, to make no mistakes. I wasn't a student. I was a fraud.

Tennant knew. The entire faculty must know. Our files were like tea leaves, our destinies written there in the records of grades and test scores and recommendations. I had a dirty little secret: I was an alternate admission. My seat had been offered to another student first; it had come to me by default. The whole application process had convinced me that I shouldn't be here now. My checkered undergraduate career, my age, the three demoralizing applications—all this told me that I wasn't going to make it.

And yet, I had to.

Over the last several years, I had met plenty of people who had said to me in one way or other that I would fail. Everyone I knew seemed to know someone who had wanted to be a vet, who had tried and tried and tried again and could not get in. They had been eager, even happy, to share these stories, as if the failures of their brothers, neighbors, cousins, and friends would comfort me somehow.

So I'd gotten quiet about this crazy goal of mine. I'd learned not to tell. It elicited too much tongue clucking and sympathy. There would be plenty of sympathy and clucking, too, if I flunked out and crept home with my tail tucked.

After the welcoming—and not-so-welcoming—remarks, the faculty led us on a tour of the anatomy building, our new home.

We fell into smaller groups and sifted rumor and hearsay as we went through the study cubicles, the stable and kennel, and the gross anatomy laboratory. I walked alone in the crowd and listened.

"He's just trying to scare us," said a slender blond woman in green shorts and a sleeveless T-shirt. "Nobody flunks out now. We're over the hurdle. They're on our side now."

Before I could ask her how she knew that, how she could be so certain, word sifted to us from the front of the group, borne on the wind like distemper germs, that, oh yes, you *can* flunk out. Somebody knew somebody who had. A couple of people flunk out every year.

"Not *every* year," the blonde argued. "Besides, if you flunk a course, they let you make it up over break and retake the final."

"Which you then flunk," another woman chimed in. "Nobody ever passes the makeup. They rig it so you work your butt off and you're out of here, anyway."

"But they give you special tutoring if your grades are low," someone else said.

"That's right," said the blonde. "They do." She looked as though she had been vindicated.

"Why should we flunk if we study?" an Asian woman asked impatiently. "I think it's been established that we're all smart enough, if we make the effort."

The voices came from all around me. I turned from the Asian woman to the blonde, who shrugged. I felt as if I were tumbling through the looking glass—curiouser and curiouser. I wondered where they got all this information, all these opinions. At least I wasn't the only one worrying.

"The real danger is suicide," said a tall good-looking cowboy, and then he laughed as if he'd made a joke. I laughed at this myself. Vet school might kill me, but I sure as hell wasn't going to kill myself.

As we passed through the double doors into the gross lab, someone in front sang out, "Oh, good! The gift shop!" The enormous room, with its high ceiling, gleaming linoleum floor, and shining stainless-steel dissection tables, was outfitted to sell us the books, smocks, dissection kits, and name tags we had ordered over the summer.

I had checked every box on the form, determined not to let false economy undermine my career as a student. The five hundred dollars' worth of books weighed over one hundred pounds, and I carried them in three loads to my desk in study cubicle D. We were assigned alphabetically to our desks—seven rooms, eighteen to a room. I introduced myself to Jimmy Fulmer and Adam Gerhardt, whose desks were to either side of mine. I stacked my books, containing their thousands of secrets, onto the shelf above my desk, arranging and rearranging them, stalling, waiting for my cube mates to leave. As soon as they were gone, I slipped into my green lab coat. I looked down at my name; "Gage" was embroidered in red script on the left breast. I closed the sliding glass doors of my bookcase, stepped onto my chair, and looked at my reflection. The beaming—and suddenly beautiful—would-be Dr. Gage. I heard voices in the hall and stepped down quickly, lest anyone catch me admiring my future self.

Back in the gross lab, I stood in line to buy the additional sixty dollars' worth of class notes we were said to need, in another line to have my picture taken, and in yet another line to buy vet school T-shirts from the sophomore class.

The room was loud with talk and laughter as we began to meet one another, and after awhile, the class began to lose its amorphous blondness, its generic whiteness. I noticed a shorthaired, Levi-clad woman pull a can of Copenhagen from her hip pocket and tuck a pinch of the tobacco into her lower lip. I had left my own tobacco in the truck, not wanting to give a bad impression the first day. Her Copenhagen can seemed a sign to me. I threaded my way through the crowded lab and introduced myself.

"Lisa Dalton," she said, extending her hand. She seemed to be taking my measure. "Care for a dip?"

"Thanks." I pinched a bit of the sweet, moist tobacco and slipped it between my lip and gum. Dalton, as I would always call her, grinned broadly.

"I wouldn't have taken you for a round-canner," she said, a

8

reference to the Copenhagen can that wore an identifying circle in the hip pocket of everybody who carried it.

Dalton seemed to know the lay of the land; who was who on the faculty—who was tough, who was boring, who hated women; which hallway in the maze of the anatomy building led where; which books we'd really need and which were to be set aside for "reference." Her best friend was a fourth-year student, and Dalton had assimilated plenty of savvy in the two years they'd lived together. A Colorado native, she was a CSU graduate and a Rocky Mountain woman, a good ol' girl of the first order, hardworking, hard-playing, and tough-minded. She had the air of someone who knows what she's in for and knows that she's equal to it.

"I'm a little nervous about all this," I said.

"That's bullshit," she said. Dalton did not suffer fools gladly.

Lloyd's place—our place—was seven miles from campus, north and east, out where town turned to country. I drove past pastured horses and cattle, past sheep and pig farms, to the old green house with its lilac bushes and screened-in front porch and five cats, two dogs, and three horses, which I was to feed and water morning and night in exchange for my share of the utility bills. Lloyd's schedule as a junior included hospital duty and erratic hours, and he was relieved to be out from under that chore. For my part, I was happy to save money any way I could.

The late-summer flies floated on the air, and the horses settled to their supper. The gathered heat of the afternoon reflected from the earth. The slanting rays of sunlight deepened the red coat of the sorrel gelding, the black of the mare, the gray of her yearling colt. The whole world was still and calm, the only sounds the steady chewing of the horses, the slow swishing of their tails, the fall of water from the hose into the trough. I felt myself relax.

As I turned off the faucet, I heard Lloyd's truck coming down Douglas Road. A 1971, the blue and white Chevy wasn't much newer than old Blue, and it, too, was in dire need of a muffler.

Lloyd honked twice as he pulled into the driveway. I walked over to meet him.

"Well, Retta," he asked, "how was the first day of school?"

"Fine."

He was a bit younger than I was, but his thinning hair, his status as a junior, and his avuncular manner made him seem like a big brother.

"So, did you join SCAVMA?" He was president of the CSU branch of the Student Chapter of the American Veterinary Medical Association.

"Yes, sir, of course."

"Good girl. We'll get you on some committees, get you active." He led the way in through the back door, and I followed him down the hall to his room. "Want to come in with me and help me set up?" SCAVMA was hosting the get-acquainted dance that night.

He stripped to his underwear and dropped his jeans and knit shirt onto the floor.

"I was going to write a couple of letters."

"Okay," he said. "Suit yourself." He disappeared into the bathroom and closed the door.

I went into my room and opened the closet. I had felt overdressed—and out-of-date—in my first-day skirt and blouse. Everybody else had been in jeans or shorts. I took out a flounced red dress that I had worn when I waited tables in a Mexican restaurant. I held it against myself and looked in the mirror.

The bathroom door opened and Lloyd came back down the hall, dripping wet, a towel wrapped around him. He looked over at me. "Change your mind?"

He was in the process of remodeling the house, and neither of our rooms had a door. So when he went across the hall to dress, he kept talking, reminding me how important it was to join committees and clubs and service organizations.

"We need to get you busy," he said again. He came out of his room, tucking his white shirt into his trousers and slinging a tie around his neck.

I followed him back to the bathroom and stood in the doorway while he scrunched down in front of the mirror to tie his tie. "It seems like I *am* going to be busy. It seems like studying's going to take every minute. Won't it?"

"Doesn't have to. You *can* study constantly, but . . ."

"But what?"

He looked at me. "Retta, do you know what they call somebody who gets C's in vet school?"

I shook my head.

"Doctor."

"But . . ."

"Grades don't matter." He cut me off before I could protest that I was worried enough about being able to make those C's. "Hell, you can graduate with eighteen hours of *D*'s. Did they tell you that?"

"Yeah, I heard that."

"So relax." He put his hands on my shoulders. "Okay?"

I nodded. He thinks I'm as smart as he is, I thought.

"Gotta run. See you at the dance."

I listened to his truck as he pulled up onto Douglas Road, as he went through the four gears and away, and silence again closed in.

I had brought home *Miller's Anatomy of the Dog,* intrigued by its dozens of diagrams, already in love with its slick, cool pages. I opened it now at random to the muscles of the thoracic limb and the diagram labeled "Schematic cross section of forepaw through accessory carpal bone." I flipped forward a few dozen pages to a diagram of the "Frontal section of head and neck through the digestive tube, ventral aspect." More than 1,100 pages of facts, which was only *one* part of *one* course.

I wished that it had already begun, that I could sink into the pages of this book, the pages of the other ninety-some pounds of books and be filled by them, that the echoes in my head would be from outside, would be information, would be what I so desperately wanted and needed to be filled with, and not the questions and doubts that echoed there now. I wanted to get on with it, to be submerged in it. When my head hit the pillow at night, I wanted my last thoughts to be a review of the superficial antebrachial muscles of the dog, and not a second-guessing of the rules we were to play by, or a voodoo analysis of something a professor had said in passing.

Perhaps I should start this minute, I thought. I opened the book to page one, chapter one: "Classification and Natural History of the Dog."

I read the first page, the taxonomy of the dog: Carnivora (order), Canidae (family), *Canis* (genus), *familiaris* (species). A summary of its evolution: Dogs dated back 70 million years to the late Cretaceous period, to the genus *Cimolestes*. A summary of the changes of 40 million years ago, of 20 million. The next page was a breakdown of the family Canidae and the genus *Canis*, and included the Latin names for the wolf, coyote, red wolf, and four kinds of jackals.

I looked back over those first three pages and wondered what, if anything, I needed to know of this information. It would take some study to commit to memory just this general background material. I closed the book. I would have to take it as it came and try not to make myself crazy before classes even started.

I wandered through the warm, open house. A breeze stirred the living room curtains. The tired old couch was covered by a blanket that had itself seen better days. The coffee table was a muddle of books, journals, loose papers, and bones.

The leg bones of the horse, specifically. Lloyd had gathered them from the hospital, from necropsy, and stripped them of all soft tissue. Now he was assembling them again—a foreleg and a hind leg—to have on hand some future day when he was in practice and needed to show some client just exactly what was wrong with her horse. These scattered bones were to be his models, but for now they were just a jumble.

I sat down and picked up a dark and horny hoof, its layers like shell. I ran my finger down the smooth, hard length of a cannon bone. It was creamy white and beautiful to feel, heavy in my hand, as though in its density it held something yet of the life it had once had, this piece of dead horse.

I leaned back on the sofa and thought suddenly of another horse, another dead horse that I hadn't thought of in years, one I could, in fact, only dimly remember.

I was four years old, and he lay beside the dirt road that led from Blanding, Utah, west into the mountains where the United States Geological Survey was drilling in search of uranium deposits. It was 1955. My father, Charles Gage, was a skilled laborer for the USGS, and we lived a nomadic life, a band of government gypsies that moved in small trailer houses from one site to the next, where the women and children created a village and an instant community and the men drilled into the earth until they knew the extent and grade of the uranium below, the feasibility of mining. And then we moved on, all around the region known as Four Corners—where Utah, Colorado, New Mexico, and Arizona meet.

We were headed this particular day to a new camp, a place called Deer Flats. Daddy drove; Mama sat beside him. In the backseat, Nancy and I watched the pines and sagebrush pass by the open window.

This horse, a big bay, was a draft horse, a mine horse, Daddy said, who had worked some other, unknown mineral excavation in these mountains. How he died—of injury or disease—we never knew. But there he was, his carcass still covered by hide and hair, an enormous hulk not far from the road.

Nancy looked away, but I leaned out the window and stared, turned to watch him through the dust that billowed up behind us. My memory of this is visceral—the angle of my head, the feel of the window frame against my chest as I craned to see the last of him. The details come from my mother's memory and her retellings. When I could see him no longer, I turned to my parents—according to family lore—and said, "That's my horse. Someday, he's going to get up, and I'm going to ride him."

Our camp was some distance farther, and I saw the horse only from the car when we passed by on our way to Blanding for groceries once or twice a month. The long grasses must have covered the work of coyotes and buzzards, for my memory is only of his huge brown body lying in the meadow, as though he were asleep.

Summer ended. Nancy went to live with Grandma Gage in Grand Junction so she could go to school. The snow fell deeply and did not melt the whole winter long. Horse and field lay covered with a thick white mantle.

In the spring, the snow melted and the grass turned the pale and tender green that it does in the arid plateaus of the West. Through those green blades arched the horse's rib cage, his bones, white and clean and lovely. To me, that skeleton wasn't frightening. Those bones were simply my lost friend, my horse. His essence resided still in the long curve of ribs, the hollowed skull, the disorder of limbs and vertebrae.

"Look!" I cried, pointing through the window. "Oh, look! There's my horse!"

My first horse was only bones, and now I had come full circle to this charnel house and this other dead horse with *his* long, lovely bones.

What a strange little four-year-old I must have been, so easy in the presence of death, as though I had known, those thirty years ago, that that dirt road to Deer Flats, Utah, would lead here, to Douglas Road, and into town, to College Avenue, to the doors of the College of Veterinary Medicine. As though I had known all along that I belonged here among the bones of dead horses.

CHAPTER 2

Knockin' on Heaven's Door

THE day after the dance was like New Year's Day, with requisite resolutions, hopes, and hangovers. A day for repairs and reflection. The night before had been sweet as the smoke of a last cigarette, and as heavy with meaning, pumped with fear and adrenaline and Coors beer.

When Lory Student Center closed, I went with Lloyd and his friends to an all-night truck stop, where we drank strong hot coffee and ate eggs and pancakes and swapped jokes until nearly 4:00 A.M. I was Cinderella, way past midnight and still dancing.

But now, the sun was up and the fairy tale princess was face-to-mirror with herself, a little surprised to see how old that face had gotten.

By the time I'd had a couple of beers at the dance, I felt as young as everybody else looked. So it was an awkward moment when Brigit Finley, one of my new colleagues, asked me whether I was on the faculty. "No, just a freshman," I answered; I felt strangely embarrassed.

Brigit had a sweet, open face and softly curled blond hair. She was on track, fresh out of college, barely into her twenties. "You've been out of school quite a while, I guess," she said, by way of changing the subject.

Though I was just thirty-four, my face registered a life spent in the New Mexico sun and wind, a teenage cigarette habit, and a genetic predisposition to wrinkles. The lines in my face testified to my foolish and favorite beauty ritual—the suntan. To Brigit, I may have looked downright elderly.

Still, there *was* a great distance between us. As Indiana Jones says, not years, but mileage. Brigit and I had grown up in different eras, in different Americas, something that I wouldn't really understand until a Sunday afternoon four years later when I happened to be touring an open house.

This house had a special feature. I went into the earth, down a dozen concrete steps, to a landing, where I turned and went down a dozen more, where I turned again and entered a square concrete room like the inside of a gray brick. The room was empty and cool, though it was July and hot outside.

The real-estate agent was saying that this would make an excellent wine cellar, and how the owner had dug it himself, back in the fifties. The agent was young, Brigit's age, that magic decade younger than I. He was affable and easy in his skin. While the room was not charming, he was charmed by its quaintness. It was a curiosity, a relic of a past age. He said he'd never been in a bomb shelter before.

"*Fallout* shelter," I said. He said, "Huh?" and I explained that it would have been no good at all against the actual *bomb*; it was meant as protection from the radioactive fallout, a place to wait for the world to cool down. He said something like "Oh, right" and that it sure would make a great wine cellar.

No doubt.

I, too, had never seen a fallout shelter, and though the air seemed fresh enough, I was starting to take deep breaths. This wasn't claustrophobia. I was just scared.

I could imagine the bunk beds, the water cans, the tins of food, the card table and folding chairs, the books and puzzles, a radio. I had imagined it all before. I imagined being locked in there with the hatch closed, not knowing what the world looked like, what was left, when or if we could ever go back outside, who or what might be just outside the door, with round, haunted eyes, wanting in.

"You could even use it for an office—it has a ventilation system," the real-estate agent was saying as he led me up the steps. "I think it's kind of cool."

He didn't have air-raid drills when he was in school, I thought, then I asked him.

"No," he said, "I missed all that hysteria."

There was nothing to suggest that this was the home of a fanatic, a hysteric, however. It was a modest frame and stucco house, with three apple trees on one side, a small vegetable garden on the other, and a fallout shelter in the backyard. The guy who had dug that enormous hole and lined it with concrete wasn't a crazy man, but simply a man born on the other side of those ten years that separated me from that real estate agent, me from Brigit.

They were babies in 1962 when Chet Huntley and David Brinkley showed us the fuzzy black-and-white photographs of the Soviet nuclear missile bases being built in Cuba. Labels and arrows pointed to the warheads. When our President-prince, Jack Kennedy, issued the ultimatum to the evil Khrushchev and ordered the naval blockade. When Russian death ships sailed toward Cuba and we hung between peace and annihilation. When we sat in school, waiting, knowing those ships and our ships were out on the blue ocean, pointed toward one another, getting nearer and nearer, and knowing that the President's long, trembling finger hovered above some black button on some black box that held our deaths, and wondering why we were in school and whether we would have time to get home before the end of the world—before the bomb.

The Bomb was what we called it—first cousin of Little Boy and Fat Man, who were our own big brothers, born in New Mexico almost twenty years before. We understood that the devastation of Hiroshima and Nagasaki was but a teaser of the explosive power in wait for us when the bombs began to fly back and forth between here and the Soviet Union, the finale of everything.

On Fridays at midnight, we watched monster movies on TV. The Blob, the Fly, the Thing, Godzilla—these were the contaminated and damned mutant children of the Bomb.

17

We knew these monsters weren't real, of course. "The Huntley-Brinkley Report" was real, and the pictures of Hiroshima, and the ships off the Cuban coast, and thalidomide babies with arms like little flippers, and the uranium-ore trucks that thundered down NM State Road 509 past the café and gas station and trailer where we lived, and the thick dust that rolled off that ore and hung like a dry fog above the desert floor.

We lived under sentence of death, and the future wasn't real, nor very long, either, not as we understood it.

I graduated from high school in 1969 and moved into the dorm at the University of New Mexico in Albuquerque. When the times began a-changin', I was ready to seize the day and do it if it felt good. If I missed curfew, I stayed up all night. Drugs called Windowpane, Sunshine, White Cross, and Black Beauty were jet fuel. The war in Vietnam became our rallying point, but it didn't make us what we were. The Bomb did that; we were its mutants, just as Godzilla was.

Sometimes I went to class, sometimes I didn't. I fell in love with tall, golden Stan—so vain that he wouldn't swim in chlorinated water, lest he bleach his tan—and moved into his small apartment, next door to Laura, who was beautiful and wild, and her husband, Steve. The four of us, plus their baby, Nicole, were inseparable. One day, Steve said there was a rock festival in Louisiana and suggested we go.

I'd never been to the South, and I'd missed Woodstock. We got in somebody's van and headed for the Celebration of Life. We didn't look back.

When I finally did look back, the seventies were almost over, and I was in Sitka, Alaska, "sittin' on the dock of the bay, wastin' time," older than I had ever expected to be. I was living with my dog, Coyote, in a camper shell on the back of a pickup truck in the cold, wet, and beautiful originally Russian town tucked between mountains and the steel-gray Pacific, while my husband was out to sea on a salmon boat. The sky was always close, as if Sitka really were near the top of the world, as it looks on the globe. The long summer hours of daylight were a perpetual dusk. The colored pencils Nancy had sent for Christmas were too garish for this place where the sun didn't penetrate and the wet air muted sound and softened all the edges.

Stan was long gone, off in some other life. Steve and Laura were divorced, and she and her daughter were living in Santa Fe. And I was the wife of an itinerant jack-of-all-trades mountain man named Alan. He'd been a lumberjack and a gemstone trader. Now he was a fisherman and I was a part-time waitress with lots of time for thinking.

The end of the world didn't seem to be coming, although Alan, with his fundamentalist Christian upbringing, was calmly confident that it was. It seemed to me, though, that there might be quite a bit of life to live before then. I was thinking more and more about half a lifetime ago and a fourteen-year-old girl who had wanted to be a veterinarian.

I met Alan's boat. He held my hand as we walked down the pier, and I waited until we were in the truck to tell him that I had decided to go back to school.

He was a taciturn man with biblical notions of marriage and the roles of men and women. He listened to me, no betrayal of emotion on his beautiful face, which, like mine, was weathered beyond its years. I knew we would have to make sacrifices, I said. I touched his hand and he wrapped his fingers around mine. I knew that it meant settling somewhere for a while—for years—while I got my bachelor's degree and then four more years while I was in vet school. He'd have to take a real and ordinary job. There would be neighbors and traffic and noise. I knew it would be hard for him, I said, but it wouldn't be forever. I painted an idyll of our post–vet school life: a log cabin somewhere outside a small mountain town. We would live a life of simple virtue and rustic charm. Finally, I ran out of things to say and fell silent.

I thought I had anticipated and answered every objection he could raise, but what he said was, "You're not smart enough to be a veterinarian." He said it as if he were stating any known fact in the universe. I was stunned.

"I know I'm ignorant. I know I'm starting from scratch, but, Alan, I can do it."

He shook his head. He had nothing more to say.

Of course, there was more talk in the next few weeks; few marriages end that quietly. Before the summer was over, however, I left him and Coyote and Alaska and headed south to live with Nancy and her kids in Albuquerque and pick up where I'd left off at the University of New Mexico.

Three years later, I was finally closing in on my undergraduate degree. I mailed my first application to Colorado State University's College of Veterinary Medicine and began to wait.

I tried to keep my hopes in check, while my friends worked to keep them up. Jill Henderson, the equine vet I worked for, had written me a "she walks on water" recommendation. Nancy's boyfriend, Jay, who had coached me through calculus, had never heard the words *you can't* when he was growing up. Success was his family religion, and he offered it to me.

My family religion, though, was in my bones: Dreams come to smash.

Daddy was a dreamer. "You'll never get rich working for wages," he'd say. So he and Mama worked every waking hour in the gas station and café they opened in the uranium fields of Ambrosia Lake, New Mexico, when I was seven. They worked like ants for five years and took what they'd accumulated and moved to Chama, a small village near the Colorado border, opened a gas station there, and waited for the boom that was supposed to come. Everybody said there was money coming from Texas, or somewhere, to build ski lifts and resort hotels. Chama would be the next Aspen, or Taos, or Purgatory.

Twenty-five years later, the money hasn't come. Mama lives in the same ten-by-fifty-foot trailer parked at the edge of the asphalt driveway of the gas station that's been closed for many years. Daddy lies buried in the National Cemetery in Santa Fe, dead of alcohol and disappointment.

That lesson is in the bones, and it doesn't come out.

And yet, you are the star of your own life. Our culture tells us that we can win. From Cinderella to Elvis, the underdog rises. There are new fairy tales in every issue of *People*. We enter the lottery and fund whole states with our hopes, because the world whispers in our ears, "It can be you. It can be you." I'd been down, turned around, and now I was a college graduate. What are bootstraps for, if not to pull yourself up?

The weight of that American optimism fought against my own reason, the knowledge that my recent grades were less than sterling, that the transcript of my first attempt at college was worse, that my Graduate Record Exam scores were merely average, that I didn't have a list of extracurricular activities to prove leadership qualities, community involvement, or a well-rounded personality, that I had a sorry and well-documented history of signing up for a full load of courses and then dropping one or two midway through the term. My record was one of a rather ordinary student with no intestinal fortitude.

But the record was the past, I told myself, not the future. And I was the star of this rags-to-riches tale.

But then again, too much bravura tempts the bad fairies.

That line between self-confidence and no expectations is very fine and hard to locate, but I tried to walk it.

On February 18, the letter arrived, three paragraphs long, the essense of which was no. I wrote back, asking for an evaluation of my application, and found out I had missed being invited for an interview by thirty-five points.

A perfect score was two thousand points. The grade point average was worth 35 percent, the GRE 10 percent, the application itself 25 percent, the interview—if you made the cut—15 percent. It was also possible to get 5 percent for each of three areas—resident, minority, and disadvantaged status.

I studied my scores. To my surprise, my GPA and GRE were not dreadful, at 80 percent and 71 percent, respectively. Because New Mexico does not have a vet school, its students are granted in-state tuition and resident status through the Western Interstate Commission for Higher Education (WICHE) program, so I got that 5 percent. Apparently, being female didn't count for anything.

Where I'd fallen down was on the application itself—45 percent of the possible, or 228 out of 500 points. Its major portion was a five-hundred-word essay, a personal statement about the applicant's goals and motivations. It had been hard to write, hard to know how to sound committed but not sappy, to indicate a love of animals without seeming sentimental or extremist, to appear energetic but in control, eager but not desperate.

I thought. I wrote. I thought. I rewrote. I worried. I thought. I wrote again.

Five days before the November 1 deadline for my second try, Daddy died.

I had been sixteen when he walked into the Veterans Administration Hospital in Fort Lyon, Colorado, and surrendered himself to the drying-out process one more time. He'd just come through it at the VA Hospital in Albuquerque but had begun drinking almost immediately. He'd battled the bottle his whole adult life, and there had always been months of sobriety between binges. This time, there was no relief, no remission of the hateful disease. The choice of Fort Lyon was a desperate one, for it was almost three hundred miles from Chama, on the desolate, windswept prairie of eastern Colorado, *and* it was a psychiatric hospital.

Mama was not to contact Daddy for the initial two-week detoxification period, they said. This was no problem, for she was angry and she was busy. She opened the gas station every morning as soon as she'd combed her hair and she closed it at bedtime.

After two weeks, she placed the call, asked for her husband, and waited for his voice.

Instead, a doctor came on the line and explained that Daddy's condition had not improved. He was still paralyzed and unable to speak; she should not expect full recovery.

No, she said, he'd made a mistake. *Her* husband was a patient in the alcoholism treatment program.

Yes, he said, Charles Gage.

No, she insisted, there was some mistake.

The mistake was only clerical. The mistake was that she had not been contacted when, four days into detox, Daddy had suffered a "cerebral accident" that left him unable to walk or speak or feed himself. He was fifty-three years old.

Sixteen horrible years later, Daddy came home to the National Cemetery in Santa Fe. Nancy, Jay, my nephew Dean, and I drove up from Albuquerque. Mama, Aunt Kay, Uncle Joe, and two of Daddy's old fishing buddies drove down from Chama. There was a brief graveside service. An outdoor speaker played a recording of "Taps." It was Halloween.

We stopped at the main branch of the post office on the way home and mailed my application. It didn't seem very likely, or very important, either.

On February 11, a fat envelope came. I was to present myself at 3:00 P.M. on February 27 in Room 208 of the Lory Student Center for an interview.

My boyfriend, Wes, and I played the interview game over and over. He asked me the best questions he could think of. I gave my best answers. I rehearsed in the bathroom, studying my face in the mirror as I mouthed the answers to the questions I was asking myself. I tried smiling when I spoke, drawing my brows together thoughtfully, giving the knowing nod. I worried about what to do with my hands.

In our role playing, Wes and I had posed every question we could imagine, but our imaginations had not been big enough.

"Suppose you are a practicing veterinarian," said Dr. Ted Miller, one of my two inquisitors. I nodded, supposing. "And suppose a little boy brings you his dog. It's been hit by a car and it's pretty obvious that its leg is broken. The kid has no money. You call his parents, who say that they can't afford any treatment. What do you do?"

I hadn't the faintest idea, but I had to say something. I licked my lips. "I'd explain to the boy's parents that they could make small payments every month. . . ."

"Not an option. They refuse to put any money at all into this dog."

"Nice people," I offered. The professors did not return my smile. I felt my stomach tighten.

"I suppose I could put a simple splint on the leg," I began. I knew as soon as I'd started that it was not the thing to say, but I did not want to turn the boy away, and yet I didn't want to look like a softy, either.

23

Dr. Miller cut me off again. "We don't want your medical opinion or your treatment plan, Ms. Gage. If you're admitted, we'll teach you what to do with the *leg.* We want to know what you would do with the *boy*—turn him away, or treat his dog?"

Now I was embarrassed as well as terrified. There was no question of what I would actually do in this situation, so I took a deep breath and told the truth. "I'd treat the dog."

Both men made notes on the legal pads in front of them. I felt as though I had just confessed to a serious crime. My tight control began to crack. My eyes began to water. I breathed deeply and consciously again and again.

The other professor looked up from his pad and into my eyes, which were filling fast. "Don't you think you might get a reputation as a sucker?"

"I guess I would."

"And you would *still* treat the dog?"

If I could keep the tears from falling, I thought, I might salvage the interview. "Yes, sir," I said.

Both men made another note. A tear slid down my cheek.

A month later, the letter came, telling me that my application had been denied, though I had been given alternate status. I would be notified in May if a slot opened up. In May, the skinny "no thanks" letter arrived.

For solace, I ran to my old friend Laura. She had been there for me since the seventies, and she was there for me now.

"Darling," she said, for she always called me darling, an affectation that was completely natural for her, "you look like shit." I was feeling better already. "You're positively pasty-faced. Out to the pool, and off with your shirt!" She paused in the kitchen to mix long-on-tequila margaritas. "You can't let yourself go, darling, *especially* if you're not going to be a vet."

I didn't even protest. I peeled off my T-shirt and lay back on the webbed chaise. The sun felt like a healing hand. Laura handed me a tall, salt-crusted glass and held up her own.

"Cheers."

"Cheers."

"Darling, it's time to face reality." Laura had never been soft, but the knocks of the last few years had hardened and polished

24

the veneer. She was still celebrating life, courting the sun, taking whatever drugs made her feel good, and planning to have fun while it lasted and leave a gorgeous corpse when it was over. She pulled her striped caftan over her head and dropped it onto the pool deck. Dark as she was, there were still freckles on her breasts.

"You are thirty-three years old," she said, and stopped, as if that was enough reality for now.

"Next you'll say I'm almost forty."

"You *are* almost forty, and you are making five lousy bucks an hour cleaning up dog shit, working *for* a veterinarian, which makes you crazy because every day you stand elbow-to-elbow with what you want to be when you grow up, and you *are* grown-up, and apparently the gods aren't going to let you."

When I didn't argue, she continued. "You have to quit feeling sorry for yourself and take charge of your life."

"I want to be a vet."

"If wishes were horses, beggars might ride." She adjusted her bikini bottom, checked her tan line, and rolled over. I closed my eyes. We fell into an easy silence, as only close friends can. After a while, she began again. Her voice was dreamy, but what she had to say was hard-nosed and clear-cut.

"You could be an R.N. in two years." Laura was a nurse. "With your background in science, it wouldn't even be hard. You'd start at more than double what you make now."

It made sense—except that it wasn't what I wanted.

"And you meet a lot of doctors," she added.

"Laura, you are so retro."

"They're perfect husbands—they make a lot of money and they're not home much."

Laura couldn't understand wanting to be just one thing. She liked variety, liked change. She'd been a paralegal and an art dealer, and she wasn't going to stay in nursing long, either, it turned out. Her advice was sincere, however, and it wasn't wasted on me.

She sat up and lit a cigarette. "Another thing, darling: You have to leave Wes." She referred to my rocky-road boyfriend, the man I was living with and hoped to marry. "That's nowhere." Laura could give a comprehensive critique when the spirit moved her, and apparently it had.

It was past the deadline for the University of Albuquerque's fall term, but the admissions counselor told me that there was still available space in the nursing class. I hoped my disappointment didn't show. My chemistry, biology, and anatomy credits satisfied U of A's requirements, and I would need just Nursing I the first term, Nursing II and Pharmacology the second, and then the entire second-year curriculum. I thanked her and shook her hand. The ability to compromise, I told myself, was the mark of maturity.

The course work was easy. My biology degree held me in good stead, and I had been a vet tech long enough to have changed a lot of dressings, given many shots, and placed plenty of IV catheters.

It was, in fact, too easy. In October, I began to work once again on my CSU application.

I worried about how to load it with a few more points. I studied copies of my first two applications. For the "Activities" entry, I had had to reach back to junior high for intramural basketball. I had had nothing for the "Honors and Awards" line at all. This year, though, I could claim the "Last Ass" award—a rough slab of wood, hand-lettered and hand-painted, with the outline of a donkey—which I'd "won" for finishing in last place in the burro race in Chama a few months before.

I began my essay: "Last July 15, I competed in the First Annual Chama, New Mexico, Burro Race. I finished last, but my burro and I became very close in the course of our eighteen-mile trek over the mountain: He hated me and I hated him." I'd been proud to finish at all, and I hoped the admissions committee noticed my tenacity. I hoped they noticed my good humor. I hoped they noticed, period.

In February, the same fat, "present yourself for an interview" letter arrived. I packed the still-brand-new pinstriped suit I'd bought for my interview the year before, and hoped it wasn't unlucky.

Dr. Helena Matthews called me for my interview and introduced herself and Dr. Miles Cochran, a clinician at the Veterinary Teaching Hospital. They sat down across the table from me, my file open between them.

Dr. Cochran leaned back in his chair, balanced on two legs, and fired the first question: "I see here that you're in nursing school, Loretta. How do you like it?"

"I don't. If I was satisfied with nursing school, I wouldn't be here now, applying to vet school." I winced at how that sounded, as if I thought the question stupid and the answer obvious.

"What is it about nursing that you don't like?" Before I could answer, he added, "My mother was a practicing nurse for twenty-five years."

Was he warning me? Or trying to rattle me? Why had he said that?

Idiotically, I said, "Oh, your mother's a nurse?"

"She was. She's dead."

"I'm sorry," I said, and he nodded in acknowledgment. This wasn't going well at all. Why hadn't I just answered the question instead of getting into this stupid mock conversation about his dead mother? I said something about human pain and suffering and death, how it was too emotionally draining for me. Not that I was emotionally fragile, I assured them. Not that I didn't empathize and feel for animal pain and suffering and death. I was ranting. I stopped and collected my thoughts for a moment. "I just don't like it," I said. That sounded limp. They nodded and took notes. "Besides, I like to work outside." God, that sounded stupid, said a voice in my head, but Matthews and Cochran smiled at my answer, or at my nervousness.

I laughed and shrugged. "I don't know. I just want to be a vet."

They asked me where I thought the veterinary profession was headed, whether I thought the field was overcrowded, whether I thought vet school class sizes should be cut. I had no idea, but I answered somehow.

They posed hypothetical situations that tested my loyalty to hypothetical colleagues and my attitudes about treating the animals of impoverished clients. I was improvising, but I seemed to be doing okay.

Then Cochran picked up my file and flipped through it. "I see here you worked for Tom Tromboldt. What do you think of him?"

This wasn't a hypothetical question, nor was it an easy one. I assumed Cochran knew Tromboldt, and if so, he knew Tom was subject to ugly black moods and had a nasty temper. So what was he testing—my loyalty or my honesty?

"He's excellent. He's a good diagnostician and a great surgeon."

Cochran nodded. He wasn't going to let me off that easily. "But what is he like to work for?"

"You know him, Dr. Cochran?"

He nodded again, but his face was a mask. He wasn't going to give me any help on this.

"I got along with him all right most of the time, but he can make you think hell isn't twenty feet away." Cochran and Matthews waited for me to continue. "He can be hard on people. He wants the most out of them. He has a pretty high employee-turnover rate."

"Is he hard on his clients, as well?"

"No, he's too professional for that," I said.

Cochran seemed satisfied. It was over.

By the time the letter came in March, Wes and I had split up. I had taken the rest of Laura's advice and given him an ultimatum—marriage or quits. He picked quits.

Every day, I got out of school in the late morning and drove to the house we had shared, sat on the front step with our dog, Seth—Wes's dog, Seth—and waited for the mailman. The pain of the end of romance was still fresh and bitter. I waited for that letter to save me and give me a fresh new life.

When it came, however, it was the same letter I had gotten the year before. I was an alternate—again. I stared at the single sheet in disbelief. I had done better, I thought. They had liked me, I thought. I'd gotten careless and let my hopes rise; now disappointment hit me like a physical blow. I began to cry, hard, violent sobs. Seth whimpered and licked my face, and I pulled his warm, wiggly body onto my lap and folded myself over him.

On May 3, a little after 10:00 A.M., a secretary interrupted the nursing lecture to say I had an urgent message to call home at once. My only thought was that someone had died—Mama, I thought. My fingers trembled as I dialed our number.

Nancy answered on the first ring. I was to call Dr. Helena Matthews at CSU.

There was an opening for me. Would I accept a place in the class of 1989? I thanked Dr. Matthews again and again. I called Nancy back. I called Mama. I wanted to run and spin in the air, to go down the hall, open every door, and shout my good news. I wanted champagne to drink, to splash in and pour over my head.

Instead, I went back to class. I went back to class for two more weeks and finished the term, though I didn't quite understand why. It got clearer during the long summer as Mama urged me again and again to request a delay in admission so I could finish my R.N. degree first. "You'd have that to fall back on," she said. "Just in case."

In case, of course, I couldn't hack it. In case I really wasn't smart enough. In case my finally getting in was just a fluke. Just in case—the same reason I had gone back to class on May 3 and the following two weeks. Just in case I wasn't good enough to become a veterinarian.

CHAPTER 3

———————

"You Think Like a Fourth-Grader"

THE bulk of our time that first semester was divided between
two courses, Agents of Disease and Gross Anatomy; and on
Friday afternoons, we had a two-credit course called Perspectives in Comparative Medicine, a potpourri of issues and information. Each course was taught by a revolving troupe of
instructors; change was constant. The ground seemed to shift
beneath our feet.

Exams would be frequent, and the finals comprehensive, covering material from the entire term. Finals were also "manda-
tory pass"; flunk the final, and you flunked the course, no
matter what grades you'd made on tests along the way. The
clear message was that everything belonged in our long-term
memory banks.

The faces at the lectern were often new, but the schedule was
rigid: morning lectures, afternoon labs. Mondays and Wednes-
days were for Anatomy; Tuesdays and Thursdays were for Agents.
Nearly everything we did was within the walls of the anatomy
building. Lectures in 108, labs in the gross lab. Even "cube time"
was scheduled, during which professors rotated through the
different study cubicles for review and question-and-answer
sessions.

I felt bombarded. Every fact, process, theory, and formula
seemed disconnected from the next. My background was so

slight that I didn't have hooks on which to hang all this new information. Each bit was discrete, separate, and thus seemed irrelevant. I didn't see how I could remember this stuff even until the always-approaching exam, much less through the final and beyond.

Lloyd tried to calm my fears. "They repeat the important stuff over and over again. There's no way you *can't* get it."

Repetition was the only tool *I* had, as well. Repeat the reading, repeat the lists, repeat the reviews—again and again and again. The only thing standing between me and mastery was the finite nature of time. All the hours that I could stay awake could be filled. I began to drink a lot of coffee.

Someone asked in the first Anatomy session whether we were permitted to tape-record the lecture. Dr. Teller smiled. "Certainly," he said, so kindly that it frightened me, "but I guarantee you won't have time to listen to any of this a second time." He knew what we were in for; we did not—and he obviously felt sorry for us.

Like a few of my classmates, I taped the lectures, anyway. I hoped Teller was exaggerating, emphasizing the "fear of God" factor, but he was not. The ideal plan was to listen intently in class, then take notes that night from the tapes, thus hearing everything twice. The school had anticipated this—our "minicourse" notes, pounds and pounds of them, were essentially notes from the lecture, intended to free us from the necessity of writing everything down, presumably so we could use our higher cognitive functions instead of our mere clerical skill. However, the very act of taking notes was part of the repetition that I was relying upon.

The task of remembering was complicated by the scattered and illogical nature of the names of both body parts and diseases. Historically, there had been no standard method of naming; the person who discovered or identified a structure, syndrome, or disease attached his name to it, a practice strongly discouraged by the World Association of Veterinary Anatomists today. Although we represented the new generation, there was still plenty of old baggage from the past. We had to drag it along with us; there was no way to avoid learning both names.

31

This eponymous system would plague us, too, in Agents of Disease, for individuals had plastered their names all over the world of microorganisms.

Anatomy offered at least the hope of logic. Our standard species were canine and equine; we would dissect and study the dog and the horse until our understanding was perfect. The other species would be much briefer dissectional studies, emphasizing how they differed from our "gold standard," the dog and the horse.

The course, which was actually two sequential courses—611 and 612—covered gross anatomy, histology (the microscopic study of organic tissue), developmental anatomy, and physiology of the normal organism. The latter included cell structure and function, body organization (systems, organs, tissues), concepts of microscopic organization, structure and dynamics of cartilage, histology and development of bone, mineral metabolism, skeletal muscle, comparative anatomy of the foot, arthrology (joints), thoracic limb (canine and equine), pelvic limb (canine and equine), tendons and ligaments, bony anatomy of the skull, development of the nervous system, synaptic transmission, neurohistology, neural conduction, functional classification of nerves, the dorsal (spinal) column, layers and development of the cerebellum, eye and surrounding structures, ears, motor system, cranial nerves, cerebrospinal fluid, blood supply, autonomic nervous system, and pharmacology of the autonomic nervous system.

It was daunting, but it was going to make sense. After all, the foot bone connected to the ankle bone, the ankle bone connected to the shin bone, the shin bone connected to the knee bone. . . .

Agents of Disease, on the other hand, seemed a hodgepodge of material, chopped in a way that frustrated our desire to synthesize. We began with epidemiology, a study of herd-oriented disease problems and the movement of disease through populations. We would then study the general properties (morphology, physiology, pathogenesis, geneticology, and identification) of those organisms that cause disease—bacteria, fungi, viruses, parasites, and poisonous plants.

The necessity of mastering this course was obvious, but the presentation of material was such that much of our work was to sort the relevant from the merely decorative. The unit on poisonous plants, for instance, was taught by an unbridled botany enthusiast who seemed bent on converting us to his field. Dr. Lewis's zeal for his subject approached the evangelical. He didn't seem to understand that he was teaching in a trade school and there wasn't time for knowledge for its own sake.

Try as I might, I couldn't muster as much enthusiasm for the anatomy of the sunflower as for that of the horse. I trusted that what he told us was what we needed to know, however, and drilled myself on the life cycle of the flower—how the pappus replaces the sepals, and what an incomplete stamen is—determined to master every scrap I was given. Lewis brushed off questions about antidotes and treatment. He wasn't a veterinarian, he said; that wasn't his area. "All in good time," he would say, "all in good time." For now, identifying the sixty-two poisonous plants by both their Latin and common names would be enough. For now, this would be suspended in the liquid stew in our heads, unrelated to anything else.

Virology, though, brought the study of minutia to the max. Professor Toppino typically wore a long white lab coat, and he seemed a little mad. The tasks he set for us seemed crazy, too, constant, tiny, and annoying as gnats. And like gnats swarming your face, they obscured the path.

One job was to "understand," which meant memorize, the sixteen rules of virus classification. Out of context, they made little sense: Rule number six was "the law of priority shall not be observed"; number fifteen, "the ending of the name of a viral genus is '. . . virus'"; number 10, "the rules of orthography of names and epithets are listed in Chapter 3, Section 6 of the proposed international code of nomenclature of viruses (Appendix C; minutes of 1966 Moscow meeting)."

I wondered what this information was going to mean to me if I somehow survived the learning of it and actually became a veterinarian. I wondered how to hold it in my head until the exam. I put it in the stew pot with the plants.

Least popular of Toppino's tests was "name the viruses," which consisted of listing on a blank sheet of paper as many of the 173 virus names as we could think of: lactic dehydrogenase virus of mice, infectious hematopoietic necrosis virus of fish, Lagos bat virus, Kilham rat virus. We were to learn no symptoms, no treatment, no identification, just names. Over and over and over again, I read the names, recited them, wrote them out. It was a mind-numbing task, like memorizing the books of the Bible, or the fifty state capitals, the American Presidents, Academy Award–winning movies—but there were so many more viruses.

The point seemed to be to make us submit, to make us accept the mindlessness of the task and do it anyway. The next four years would require us to do many things that repelled us. Memorizing 173 viruses was merely annoying and time-consuming, a small conditioning exercise, a first step in establishing that they owned us now. They were breaking us to ride.

I felt the first flush of anger, the first questioning of my questioners. There wasn't time enough for what they asked us to do. I threw away the meeting and lecture announcements of the equine and bovine practioners' groups that I had joined at Lloyd's urging. But under the anger, like a primer coat of paint, was genuine and relentless fear.

Just as the anorexic looks in the mirror and sees fat, I looked at myself and saw stupidity. I was a fraud. Never mind that I was here, inside, admitted, validated. Never mind that my classmates, too, seemed to flounder under the volume of reading, the masses of information, the pace of lectures, the confusion of labs. Never mind the encouraging platitudes from home; more than a state line and a few hundred miles separated me from my family. I was alone. With my colleagues, yes, who were also alone. We ran on adjacent treadmills and nurtured the perverse pride of the beleaguered. We moaned and complained in subvocal mutterings as we bent over our books and microscopes. The few, the proud, the freshmen vet students: We could bitch, but we could not whine.

I crammed my head full of unpronounceable Latin names, the growth needs of innumerable bacteria, the colors of various fungal cultures, the pathway of neural impulses from the brain to the uterus of the dog—all for the weekly exams—and despaired of ever remembering enough of it to get through the final, months hence. After each test, the brain seemed to empty, readying itself for the next big chunk of unrelated facts. Before exams, I would have to read and reread all of it, every word, and cram it back in. Nothing made enough sense to be stored in my long-term memory.

I tried not to worry—because there just wasn't time.

A day at a time, a task at a time, the object was always the immediate. To think beyond December was madness. The next test was as far as anyone could see. As if we were treading choppy water, the horizon was obscured by the next wave, always in our faces.

You were tired. Your arms and legs, your very brain, ached. You kept repeating your mantra: "I can handle this—if the waves don't get any bigger." Then a guy on a ship tosses you a life preserver. You look up at him in gratitude and slip it over your head before you realize that it's made of cast iron. That guy was Elmer Howard, professor in charge of freshman Anatomy.

I had scored 85 percent on the first lab practical exam. The second exam consisted mostly of histological specimens—microscopes set up at stations throughout the lab with slides of various tissues, along with a few bones displayed grossly and a few organs tagged in dissected animals. I thought when I finished that I had done okay—not great, maybe, but okay.

While we were in lecture in the mornings, our exams would be delivered to the cubes by the Test Fairy and placed facedown on our desks. The first student back to the cubes would yell out and let the rest of us know that the exams were graded. My gut knotted as I walked into the cube, put down my notebook, and turned over the paper: 42 percent. I was stunned. I'd flunked.

My instant reaction was that I had flunked *out*. I didn't belong here. I was out of my depth. It was over; it might be a long slide to the end of the term, but this was the decisive point, the moment I could pinpoint as the end of the dream.

Wait a minute, said a small voice in my head, as if it had been waiting for my panicked self to take a breath. Remember Day One? Remember what Dr. Howard said? You are special; you are terrific. They love you; they're here to help; they're in your corner. I listened with all my might. The voice talked me all the way to Howard's office.

"I don't know where I went wrong," I said, handing him my test paper.

He gave the paper a cursory look and shoved it back across the desk. "Look at your answers." He sounded disgusted. "Look at number seven, for example."

I picked up the test. "Cartilage?" I could see the specimen in my memory. A few round cells suspended in a gell-like afibrillar matrix. I had been certain of this answer. "Dr. Howard, it *was* cartilage." A cold terror seized me, for if I was wrong about this, I was truly lost.

"*Hyaline* cartilage." His voice was weary. "I could get any idiot off the street to tell me it was cartilage."

"Then I need to be more specific." It was half-question, half-statement.

He just looked at me, expressionless, for a long moment, and then he said, "You think like a fourth-grader." His voice was matter-of-fact now, as if he had said the most ordinary thing. My brave, frozen, ingratiating smile slipped from my face as he turned his attention to the papers on his desk. My audience with Dr. Howard was obviously over.

I picked up my exam, stood up, and thanked him for his time. Somehow, I made it out the door.

The voice coached me down the hall: Look, he was harsh, okay, but you don't have time to dwell on it. If you start crying, your eyes will hurt and you won't be able to read tonight, and you *have to* read tonight. Not everybody's going to love you,

Loretta. At least now, you know what's wrong. You just have to be more specific. Don't take it so personally. He doesn't even know you. He's just an old curmudgeon. He's trying to toughen you up, like in boot camp or something. For God's sake, don't cry! Don't be a fourth-grader! Don't be a *girl*! It's just one little test, and now you've learned something about how to take tests, that's all. You *knew* it was hyaline. You just didn't know what they wanted. There will be a thousand more tests before it's over. Everybody has setbacks. Don't cry!

By this time, I had made it to the bathroom and washed my face. Cool water and the coaching put me back together. I was beginning to convince myself that Howard was tough but fair, an irascible old bastard with a flinty exterior and a carefully concealed but warmly beating heart.

If this was a work of fiction, he would have been there on graduation day saying something suitably crusty, like "You'll do, Dr. Gage"—but with a tear in the corner of his eye. But this is not a work of fiction.

I scored just above the class average on the next exam, but this relative success seemed as random and unrelated to my efforts as the previous failure had seemed. At the end of any given test, I put down my pencil and was flooded not with relief but with dread. I could not judge how well or how poorly I had done. I had no barometer; I was flying through a fog without instruments.

One early afternoon, I walked past a small side room just off the gross lab and saw Dr. Howard conducting a review session for a half dozen or so of my classmates. I hesitated outside the door and listened; he was quizzing and drilling the students on the canine thoracic limb, material over which we were soon to be tested. I thought quickly. I could use a review of this material, and, I reasoned, if I joined the session, it would show Dr. Howard that I wasn't pouting, that I was eager and willing to do whatever I could to master anatomy. Yes.

I slipped quietly into the back of the room and sat down next to Jeanette Hay. Howard's eyes met mine and he abruptly stopped his lecture. "Yes?" he said.

My classmates shifted in their seats to look at me. I smiled a bit uncertainly. "Sorry to interrupt. I just thought I'd sit in."

Howard's eyes grew hard and narrow. "I don't recall that you were invited," he said. Then he shouted, "Get out of here!" In the confines of the small room, his voice felt like a physical attack. I was crying before I was out the door. A few controlled steps beyond, I began to run like a wounded animal, outside, into the chilled autumn air, across the field to the parking lot, and into my truck. I wanted to keep running, to turn the key and drive away, off the campus, east to the interstate, south to New Mexico, to home.

The coach in my head was silent.

Gradually my sobs subsided. I blew my nose and wiped my face. I had work to do. Through force of will, I went back across the field, through the outside door, down the opposite corridor, as far from Howard as I could get, and into my study cubicle. I opened my notebook and forced my eyes across the page, reading the words again and again until my studies pushed Howard to the back of my mind.

A while later, Jeanette came to the doorway of the cube and tapped on the door frame. "I'm sorry he embarrassed you," she said softly.

I started to say something like "Thanks" or "That's all right," but I felt the tears welling. I shrugged and smiled. Jeanette and I were not particularly close friends, and it seemed to me very kind of her to come and say that. "Come on in," I said, and she shook her head and indicated my cube mates, who were studying near the back of the room. I joined her in the hall.

"I would appreciate it if you wouldn't tell anyone that I was in that group," she said in a voice that was almost a whisper.

I was confused. What did *she* have to be embarrassed about?

It was a special group, she explained, just those who were flunking Anatomy. Nobody else was supposed to know about it.

"Oh," I said. "I'm not doing so well myself."

"You're not flunking, or you'd be in that group."

Jeanette looked as bad as I felt. "I didn't realize . . ." I began.

"I know you didn't. And he didn't have to be so rude. We all felt bad for you."

We hugged one another, two miserable women trying to hold on to some self-worth in the face of this horrendous semester. "You'll be okay, Jeanette. You're smart enough, or you wouldn't be here. You know that." I heard my coach talking, giving Jeanette the pep talk, the platitudes, the words I so often told myself. Jeanette nodded.

I think she avoided me after that, though it might have been my imagination. But I was privy to her dirty little secret, and we all guarded ourselves here, pretending we were tough soldiers, pretending we were just fine. We were all so used to academic success. Most had been at the top of their college classes. For their whole lives, their identities and self-esteem were grounded in their braininess, their ability to master whatever course work was thrown at them. We judged ourselves by our grades.

Howard had hurt my feelings, but if I hadn't stumbled upon that exclusive review session, I might never have known that I wasn't so alone as I felt. I wondered how he treated these students who were on the verge of failure. Did he heap his scorn on them, call them fourth-graders? Or was that ridicule reserved for me? Of course, I never asked. Etiquette proscribed it. We would not mention the unmentionable.

Horses are said to have five hearts, meaning that their four legs are as crucial as the muscle pumping blood through their body. They are heavy, big-bodied animals; their legs are fine and complex and make them vulnerable in the extreme. So when Anatomy turned to the equine limb, I was properly convinced that the material was complicated and critical. Mastery was essential, but gross lab sometimes seemed designed to frustrate rather than facilitate that mastery.

We dissected in alphabetically assigned groups of four, and I was on a team with three men who seemed comfortable with a pace that, for me, was too fast. Fear made me feel I must study each layer of tissue again and again and test myself until my knowledge was perfect and my recall instant and easy. When

Barry or Dale or Adam would say, "Okay, everybody got it?" and the other men would nod, and we would cut away the muscle, veins, arteries, and nerves to expose the next layer, I was silent, though I never felt I had "gotten it," not well enough. I hadn't taken it to my heart and made it mine. And there was no going back. When the tissue was gone, it was gone. Diagrams and photographs in the text were a poor substitute for the actual animal.

All specimens were stored in the cooler, of course, when we weren't working on them, each guarded by a hand-lettered sign: TOUCH MY LEG AND DIE. HANDS OFF!!!—THIS MEANS *YOU*. ONLY FOR DISSECTION GROUP 12. The specimens were as precious as anything we owned.

Our work on the equine was from the ground up. The hoof itself consists of three layers of wall: stratum externum (a.k.a. stratum tectorium), stratum medium, and stratum internum (a.k.a. stratum lamellatum). This wall encased connective tissue, corium (dermis), digital cushion, distal or third phalax (coffin bone), most of the lateral (collateral) cartilages of the distal phalanx, distal interphalangeal (coffin) joint, distal extremity of the middle phalanx (short pastern bone), navicular bone, bursa podotrochlearis (navicular bursa), several ligaments, tendons of insertion of the common digital extensor and deep digital flexor muscles, and the attendant blood vessels and nerves.

One of the Anatomy instructors, Debbie Sanford, was only six years beyond her own freshman year, and she was sympathetic to my terror. One afternoon, she said that she had two equine limbs to prepare for a demonstration and she'd be coming to the lab the next morning at four-thirty to dissect them. If I'd like to assist her, she'd be happy for the company.

I often worked in the cube or the lab until late at night, but it was strange to *arrive* in the black silence of 4:00 A.M. Empty of students, the gross lab was cavernous. What had become routine—walking into a cooler full of stiffened dogs, past a row of hanging cows, horses, burros, and llamas—was suddenly eerie again. The defenses of reason relaxed by sleep, the imagination jumps at the shadows. It's your own mortality, the monster under the bed, that rises up and looks at you through the glazed and clouded eyeballs of the dead. Debbie felt it, too. Whistling past the graveyard, we laughed at our uneasiness—what girls we were underneath the grown-up scientist veneer!

But once the lights were on and we had our specimens on the table, once the big metal cooler door was shut on its horrors, we relaxed. Day and night were the same in the windowless lab. The work drew our attention and the grogginess of sleep disappeared.

Debbie worked carefully and methodically through the layers of skin and muscle, taking time to point out blood vessels and nerves, letting me test myself against her knowledge. A gentle tutor, she answered my questions patiently. As we worked, we traded little bits of our personal lives, as well. She talked about her husband; I talked about my broken relationship with Wes. Two hours passed quickly, and at 6:30, Professor Howard walked in.

Reactive as a rabbit, I tensed. But, like a rabbit caught in the glare of headlights, I had nowhere to run. His footsteps were loud as he crossed the floor toward us. The coach inside chided me and told me to relax: At last, he'll see you as a serious student; he'll notice the extra effort you're making. I smiled tentatively.

He ignored Debbie. "What are you doing here?" he demanded.

"I asked Loretta to help me," Debbie said, but he cut her off, and I saw that his brusqueness was not reserved for me.

"That's ridiculous. She slows you down, and you need to get this done." His tone did not invite discussion.

To me, he said, "If you're so eager to dissect a leg, you have one in the locker. Work on it."

"Yes, sir," I said. I thanked Debbie for her help and walked past Howard out of the lab. My lab partners wouldn't appreciate my hacking on our specimen by myself. I crossed the lawn to Lory Student Center to wait for the day to begin. I felt rotten, but I didn't feel a bit like crying. I guess I was toughening up.

A relief from the memorization and ID work that comprised much of the term was a paper assignment in immunology, one of the units in Agents. I went back to my notes to double-check Professor Kearns's directive: "Topic—your choice."

Leaving the anatomy building and driving the two miles from main campus to the vet school library, which is housed in the Veterinary Teaching Hospital (VTH), reminded me that there *was* a future and that someday I'd be out of the classroom and into the clinic. The relaxed atmosphere in the one-room library also promised that life would get better. Students were talking in normal voices. Occasionally, someone laughed.

I had no ideas for this paper, so I browsed, reading the spines of the shelved books, until I happened on a big wooden book-case filled with issues of the *American Journal of Veterinary Research*. I took several issues to a study carrel and began to flip through them. Almost immediately, I found an article of real interest to me, a comparison of the effectiveness of oral versus injectable ivermectin as a means of worming horses. When I'd teched for Jill, she had used the injectable form with no problem, but it had since been pulled from the market because of adverse reactions, including bacterial infection at the injection site.

The article was informative and well documented; it mentioned an occasional anaphylactic reaction to the injectable form. This reaction could cause violent seizures and even death. The bacteria associated with site infection was a clostridium, and all I really knew about it was that it was serious trouble.

Suddenly, and for the first time, I found myself looking forward, beyond Christmas break, to the next semester and the unit on bacteriology. This seemingly random deluge of facts called first semester, which seemed as tangled and hopeless as a skein of knotted yarn, was going to straighten out and be knit into something clean and useful. I had only to trust and keep slogging and it would someday make sense. I saw a brief but very bright light far, far down the tunnel.

I found the sources listed in the article, photocopied the pertinent pages, and drove home, energized, almost euphoric.

Lloyd was still out, which meant I could break house rules and let a cat in for the night. Sister, the cantankerous tortoise-shell, darted in the door, and I conveniently ignored her until we were tucked in bed. Cuddled with my stowaway, I read up on ivermectin.

The next night, I wrote the paper, understanding all of it and feeling, for once, on top of things. It was the final task in the immunology unit, and I dropped it at Dr. Kearns's office the following morning with a sense of well-being and completion.

A week later, the paper grades were posted. As always, a crowd formed around the bulletin board, and I lined up for my turn. My Social Security number—by which grades were always posted—was near the bottom of the sheet, with those of the other New Mexicans. I scanned the page, checking the class effort as a whole. We'd done a good job; most scores were in the 80s or 90s. But one grade stood out, and it was mine—12 percent. I held a notebook under the line to be sure I was reading straight across. Twelve percent of the possible 40 points meant that my paper had earned 4.8. Five points? That was unbelievable. That was ridiculous.

The coach started coaching hard and fast: Okay, there's obviously been a mistake. Maybe it wasn't as good a paper as you thought, but it wasn't a 12 percent paper, not by any nightmare reckoning. It's a clerical error. The paper was clear, well documented, to the point, and interesting. He wrote down the wrong number, that's all.

There wasn't time to go to Kearns's office; the neurology lecture began in five minutes. Stunned and trying not to be, I went into 108 and sat down. Jimmy Fulmer turned in his seat. "How'd you do on the immunology paper?"

"Oh, are they posted already?" I lied.

"Yeah, they're posted." Something in his tone made me wonder whether he'd seen me checking the board.

"How did you do?" I asked.

He winked. "Ninety-three percent. Everybody did pretty well, I think."

And then Dr. Miller took the stage, saving me from saying more. I hoped he could save me, as well—with the energy of his lecture—from spending the entire hour reliving the writing of the damned paper and trying to remember its every point, word, and reference.

No problem. Ted Miller's neurology unit was nicknamed Kamikaze Anatomy, for he was as ardent and obsessed as a Japanese fighter pilot. He paced—or, rather, raced—the length of the platform and up and down the steps of the hall, firing questions, pausing only briefly while someone struggled for an answer, then firing at another. It was a performance as well as a lecture. He wouldn't allow anyone's attention to drift. I gladly gave myself over to it.

Too soon, however, the hour was up, and I crossed the now-brown lawn to the microbiology building and Dr. Kearns's office. I hoped he was in, and I hoped he wasn't.

It was an overcast day. The hallway was gloomy, and a sliver of light fell from his barely open doorway onto the tile floor. I tapped lightly and the door swung open.

"Yes?" He barely raised his eyes from the stack of papers on the desk in front of him. He looked so busy and focused that I was momentarily sorry to interrupt, but I reminded myself that my schedule had been interrupted, as well, because of *his* mistake.

I introduced myself and he nodded, motioned me to a chair. I slid my backpack from my shoulder and sat down. "It's about the paper," I began, but he cut me off.

"Those were pretty good," he said. "I was happy with the performance of the class as a whole, except that some idiot wrote a paper on worming horses, and it had absolutely nothing to do with immunology."

I had to admire Kearns's adroitness. He smiled. He had me against the ropes, and he knew it. I smiled back.

"Well, that explains it," I said. "I'm the idiot." I stood up. "I won't take any more of your time. I just needed to know what the problem was."

He softened in the face of my retreat. "It would have been

a good paper for the parasitology unit," he said. The man obviously lacked Professor Howard's killer instinct.

I was stinging with embarrassment. I *was* an idiot, an idiot with a fourth-grade mentality.

I walked back down the dreary hallway, pushed open the door, and stepped outside. The low clouds promised snow. It was turning nasty.

CHAPTER 4

The First of the Critters—Blacknose

THE pens adjacent to the gross lab were temporary quarters for animals to be euthanized for study. Rabbits, goats, and hundreds of dogs rotated through this facility. A couple of llamas were housed here, destined to be used as models for drawings for a textbook of llama anatomy. Layer after layer would be stripped from their bodies as the artist/author sketched muscle groups, vascular patterns, and organ arrangements. Sometimes the pens held chickens, and the lab would be filled with the sound of their clucking. Then they, too, would be gone. Once delivered to the anatomy building, these sacrificial lambs did not live long. But two endured: Flicka and Blacknose.

Naturally, Flicka was a horse, a sorrel quarter horse, the generic red working horse of the American West, common as dirt. She had been donated to the vet school because of a sarcoid on her leg. The growth did not compromise her movement, but it was ugly, and there was no premium on red horses like her. Because of her good temperament, her life was spared and she was not used for baby surgeons to practice on. Instead, she was used to teach first-year vet students to feel muscle groups, to hear chest sounds, to locate organs, veins, arteries, and nerves in the living horse, and to teach the novices among us how to pick up horses' feet, open their mouths, put on their halters, lead them, and how to behave and move without causing them to startle.

Blacknose was a greyhound. Like all her ancient breed, she was lean and elegant, her Egyptian ancestry evident in every long, graceful line of her body. She looked, quite simply, like a hieroglyphic. This splendid animal was here to teach us the anatomy of the normal, healthy, living canine.

I suspect that, more important, she was kept simply to *be*, to be alive, to relieve us of the relentless procession of dead animals that made up gross anatomy lab, to stand as proof that we didn't kill every single creature that passed through our doors, to remind us that our work was about life. She was there, in part, to help us keep our hearts from calcifying.

She was a brindle and, like Flicka, possessed a sweet nature and an eagerness to please that had saved her when lab coordinator Jake Wilder had had to choose just one dog to live. She was full of something that the International Committee on Veterinary Anatomical Nomenclature had failed to label, a property called "heart" in the common tongue.

Heart is common to storybook racehorses, a bit of soul that makes them run even in great pain and sometimes makes them win against better horses. It's a quality that compensates for mere physical liabilities. I've seen horses with heart, horses that ran with their knees full of bone chips, horses that ran with blood flowing from their nostrils, horses that ran unto the death. Animals with heart will do that, ignore their pain and give their all, but the winning is mostly in the storybooks.

And so it was with Blacknose—heart aplenty but not a winner on the track. She was fast as Pancho Villa's horse, but she wasn't fast enough, not even close. If she had been, she wouldn't have been here, living in a cinder-block cell off the gross anatomy lab. She would have been racing still, or bearing litter after litter of pups, from which the fastest would be kept for a short life of racing or a longer life of breeding, and the slower ones culled for dissection at a veterinary college or experimentation at a drug company or medical school.

The inherent elitism in this animal world where the imperfect are expendable is antithetical to human medicine—at least in theory. But here before us every day was living—and dead—evidence of a variation on Darwin's law: the survival of the fleetest.

So Blacknose was a slow greyhound. Except there's no such thing, and taking her out for her daily air and exercise was a challenge for her handlers, freshman vet students. Early in the term, one of my classmates had thought he had the solution: riding Flicka and ponying—or leading—Blacknose on a longe line. Dog, horse, and man were happy, but word got back to Dr. Howard, who made it clear that he would not tolerate this foolhardy invitation to disaster.

My turn came on a warm Indian summer afternoon. As soon as we left the building, Blacknose strained at the length of the line and begged to run. Her feet clawed the ground as she fought for freedom. I walked faster, to no effect. She pulled as hard as ever. I jogged, to no effect. I ran, for the short bursts I could manage, and still she strained for more, keeping the line taut between us.

Greyhounds are larger than I had thought, and all of their body is muscle (their low fat ratio, I would learn, makes them difficult to anesthetize and slow to recover from anesthesia). Her power, low to the ground and focused in a way that people rarely focus, drove her like the single-minded force of nature that she truly was. She was strong and greedy for movement; she was pure appetite.

Awkward and clumsy, I leaned back against her strength. It is not easy to contain an animal that wants to be free, and she seemed to me as cruelly bound as a caged bird, constricted to tiny hops. She was bred by humankind for the one thing she was now not allowed to do. She didn't need language to tell me that what she felt was pain.

The anatomy building is on the southwestern part of the large campus, where foot traffic is light and the lawns are as big as parks. I knew that some students—maybe most of them—let Blacknose off the line, although of course it was against the rules. She came back when called, everybody said.

I quickly tired of her relentless pulling and of her frustration and unhappiness, too. I stopped and called her name. She trotted back, as if she knew freedom was at hand. I gripped her collar and spoke seriously to her. I could understand something of her language and maybe she could understand something of mine. "You have to come when I call you, Blacknose. You have to. Promise me you will." I read a promise in her eyes. "And stay on campus—no crossing streets." We were pretty far from city streets and highways, but "far" for me was but a little distance for this dog.

Still, I had decided. I opened my hand and let go of her collar. "Okay," I said. She stood stock-still for only an instant, then bolted, as if from a starting gate.

I watched as she broadened the distance between us. I feared she was gone for good, but fifty yards away, she began to circle, governed even in her freedom by her obedient nature. She flew over the field and I turned in a circle to watch her pure beauty. I watched long after I'd begun to feel the chill of late afternoon. Finally, however, I had to call her in, for I had work to do, and minutes got precious when the day waned.

I saw that she heard my voice by the tilt of her long head and the slight slackening of her gait. She ran a bit longer before pulling up and trotting to me, her instinct to run subdued by her also-bred-in-the-bone instinct to obey.

I slipped the catch of the lead through the ring on her collar and patted her head. She was panting hard, out of shape, for she couldn't maintain athletic fitness in just one short outing a day. Her pink tongue lolled from her mouth. The skin bunched and crinkled at the corners of her mouth and around her eyes, as if she were smiling. Perhaps she was.

We walked for a while, until she'd cooled, and then I took her home to her cinder-block and chain-link pen. The adjacent pen was full of greyhounds just like her except they'd be euthanized the next day and turned into specimens. I fed them all, scooped up their feces, and hosed down the concrete floor. As I left for the evening, I stopped one last time to reach over the wall and pat Blacknose's pretty head. I put aside the complications and contradictions inherent in this schooling and in this strange profession. For now, I would be the best friend I could to this one dog and try not to think about the others.

A month or so later, I was studying late in the cubes when Jimmy Fulmer came in and said that Blacknose was missing. That afternoon, like most days, her student handler had let her off the lead, and this time she had run and run and not stopped running, into the gathering night. The voice of her genetic engineering had outshouted the voice of her keeper.

I closed my book, my finger marking the place, and thought about Blacknose flying into the distance and that coming night, away from here, away from her cinder-block cage, away from the stench of formaldehyde, away from the constant prodding of freshman fingers, away from the rules and rigors of vet school, and into a world where reality was her flying legs and the ground disappearing beneath her.

Off and on that night, I put down my book and imagined, dreamily, that I, too, could stretch and run and never stop. I became Blacknose—able to run forever, never hungry, never thirsty, never feeling the bitter Rocky Mountain cold in my bones. I knew that neither she nor I could run forever, but maybe she could find a home, someone to run with her and love her, and a warm bed.

That fantasy—as well as the fears of what actually does happen to lost, runaway, and homeless dogs—was laid to rest next morning when Dr. Miller announced that Blacknose had been picked up by Fort Collins Animal Control. A cheer went up. Our dog was found.

How strange that we should care for her, when potential replacements, just as satisfactory, were delivered weekly to our back door, when it was just a random circumstance that she lived while others died. But we *did* care. She was our dog and we were glad that she was safe and that she'd soon be home with us, grateful that she wasn't hit by a car, or hungry, or frostbitten, or poisoned, or shot, or any of the horrible things that could have been.

Dr. Miller said she'd been picked up quite a ways from campus, out where Shields Avenue is nothing but country, because she "apparently got away from her handler." He waited until we stopped laughing and then said that from that day forward, *no one* was to let her off her lead, at all, under any circumstances, period. The "or else" was implicit.

And so her moments of liberty were over. They were only small moments, anyway, we told ourselves. It was insignificant, really, in the context of school and our lives. It was a very small thing that we would soon forget, for she was, after all, alive, even if she would never again run free. Never again, or at least until next fall, when the new freshman class would take over the gross lab and its chores. They would be green and frisky, just like us. And just like us, they might be inclined to break the rules.

CHAPTER 5

Contradictions

IN late September, the class had been summoned from gross lab in groups of twenty and sworn to the honor code, which had been instituted at CSU in 1907. Since we had all been operating under an honor system instituted by our mothers as soon as we were old enough to know right from wrong, it wasn't exactly news that we were expected to do our own work. The formality and solemnity of this indoctrination made it seem like some kind of initiation ritual, however.

Lloyd was one of the two junior class members of the honor board who led the session. He leaned back in his chair, balanced on two legs against the wall, and watched while Carl Ulrich, a good-looking cowboy, roamed the room and quizzed us.

"What does the honor code mean to you?" he asked the first student.

"That we shouldn't cheat on exams?"

Carl nodded thoughtfully, then moved on. "And you? What do you think?"

"It's a code of ethics that the veterinary profession has adopted."

"What're ethics?" Carl shot back at him.

"Ethics are the laws of conscience that govern a society." Ah, I thought, a gunner, one of those overachievers who had claimed the front row of the lecture hall and already begun to distinguish themselves by asking esoteric questions only peripherally related to the topic at hand.

Carl seemed underimpressed. "Okay," he said. He was no doubt acquainted with gunner types, for every class has them. He asked a few more of us, and we gave pretty answers couched in solemn, formal terms.

Carl dismissed our grand guesses and gave us his straight, unadorned definition. "We don't lie, we don't cheat, we don't steal, and we don't tolerate it in our colleagues."

His face was serious, with the enormous solemnity of a Norman Rockwell Boy Scout. We were solemn right back at him. I fought the impulse to giggle. I felt silly, slightly embarrassed, as if we had been called in to swear that we loved our mothers or something.

Lloyd broke the intensity of the moment. "It's easy to sit here and agree to live by the code, but I'm here to tell you that when push comes to shove, and you're flunking a course, and you haven't studied for the test you're about to sit, then it's not too hard to rationalize getting a little help from one of your friends. People change when they're pushed into a corner, and this place is going to push you into that corner."

He paused for a dramatic effect I didn't really need. I'd caught a glimpse of that corner already.

"But I want you to know that you can come to us and we'll do what we can to help you get through it without compromising your character. I know what I'm talking about. I've flunked tests before. I've gotten D's. But they're going to call me Dr. Worthen, anyway."

There was that line again. I admired him for telling his dirty little secret. I was glad he was my friend and roommate. I'd gotten lucky when I met Lloyd.

This swearing to the honor code was the extent of our guidance freshman year in matters of morals. Sophomore year, we would get a formal, credit-bearing study of veterinary ethics, but for now we were on our own, relying on whatever values we had, whatever relationship we had already formed with God or the force of the universe—or whatever name you had for it—to see us through this year and ease us bit by bit into the full horrors of our education.

We would not yet be called upon to kill. Our dissection specimens would be quite dead and well pickled before we lifted our hands against them. Our participation this term would be limited to those dissections and the rotating chores of feeding and cleaning up after the doomed animals until Jake Wilder could attach them to the lines that would drain their blood, fill their veins and arteries with chemicals, and reduce them to mere samples of bone, brain, muscle, and nerve. Thus we would build the calluses on our hearts as gradually as we built our knowledge and skill.

We were tough soldiers, though, and we knew what we'd signed on for. We had all studied biology as undergraduates, of course, and we'd all dissected frogs, and most of us had also cut up a cat and a fetal pig. Moreover, most of us were hunters, fishermen, and carnivores. We were not the squeamish sisters of the world. We were realists, pragmatists, scientists.

I was surprised, then, at how uncomfortable I felt standing at the stainless-steel dissection table, waiting for Jake to deliver our first specimen. This was to be a quick and dirty job, as much an introduction to our instruments, our lab partners, and the art of dissection itself as it was to the anatomy of the cat.

We waited in our pristine green lab coats as Jake wheeled a fifty-five-gallon drum into the lab and pried off its lid. The bitter aroma of formaldehyde curled out into the air and spread through the room. I held my breath as he fished a stiffened cat from the drum and set it before us.

These cats had not been prepared here but had been purchased from a commercial specimen company. They were stiffened into a variety of contortions that spoke to the volume of animals processed. It was as if they had been tossed willy-nilly into the vat, and, floating and sinking, crammed together in the preservative, they had assumed these shapes that were caricatures of life. The limbs were stretched as though jumping and bent as though scratching. The heads were tilted to one side or other, or turned as if the cat had heard a noise behind it or looked up from licking its back—except they were so stiff and horribly dead. Their coats were wet, clumped, and spiky.

Our cat was a gray tabby.

I pushed from my mind images of the diabolical processing plant where her life had ended. It was a cat no longer, just a learning tool and nothing more.

Dale Grant turned her over and made a long abdominal incision. We spread apart the pickled, leathery skin and began.

The canine specimens were, for the most part, uniform. Greyhounds like Blacknose, most were brindled; some were black, others white. Killed on the premises, they were fixed in identical poses, the four legs straight out, the head centered on the spine, as though manufactured. It was a comfortable illusion but one we could not sustain, for, just as we cared for Flicka and Blacknose, we would each take our turn caring for the dozen or so dogs that were delivered weekly during the racing season from a track called Cloverleaf, just south of town on I-25. There was no luck for them in the four-leaf clover. Running for their lives, they, like Blacknose, were just not fast enough.

They were the canine equivalents of the hundreds of young basketball and football players shunted through U.S. colleges, trained only to play, and then culled from the NBA or NFL drafts, or, after training camp, returned to the streets, untrained for anything except their sport, and not wanted there. Except we *kill* the dogs that can't make the pros.

The routine for handling this steady stream of dogs was for a pickup truck with a camper shell to pull up to the back door of the lab. A student would unload the dogs into the pen next to Blacknose, where they stayed until Jake had a chance to euthanize them. If he was delayed, the student would feed and clean up after them. They didn't go out for exercise. Their tenure would be short.

You reminded yourself that they weren't killed *because* of us. Vet school or no, they were destined for destruction. The morality of that was beyond consideration; the situation was a given. You could hate it, but you couldn't change it. So you slipped it into a compartment of the brain where you never entered, where you kept the monster under the bed, your own death, and the end of the world. If you were smart, you left it alone.

The smaller question was how to treat these animals that were just passing through. Humanely, of course, kindly. But did you talk to them, pat their heads, scratch their ears, and open yourself to extra pain? Or did you deal with them as mechanically as possible? You didn't actually pose the question, but it arose, and you answered from the gut without deliberation.

It was my turn. Jake told me not to feed the dogs when they arrived. He was running a bit behind schedule, but he'd process them before he left for the day. So I signed the delivery slip, led the dogs two at a time into the pen, shut the gate, and shot the bolt, quick and efficient as a robot. As I turned to go, however, I looked for just a moment into their twelve upturned and expectant, frightened, and hungry faces. And I was doomed. I went back into the pen.

One by one, I removed their muzzles. I filled the bowls with dog food. I called them good dogs and praised them. I touched their heads and ran my hand down their long, warm backs. Their long greyhound tails whipped back and forth, and they ate their last supper.

Jake came for them before they were finished, and he looked at me, at the feeding dogs, and then at me again. I was silent and so was he. I could imagine what he would say; he could imagine my answer.

"I'll get to them later," he said finally. "Want to go get a beer?"

"Yeah," I said. "I do."

"I thought you might."

We walked to the pub in the student center, sat down, and ordered our beers. I waited for my chewing-out; it didn't come. We talked about a lot of things, but not about the dogs and my disobedience.

Jake Wilder was my idea of what a vet should be—although he wasn't one—and what a teacher should be, too. He's bright, with both academic savvy and common sense. Officially, he was the laboratory coordinator, but he was tutor, friend, and mentor, as well, to any freshman who needed his help.

He would stay into the evening if you needed help, sitting on one side of the double-headed microscope and coaching you through the histopathologic study of tissue, scanning slides for specific cell types, making certain you could identify the traits of different tissues and distinguish among them—hepatocytes, adipocytes, connective tissue. He taught you how to take a test, what to look for, how to think through and understand the tissues—the difference between smooth and striated muscle fibers, for example—based on their function and microscopic anatomy, how to think backward: Why would things be arranged this way? Why did this make sense?

He handled the doomed animals in the same quiet, calming way he handled freshman students. He'd started as a lab assistant in 1980 and had been working ever since to find ways to reduce the number of animal specimens needed in Gross Anatomy. But you needn't know this to know he's a good man. His ethics are apparent in the sure quickness of his hands.

He was studying for a Ph.D. in Anatomy, and I'd heard the rumor that he had once applied to CSU vet school and been rejected. If that was true, it proved that the admissions committee sometimes makes big mistakes.

We talked like any two friends having a beer and passing the time. He told me how much he liked teaching, though that was already obvious to me.

"Every year," he said, "I get a whole new herd of bright young people. They're excited and they're eager and they're smart. Some of 'em, I just fall in love with." He grinned. "Well, maybe not 'in love,' but we get to be friends. It's a kick. I'm happy."

He paused, as if he was thinking it over, and then he smiled. "Oh, there're always a few who don't know jack shit, but they catch on after a while. Or else they're outta here."

I would remember Jake's comment in May when I arrived at his place in Poudre Canyon for the end-of-year party.

The log house that he and his wife, Sarah, had built on a bend in the river was big and beautiful. A band was tuning up in the garage. Some folks were playing volleyball in the yard near the house; others were playing softball in the field beyond. A pig was roasting in a pit at the river's edge. Everywhere there were students and faculty and their friends and spouses, talking, laughing, having a good time.

In the middle of it all was Jake, beer in hand, a grin on his handsome face. He wore a white T-shirt. Across his chest in black letters, it read, I KNOW JACK SHIT.

He does know jack shit, and bullshit, and dog shit, and shit work, too. He's the kind of man who doesn't value academic prowess above other kinds of intelligence, the kind who doesn't shrink from hard and dirty work, the kind of man who we, as a class, took to.

We did *not* take to Professor Kearns and his unit on immunology. Personality and style could mark a man, and Kearns was too neat, too particular, too *prim*. He began his unit with ancient history, the work of Louis Pasteur. The class was amused—and not amused.

The new—and the terror—was beginning to wear off this professional-school business, and we came to Kearns freshly annoyed and getting angry at the mounds of extraneous minutia that accompanied every unit of study. The pace was picking up, and we were too busy and too overwhelmed for the pursuit of pure knowledge.

An ugly mood was in the air.

One morning, Kearns's lecture was beginning to run over into our ten-minute break. We began to check our watches, rustle our papers, close our books, and grumble to one another. Suddenly, Josh Dabney stood up and announced loudly, "That's just about enough of this bullshit." He snapped his notebook shut and walked out.

We all turned to watch Josh's exit. The room was quiet.

Kearns, too, was silent until the door closed behind Josh, then he checked his watch, apologized for running over, and dismissed the class. His apparent embarrassment gave us just a taste of blood. Next chance we got, we went for the throat.

Previous freshman classes had had a live demonstration of the effects of anaphylaxis, but Kearns had videotaped the demonstration so that, starting this year, there would be no need to subject animals again to this suffering.

We sat in the darkened lecture hall and watched the tape. Kearns had injected two guinea pigs with an antigen to which they had previously been sensitized. For a few minutes, both pigs writhed in allergic shock, until Kearns injected one of them with epinephrine, which almost instantly counteracted the bronchial constriction and vasodilation. The pig scampered to its feet and regarded the camera with its round, shining eyes. Then, to our shock and dismay, it began to nuzzle the second pig.

For what seemed an eternity, the dying guinea pig twitched, gasped, and arched in convulsive pain. And through those long moments, the first guinea pig stayed at its side, touching, nuzzling, offering entreaty, encouragement, and comfort—if you are willing to ascribe those qualities to a rodent.

We were meant to be scientists, to observe, detach, and study. This was a rodent, a laboratory animal. And this was merely a videotape. We had accepted animal expendability as a nasty and constant fact of life, and particularly of life in vet school. We had tacitly agreed that emotion had no place here and we were prepared for physical suffering.

This caught us by surprise, however. Scientific detachment didn't quite cover the apparent psychic distress of the recovered guinea pig. Its tender response to the suffering of its mate poked through the calluses we were building around our hearts. The class groaned at the Disneyesque turn the video had taken.

I was confused by my feelings and the response of the class. I hadn't enjoyed watching the tape, yet it seemed wrong to flinch from it. Wrong, not only morally (for turning our heads did not make the suffering go away) but also developmentally, for surely it was part of our training that we should face the facts of animal pain and death and thus harden ourselves to accept those facts. Certainly, we all knew, this was not as bad as it was going to get, not by any stretch, not by half.

The next day, a petition circulated, condemning the tape and demanding that it not be shown again. The petition, I thought, must surely mark us as freshmen, as the babies of the school. It must seem like a tantrum to Kearns and the administration. Our class must seem to them like a puppy bucking and twisting at the end of a leash, fighting the inevitable, refusing to go where it was being led.

Within a few days, however, Kearns capitulated and through tightened lips announced that the tape would be withdrawn. A smattering of applause ran through the room, but surely it was a hollow victory, for now another tape had to be made in which the salvaged and doomed guinea pigs would be separated. No doubt this new tape would be easier and less distracting to watch, but the point of the protest obviously was not to spare the animals.

Rather, it seemed to be to spare future *students* the distress of watching the bonded rodents, to spare the students the discomfort of having their emotions tugged when they were working to dispense with feeling altogether. More honestly, perhaps, it had nothing at all to do with future students. Perhaps it was merely a protest of our own discomfort and conflict, our way of saying that we were disturbed by this nasty distraction, this sympathetic engagement with a guinea pig.

This was an early skirmish in the war between feeling and reason, a war that would rage all through vet school and on into the practice of veterinary medicine. The tide of the battle would turn first one way and then back the other, neither side ever vanquished. My life, my mind, had become the battleground.

CHAPTER 6

The She-Wolf of Douglas Road

THE pressures of school—the ones that backed you toward that corner Lloyd had referred to—could put a strange spin on a friendship, especially when you factored in the early hard winter of northern Colorado.

One early October Friday afternoon, the sky fell dark and low, a few dozen feet above the earth. The temperature had been dropping steadily all day, and by the time I got home, things were starting to freeze. It was snowing in the foothills; all was darkness in that direction. As the day ended, it seemed the storm itself was choking the daylight and killing it dead.

Lloyd and Jennifer were still at the hospital, and I scurried around the yard, gathering scraps of wood to feed the big potbellied stove in the living room, next to my study table. We had no woodpile, for Lloyd was certain that the scrap wood littering his five acres would keep us warm for a good long while. I wasn't so sure.

I filled my arms with broken slats, pieces of two-by-four, and busted-up wooden chairs, kicked open the back door, and crossed the kitchen to drop the light and brittle load by the old cast-iron stove. I had an Anatomy exam on Monday, and I wanted to get settled in and cozy for a long weekend of study.

This scrap wood—or *crap* wood—wouldn't burn long; I'd need a lot to get through the next two days.

On my third trip, I heard the phone. I sprinted across the yard, dropped my load of slats and twigs outside the back door, raced inside, and grabbed the phone mid-ring.

"I was about to give up on you." It was Dalton.

"I was getting some wood in. Storm's going to hit soon."

"That's why I'm calling." She paused, and that pause sounded like bad news. "I'm supposed to be house-sitting up in Rist Canyon this weekend. It's a nice cabin, with a fireplace and lots of food and good whiskey. Just a few chickens, a couple of horses and dogs to take care of."

"Uh-huh," I said. What's all this got to do with me? I thought. I was afraid I was starting to figure it out.

"They were supposed to leave me a four-wheel drive to get up there, but I can't get ahold of the guy who has it, and with this storm comin' in, I've got to get up that canyon before dark. And I was thinking that we could make it in Blue. You've got chains, don't you? We'd have a hell of a good time." She hurried through this all in a piece.

"Dalton, I've got to study. That Anatomy exam . . ." My voice trailed off.

"We'll study together, I promise. Not too much fun. Retta, please, I don't know what else to do."

"Could you try the guy with the four-wheel drive again?"

She sighed. "I'll try, but we're running out of daylight."

I noticed the *we*. It sounded like a done deal. In a couple of minutes, Dalton called back, and a done deal it was.

I gathered a few things and wrote a note for Lloyd. I tossed my books and bag into the cab of the truck and felt under the seat for the canvas sack that held the tire chains. I turned my collar up and the key to the right. The old engine rumbled and took, backfiring once. A puff of blue smoke hung in the air behind me as I pulled out of the drive.

Snow always made Dalton giddy, and she was waiting outside for me. Talking loudly and moving fast, she opened the door and tossed her bag onto the floorboard. Her Australian shepherd, Tag, climbed eager and panting onto the seat beside me.

Dalton climbed in, slammed the door, and turned and flashed me the naughty grin of a wicked child. There was nothing for it but to give myself over to the adventure.

We picked up a six-pack of Coors at a drive-up liquor store in Laporte and drove off into the mouth of the storm.

Old Blue pulled hard into the wind that ripped down the canyon. We met a few cars, coming slowly, lights on, going into town, but no one else was headed up the mountain. The snow—big flakes coming straight at us—was beginning to stick to the highway, but we didn't stop to put on the chains. We were having too much fun, sealed together, intrepid voyagers, made brave by the storm, the beer, and the weekend.

When we pulled off the highway and onto the unpaved mountain road toward the cabin, however, we knew the gig was up—we couldn't go much farther without chains. We laid them out in front of each tire and I drove slowly forward. Blue slid to the right and missed the mark. We tried again and got one. Another attempt and we got the job done, but we were wet now from lying on our backs, groping around to hook the chains. The temperature was bitter and dropping fast. The high canyon walls blocked the last of the day's light. The falling snow had thinned a bit, and high above us, the sky held only a faint tinge of pink. With the storm and the cloud cover clearing, the night would be crackling cold.

We plowed through deep powder for about five miles until Dalton spotted the place back through the trees. There was the hint of a driveway in the solid whiteness of the snow, but it was downhill to the house—and uphill going out—so we left Blue parked on the road.

The horses' tails, whiskers, and lashes were glazed with ice. Their water—and the outside faucets—were frozen solid. We found two buckets and began the trek from the bathroom to the horse trough, again and again, and replaced the frozen watering dispenser in the chicken coop with pans of fresh water. The dogs of the homestead hung on our heels as we worked. I was sobering to the misery of what seemed a deep winter night. It was pitch-dark when we finished.

The porch was stacked with dry cedar and piñon and we soon had a fire going in the Franklin stove. We poured ourselves shots of Jim Beam, toasted our well-done chores, and agreed that we'd earned this one night away from the books.

In the last few weeks, Dalton and I had begun to find that common ground of real friendship, and we relaxed together, feet stretched toward the fire, Tag between us, and talked about our professors and classmates, our families, our past lives and our futures. I told her about Wes and Alan and a few others I'd run with and been hurt by. She told me about a time or two when her heart had gotten stomped on. We talked into the night, until the fire was low and the bottle dry.

Morning came hard and early, finding us hungover and cold. While we slept, after the fire had turned to cold ashes, the inside pipes had also frozen solid. A lot of snow makes a little water, and it took a big chunk of the morning to melt and carry enough for twenty chickens, three dogs, and two big horses. The glare off the snow burned an ache right into my eyeballs.

We opened our books in the early afternoon and Dalton began to quiz me for the upcoming test. I whimpered. I was tired. I felt sick. I wanted to be alone. We retired to opposite corners and tried to work. Before long, it was time again to haul water, though our constant roaring fire had by then thawed the indoor plumbing.

We ate, studied, and slept. Sunday morning, we were a little stronger than the morning before, but as the day slipped toward evening, I slipped toward panic. The Anatomy test was at 8:00 A.M., and my brain still felt packed with cotton.

Monday morning we fed and watered the animals in the bitter-cold darkness. It was 6:00 A.M. when we hiked up to the road where we'd left the truck sixty hours before. We stowed our gear, scraped the windows, and climbed into the cab. I turned the key. Nothing. Not a sound. Silent as the snow that entombed us. Dead.

About thirty yards beyond, the road took a downhill turn for what looked like a promising distance. If we could just push Blue to the edge of that hill, we could get rolling and have a chance to pop the clutch and start the engine.

Dalton went around to the tailgate and I leaned into the door frame. On the count of three, we pushed with all our weight and strength. There was just the slightest give. We tried again. We heaved and pushed and groaned, but the snow was deep and Blue was an old truck and heavily made.

Breathing hard, we leaned together against Blue. I could feel sweat running down my back, under the layers of long johns, flannel shirt, sweater, and down vest. We listened for traffic. All was still. About a quarter-mile away, smoke rose from a barely visible chimney on a snow-packed roof. We were short of options and running out of time.

Followed by the three dogs and breaking her own trail, Dalton went for help. I watched her disappear into the pines and wished I'd gone with her. It was so still in the snow-hushed canyon. I could almost feel the minutes passing. It seemed like a long time before I saw her coming back through the trees.

The neighbors would help us, she said, when they finished breakfast. We sat and waited. There was nothing more to say.

Finally, the fellow arrived in his Land Rover. Neither of us had jumper cables, but he said he could push us to the crest of the hill. I stayed behind the wheel and Dalton got out to check the bumper-to-bumper alignment. It was a good fit and the Land Rover dug in, a steady slow push to the crest. Blue and I took off under the power of gravity. I heard a honk and looked in the rear-view mirror, to see the neighbor wave and turn back toward home. I was on my own.

It was a good long hill, but I was nervous. I would have to judge everything just right. I'd have to get going fast enough to make the pop work, but I'd have to pop it before I ran out of hill—at just the perfect moment. And I had to keep from getting stuck.

I gathered speed. Half snow-blind and mesmerized by the pure blue-white vast and silent space before me, I began to fly. The bottom of the hill was rising toward me. There was no sound, no trail, just white silence and speed, and me in the middle of it.

I took my foot off the clutch pedal, and old Blue groaned and backfired. I held my breath. The truck shuddered and coughed. I pulled out the choke. Blue sputtered. I plunged the choke lever halfway home. Blue coughed again and died.

There was still a bit of hill left, so I depressed the clutch, and we began to roll, slowly, then just a bit faster, and I popped the clutch again. Blue revived for a moment. A huge blue cloud rose behind us. I revved the engine. More noise, more oily exhaust—it was working! Powered by its own wonderful engine, Blue gathered speed.

Unaware that the road looped back around to the highway, I was looking for a place wide and safe enough to turn around. From Dalton's point of view, I was merely disappearing into the sunrise. She loped behind, yelling and cursing, but Blue's unmuffled and backfiring motor was all I could hear. The old truck was running stronger, but I was afraid to take my foot from the accelerator. Finally, I saw a place that looked solid and wide enough to attempt a turn. I eased over, and the snowpack held. I rolled down the window to look back, and then I saw Dalton, waving her arms frantically. She was shouting.

"What?" I yelled.

"Wait for me!"

She stumbled down the hill, plowing through the new snow, clumsy in her boots. Tag romped beside her. When she got to the truck, she hung on to the door handle, bent over, breathing hard for a long moment. Then she and Tag climbed in. When she caught her breath, she started cussing.

"Goddamn it to hell, don't you know shit about driving in snow? If you'd backed into that ditch, we'd be here till spring. Goddamned stupid bitch!"

"Well, I *didn't* back into the fucking ditch."

"Because I stopped you! Why in the hell wouldn't you wait for me?"

"Because the damned truck was acting up!"

"What kind of fucking idiot do you have to be to go to the fucking mountains in a fucking blizzard with a fucking worn-out battery?"

"What kind of fucking idiot do I have to be to go to the mountains in a fucking blizzard to do my fucking friend a fucking favor?"

We turned onto the highway and drove down the canyon, silent in anger. We were tired and cold, our bodies were dirty, we weren't ready for the exam that we were going to be late for, and the road was icy and treacherous. I drove too fast and dared her to say another word. She didn't. I didn't. We'd both said plenty.

We drove straight to campus, for it was after eight when we reached the city limits. There didn't seem to be a parking place within miles, so I pulled up to the front of the anatomy building and let Dalton out.

She slid from the cab and Tag followed. With her backpack slung over her shoulder, she sprinted to the door and didn't look back.

I turned into the faculty lot and pulled into a space reserved for some professor. So be it. Fuck the professor. Blue Monday, and it was every woman for herself.

The test questions hadn't looked all that good that cold, blue Monday morning. In fact, they didn't resemble anything I'd ever seen before. Instead of the uncertainty I usually felt after an exam, this time I *knew* I'd scored low—below the class average, it turned out, which was none too high to begin with. I'd gotten a parking fine and knew that before long I'd have to break into my skinny piggy bank and buy a new battery for the truck. And worst of all, the one good running buddy I'd thought I had wasn't saying much, when she bothered to speak to me at all. Somehow, it all seemed of a piece with the more mundane miseries of the winter-like weather that had settled in like arthritis, monotonous and boring, but painful, nonetheless.

I had to take an ax to the horses' water in the mornings now, break up the ice, scoop out the chunks, and haul warm water from the bathtub to refill the trough. The horses crowded me, their breath forming huge white clouds as they shoved one another aside to tear bites of hay from my arms before I could throw it into the manger.

The gray colt was long on energy these cold mornings and short on manners. Lowest in the equine pecking order, he had no one to bully but me, and I had to be careful of his heels, for he liked to spin and kick like a rodeo bronc.

I began to have a brief but vivid fantasy: that the flashing black hooves of the spinning gray colt caught the side of my head, that I fell unconscious to the ground, to wake much later in the hospital, broken but warm. I'd missed too much work to catch up, and my professors sent me home with their sympathy and affection, telling me to mend, rest, and come back next August to start fresh. I wouldn't fall behind then, I thought, if I could just get rested and warm and start over. I wouldn't let myself get so tired. I wouldn't make fourth-grade mistakes if I had a second chance.

Such was my fourth-grade fantasy, which I rehearsed and embellished every morning as I fed the horses and struggled up from the grogginess of sleep.

I hadn't gotten around to buying that new battery on the clear, brutally cold morning when the old one finally and forever died. I turned the key—one groan and nothing more. Jennifer had already left for the hospital, and I'd heard Lloyd come in sometime after two. I didn't have the heart—or the nerve—to wake him. The sun was bright on the southeastern edge of the cloudless sky and there were only scattered patches of old snow on the shoulder of the road, so I decided to ride my bike the seven miles to campus. I'd done it often that fall, and I figured I'd warm up as soon as I started pedaling. The day might even warm up, too, I thought, but I was wrong about the day.

Pedaling homeward late that afternoon, north on College Avenue toward the Wellington Highway, I was trying to beat the darkness. I hunched into a wet wind that had come up about 2:30 and now shoved my breath back down my throat. My teeth ached and my hands were numb in their cotton gloves. The moisture in the wind was rapidly turning to snow or sleet, something vicious that I squinted against.

Semitrucks on the run to Cheyenne hit their highway speed at the edge of town, and when they passed, sprays of crystal ice flew up from their wheels and peppered me like buckshot. I fought to stay upright as the draft from one after another of those eighteen-wheelers shook me like a paper doll. And then suddenly, an enormous chunk of glacial ice dislodged from under a mud flap and careened across the shoulder of the road in front of me like a giant hockey puck.

That could have killed me, I thought, and suddenly I began to cry. I wished it *had* killed me. I wished that one of those trucks would just suck me up and slam me back down on the pavement and that it would all be over. It would be so easy to let go of the handlebars, I thought, and let whatever was going to happen happen, just to quit the struggle. Or to turn the bike just a bit to the left when the next truck thundered past. As if I were standing outside myself and looking from a high distance on this scene, I felt pity, such sorrow for my poor self, as if I were somebody else.

I stopped and stood on the shoulder of the road, straddling my bike, howling and sobbing into the wind, cursing the storm and the truckers and the high Colorado terrain, cursing Elmer Howard, cursing my weakness, cursing the College of Veterinary Medicine, the whole profession, and cursing myself for wanting it so badly.

I left my bicycle by the barbed-wire fence that paralleled the road. Soon the snow would cover the bike, but I didn't particularly care whether or not it was there when I came back. I started walking, plodding along like a refugee. I'd made it a couple of miles and turned onto Douglas Road when Lloyd picked me up and took me home.

"I'm just so tired," I said.

"I know you are."

"And I'm scared."

"I know." He squeezed my shoulder with his big hand. There was nothing I could say that he didn't know. I was feeling nothing that he hadn't felt. I forgot sometimes that I wasn't alone, an anomaly, a psychotic weirdo masquerading as a student. Yet there were times when I did truly understand that we were all in this together.

A strange thing happens in the gross lab from time to time, more often than you might think, but I saw it only once, deep in the night. Sleepy students are bent over dogs that have long ago been hacked to bits or over horse legs that are now only scraps of muscle and bone. We are tired. The lights are too bright and the air is stale with formaldehyde and the faint stench of putrified flesh.

Somebody stands up, goes into the cooler, and chooses a mount, a preserved and partly dissected horse or llama, cow or burro. He hauls it into the lab itself, the dead animal hanging from giant hooks in the leathery flesh of its shoulder and hip. The student tugs it along as it swings on chains, attached to wheels that roll in the tracks in the ceiling.

We look up from our work and watch as this cowboy climbs onto a dissection table, swings a leg over, and straddles the cadaver. One by one, we, too, rise up. We grab a leg or push the dead butt of the beast until the cowboy and his mount fly around the room, faster than the Cisco Kid, brighter than Brom Bones.

Then somebody else goes into the cooler and gets another dead thing. You look into the blank and clouded eye. You look at the shrunken black lips pulled away from big yellow teeth in a grisly grin. You laugh. It's a midnight rodeo, and you beg for your turn, as if you were a kid again and this were Disneyland; as if you were—as if we all were—psychopathic maniacs in professional drag.

It happens, but only at that special time when the right side of the brain demands its own time, whether invited by sleep or not. It happens, but only when dream becomes hallucination, and hallucination becomes reality, and reality becomes a dream. You have to drive straight off the road of reason to get there, past the roadblocks and beyond the limits. It happens. It did happen. I might have thought I dreamed it, but there are photographs. It seemed so normal, almost wholesome, and comforting, too. If we were all crazy, then I was okay.

The tension, the cold, the conflict, the failures and fear of yet more failure, the crush of work, the lack of time, the fatigue, the sleeplessness, the humiliations, the frustration, the fights with faculty and friends and self—they all accrued so slowly. The strange became normal. You hardly noticed you were nuts. You dealt with everything as it arose—each exam, each storm, every doubt, the moments of self-pity and suicidal despair—and then you put it behind you and dealt with the next one.

November had been fierce, but it was almost over. December and the first round of finals were approaching. In spite of the weather, there seemed to be some thawing between me and Dalton. My grades were hovering right on the line between C and B. I'd gotten Blue a beautiful and trustworthy battery. I was still standing. It looked as if I was going to make it to Christmas break. I was okay, I thought, or at least I thought I was *going* to be.

I awoke one night right before finals, not knowing what had awakened me. I lay in the dark, listening to the silence, and I felt suddenly that my hands were wet. My face was wet, too, and I touched it with my fingers. In the dark, I rubbed my thumb across my fingertips, feeling a thick, sticky wetness. I touched my face again.

I bolted up in bed as adrenaline jolted my heart. I groped for the reading lamp beside the bed and switched it on. I stared at my hands. They were bright with blood. My chest tightened and I fought to draw a breath.

I'd seen this scene before, the most frightening moment in any horror movie, when innocence gives way to knowledge of the most sinister kind—a real and normal person discovers he's a monster.

The blood on my hands, was it the blood of my victim? Had I risen from my sleep to feed upon another creature? Had I returned from the hunt and fallen back to sleep—to my other reality—with the gore of some child or dog or rat clotting my face and my hands?

I stood up and walked slowly down the short hallway to the bathroom. I stood in the dark before the mirror, braced for the sight of my reflection in the glass, for the sight of fangs and a hairy gray muzzle where my face should be. I braced to see a monster, the she-wolf of Douglas Road.

I reached up and flipped the switch. Light banished the darkness, and there I was, my own self. Of course. No elongated muzzle, no pointed ears, no yellow eyes, no sharp incisors. Only me, but with both cheeks gouged, three furrows down each side, seeping clear serum now, the blood crusted along my jaw and into my hairline where I had wiped it.

I looked again at my bloodied hands, then back at my face, still trying to understand that I was the instrument of this destruction. I had torn open my own face. I had no memory of a dream, no memory at all. It was almost easier to believe that I was a werewolf, easier to believe that some supernatural force had taken me over and was my bitter enemy, even as it shared my body.

I splashed cold water onto my wounds, washed away the blood from my hands, blotted my face with a towel, and looked deeply into my own eyes—brown, not yellow.

"You're sick," I said, and I nodded back. "You need to get help," I said. I nodded back. "You need to talk to someone, a counselor, a psychiatrist."

I shook my head. No. I had no time for that.

Another voice inside me said the world is full of scratches, you'll heal, a couple more weeks and you'll have a vacation, you can rest then all you want, talk to Laura, she'll be your shrink, but you've got a lot of ground to cover tomorrow. Could we please just go back to bed and get some sleep?

I nodded, shut off the light, and walked back down the hall to my room, lay back down, listened for a while to Lloyd's slow, steady breathing, and put this behind me, filed away someplace in the back of my poor brain.

I closed my eyes and willed myself to sleep.

One day followed the next. Civility, grooming, meals, and sleep fell by the wayside. We grew tired, pale, and bitchy. We went to class and review sessions, huddled in our crowded cubes, found secluded corners for reading notes and catching an occasional fifteen-minute nap. We drank coffee, ate candy bars, and counted down to Wednesday, December 18, the day of the first final, Anatomy. The Agents of Disease and Anatomy lab exams would follow on Thursday and Friday.

And then, unbelievably, the first semester was over. Somehow, all 125 of us passed. We were one big step closer to being doctors, and we shared a subdued euphoria. We could do this, and we were beginning to believe it, too.

There was a big vet school party after exams, but I didn't stay for the celebration. I caught the Fort Collins–Denver airport shuttle, slumped into my seat, and watched the dreary winter-dead landscape pass the window. I was one-eighth of the way to being a vet, too tired to exult, too happy to sleep. It felt strange to be heading back to Albuquerque, as if years, and not just months, had passed since I left. Part of me wished I had stayed for the hoopla, to mark this passage with Dalton and my other running buddies, Mae Daniels, the Blackfoot Indian from Montana; Eric Ferguson; Jimmy Fulmer; and Elaine Davis. I would miss them; the four-week break that loomed ahead seemed like a long stretch of time. This semester had changed us all a little bit and made us more like one another, just as it made us a little different now from our families and other civilians.

Lloyd had said that the exams, the pressure, and the lack of sleep become just a blur in your memory but that you remember the parties in vivid detail. I would be left with only the blur.

I was eager to get the hell out of Dodge, however, even though I was going to have to wait tables during the break.

Physical work would be welcome after the mental strain of this semester. And, too, I was going home in something like triumph—I had survived, even prevailed. I was going to be a veterinarian. It had been a hope; now it was a conviction.

I wasn't sure what I would say when people back home asked how my semester had been. I didn't think I could explain it, so I guessed I would just say it had been fine. Hard work, but fine. Looking back, it seemed almost as if that were true. It had been just fine.

CHAPTER 7

The Second of the Critters—Tipper

THIS was a beautiful horse, my sister's boyfriend, Jay, asked me to believe. He was getting old, yes, but wasn't he *fine*? He needed the caked mud washed off his legs and flanks, sure, and he needed a good brushing. He needed his mane and tail combed out, but then—wouldn't he be the absolutely perfect Christmas present for Nancy?

The world and everything in it had gotten just a little out of whack these last four months. Jay apparently had gone crazy. He was making this wacky, grand, expensive, stupid gesture to make my sister *happy*. The pursuit of happiness, that American ideal, was a wild luxury I couldn't comprehend. I wondered what he did all day long—what he did with his hours and hours of time—that he had the leisure to think up this bizarre plan, to ferret out and procure this worthless nag. I was having a hard time talking to Jay. There was the illusion that we shared a language, but the meanings of the words were twisted peculiarly. Words such as *beautiful*, for instance, no longer held a common meaning for me and for him, nor words like *happy* and *perfect*.

I leaned on the pipe-rail fence and watched as he buckled the brand-new bright Christmas-green halter on the head of the old sorrel gelding. As he led him from his pen, Jay told me all about this magnificent animal: He was a registered quarter horse; his name, too, was Jay—Jay Coppertip; he'd been a race-horse and a champion roping horse, carrying his rider to the National Finals.

This fine horse walked with the short-strided, tender-footed gait that could mean navicular disease, and with each step, his right hind leg jerked backward a few inches and then forcefully slapped down. Man and horse stopped in front of me. "Well?" Jay was beaming.

"Well . . ." I smiled back weakly.

"I know he's got some problems."

Yes. He had problems, big problems that had turned a great athlete into a crippled has-been. The hind leg suffered from fibrotic myopathy, a mechanical lameness caused by a muscle injury that calcifies as it heals, permanently limiting the range of motion. It looked ugly when he moved, but it wasn't painful. The front lameness, though, was more troubling. Navicular disease is chronic, incurable, and painfully debilitating.

"She won't be using him hard," Jay said. He was pleading with me to agree, to confirm that he'd done the right thing.

He had called me in Fort Collins in late November to tell me about his wonderful plan to get my sister a Christmas horse—and to ask my advice, for he knew little about horses and I knew a bit more. We both knew a lot about my sister. She had fallen from a horse seventeen years before and shattered her elbow. She hadn't gotten back on immediately, as one is supposed to do. Instead, she had spent two weeks in a hospital. She still loved horses, but she was afraid of them now—at least afraid of riding. So it was essential that the Christmas horse be gentle, well broken, and tractable.

And it had to be cheap.

Horses weren't inexpensive, however, even the cheap ones. The purchase price of a horse is a pittance compared with the expense of keeping one—feed, stabling (for Nancy and Jay lived in the middle of Albuquerque), vet bills, tack, farrier, trailer.

I'd told him then that he was out of his mind. He'd seemed not to hear the edge in my voice that should have tipped him off that I was annoyed, that I was incredulous that he would call, interrupt my work, and bother me with this foolishness. This was frivolous, and my life was serious. He'd seemed not to hear all that in my voice, though, so I'd sighed and told him all the reasons why getting a horse for Nancy just wasn't a practical idea. I had sounded like my mother reciting the multitude of reasons that Nancy and I couldn't have a horse all those years ago when we were kids.

Jay was obviously going to get Nancy a horse whether I thought it was rational or not, so I'd reluctantly agreed to look at horses with him as soon as I got home for Christmas break.

It turned out that he hadn't needed me, after all, for when he found this horse, he jumped the gun. It required no expertise, only moderately good eyesight, to see that this horse was in bad shape. Jay, however, was looking at the animal not with his eyes but with his heart.

It's dangerous to be naïve, romantic, pigheaded, and impulsive, and Jay was all of that and more.

He had been to every stable in town looking for just the right horse. One day, a woman called him back to say she had just the one, an older gelding with some minor hoof problems that made him unusable for hard ranch work. Actually, she said, the owner had been ready to send the horse to slaughter—where he'd get seventeen cents a pound. But the fellow had great affection for the old guy and was willing to give him to Jay for nothing.

So Jay had saved the horse's life. And there was no going back, for Jay already loved him.

"He'll make a good pleasure horse, don't you think?"

Jay was so proud of his find that I couldn't stay angry.

"He might . . ." I said finally, "with corrective shoeing." I was not optimistic. Shoeing can help, but there is no cure for navicular disease. "I do know a blacksmith I can call."

"Great!" Jay believed in miracles.

The next day was Sunday, December 22, but because of the logistical problems of having Santa Claus deliver a horse, it would be Christmas Day at our house.

Amber and Dean, Nancy's kids, left early to bathe and

groom the old red horse. That afternoon, we conspired to strand Nancy at the house. I borrowed her car and parked it around the block, where Jay picked me up. We headed to the stable to meet my friend Susan Keeney and get her truck and horse trailer.

The horse *did* look better after his bath, and he walked into the trailer without protest. He *was* quiet and obedient, I had to admit.

Jay's friend Hank Bailey, decked out in his Santa gear, met us on the back street and led the horse down the alley and onto the lawn.

It was midafternoon. Carlisle Boulevard, always busy, was crowded with cars, and the sight of Santa and a horse in the middle of the city slowed them all down. People honked and waved, but the old gelding stood calm as a circus pony while Santa held the lead rope and shouted "Ho-ho-ho" to the passing traffic.

Santa knocked, and when Nancy opened the door, she stood stock-still, staring at us all as though struck dumb. But after just a moment, thank God, she burst into tears, and then everyone began to talk at once, Jay explaining the horse's history and his minor medical problems, Amber telling how we'd worked to keep the secret, Dean saying what a filthy mess the horse had been just that morning. Santa turned and waved at the passing cars.

Jay boosted Nancy up onto the big red horse and she sat there for the longest time, tears running down her face, while the horse grazed on the winter-brown lawn.

She called him Tipper, for Coppertip, and for the white flecks that freckled his back—a condition, I was to learn, called reticulated leukotrichia. She gave him another nickname, too—Feo-Face, for *feo* means "ugly" in Spanish, and the first time we saddled him up, he showed his ugly side.

When Nancy tightened the cinch, Tipper twitched his nostrils almost shut, pinned his ears flat, and swung his head toward her, open-mouthed, to bite. The lead rope tied to the hitching rail held him, but Nancy jumped back, startled at this show of temper.

Then she laughed at herself, took hold of his halter strap, and patted his big face. "Poor old Feo-Face," she said. "You can't help it, can you?" She was right about that; he'd no doubt gotten his foul temper the same way he'd gotten his ruined feet—from hard treatment and misuse.

Susan had loaned Nancy her saddle and bridle until she could get her own, so we tacked up the old horse and led him to the stable's riding arena. Nancy climbed into the saddle.

"He's tall," she said, and he was—sixteen hands. I could tell she felt a long way from the ground. "Well," she said after a moment, patting his neck, "here goes nothing."

She turned him to the right and they began a circuit of the arena. His walk was slow and his pain obvious. Halfway around, Nancy dismounted and led the horse back to where I stood. There were tears in her eyes. There was nothing to say.

We led him back to his pen and took off the saddle. Nancy brushed at his clean red coat, though it hardly bore the mark of the saddle. Finally, she turned to me. "If we don't keep him, he'll go to the slaughterhouse, won't he?"

I nodded. The brutal truth was that there are lots of horses in the world and feeding them is expensive. Better horses than Tipper go to the killers every day.

"Would he be better off dead?"

I shrugged. "I don't know how much pain he's in when he's just standing. And how can you judge a horse's quality of life?"

"I don't know if I could stand to have him put down, anyway." She paused. "And then there's Jay. . . ."

Yes, then there was Jay.

I rushed to offer hope when there wasn't much to offer. "Let me call the blacksmith and get his opinion, okay?"

"Okay." She didn't sound too convinced.

"You could also give him bute when you want to ride."

"Bute?"

I explained that phenylbutazone was an anti-inflammatory that relieves but doesn't eliminate pain, and it can cause ulcers. Nancy looked truly discouraged. "There *is* a radical treatment, a surgery called nerving."

"But . . . ?" She knew me too well; she knew there was a catch.

"It's expensive. And, since the digital nerves to the caudal portion of the hoof are severed . . ." Nancy gave me a look that said, Please speak English. "Cutting these certain nerves eliminates pain sensation in a portion of the hoof, so the horse can sustain an injury you might not notice. He can lose his whole foot before you know it."

"But if you were very careful and checked his feet every day . . ."

"That would help, sure." I could see the wheels turning in her head. "Nancy, it would cost about eight hundred dollars."

"I see." Both her children were in college—and borrowing the money to be there. There simply wasn't eight hundred extra dollars to be had. "But the corrective shoeing might help?"

Like Scarlett O'Hara, Nancy was willing to worry about this tomorrow.

And I was ready to get back to my books and my bones—disembodied from a living creature and its pain, and discrete, too, from human hearts that broke on account of the poor dumb critters.

Sam Cooper was the best blacksmith in town—and the busiest, but he made time to do me the favor of looking at my sister's new horse. He studied Tipper's gait as I led him away and back again at a walk and then at a trot. He said nothing, nor could I read his tanned and handsome face. He applied the hoof tester to each hoof and, without a word, registered Tipper's discomfort. He finished his quiet and thorough examination before he gave me his assessment: Most likely Tipper was suffering from navicular disease.

He's a kind man who admires and respects, even loves, horses, but he's not sentimental. He's seen too much. "Your sister would be better off with another horse," he said.

"This is the one she's got."

He nodded. He'd seen enough of people, too, not to waste his time trying to change their minds and notions. "Okay, then, I can put pads on him and build a pair of shoes that will relieve some of the pressure on the navicular bone."

"Okay."

"But I can't make him go sound."

"Okay. Whatever you can do."

So he built those shoes, cut rubber pads to help cushion the soles, and filled the space between hoof and pad with oakum.

When he was done, I led Tipper out and back again while Sam studied him. "Some better," he said. The improvement was subtle. "But I'm afraid it might be too little too late."

Sam invited me to ride along in his battered green truck as he made his other rounds, and I told myself I could learn a lot by watching him. After thirty-some years as a farrier, he knew more about hoof problems and lameness than most vets. It would be educational.

It was a warm December day and I had a good time. Sam showed me his technique for treating an abscessed hoof, carving it open to drain and applying "hot" iodine. He showed me how to make a sturdy, inexpensive bandage out of a disposable diaper, an old inner tube, and duct tape; how to recognize the white-line separation that might signal laminitis; and how to tell from the way a lame horse bobs its head, hikes its hip, or sinks into the fetlock just which leg is hurting.

Sam was a good teacher and an easy companion. In his leather apron, he seemed to belong to another, more romantic era. With his blue eyes and short-cropped gray hair, he reminded me somewhat of Paul Newman.

By the end of that good day, we were buddies. By morning, we were lovers.

We were together those few weeks whenever I wasn't at work, days as well as nights. I rode along on his rounds and ignored the guilt I felt at leaving unopened the pile of books I'd carried home with me. We washed the truck and had a water fight. We built a fire and dried each other off. We went to dinner and held hands under the table. I wore my hair loose. I baked him a pie.

It was vacation, I told myself, time out of time.

* * *

As for the old lame horse that had brought us together, Nancy went out to the stable several times a week and brushed him, cleaned his feet, turned him out into the arena so he could roll in the sand, and took him for short walks down the ditch, where he nibbled the winter-dead grass along its banks.

She finally had a horse of her very own.

And I had a boyfriend, at least for this little while.

CHAPTER 8

To the Bone

SECOND semester, we hit the deck running. The term continued the work we'd already begun, with Functional Anatomy, Agents of Disease II, and their respective labs. In addition, there was another term's worth of Perspectives, with its potpourri of speakers and topics, and an introductory course in radiology.

There was a new roster of professors, too—among them Scott Gossett, biochemistry cowboy, who wore his blue jeans tight and his cheek packed full of Copenhagen. He strutted the stage with the arrogance of a bantam cock. He was a fairly young man with a shining bald spot, but he seemed to have old-guard attitudes, especially about the place of women in veterinary medicine. He seemed to think it was right behind the reception desk, and then only if they were too old, ugly, or disagreeable to catch a husband; *wives* belonged in the kitchen or the bedroom. Gossett had been the pre–vet school admissions adviser of my friend and classmate Elaine Davis. His advice to her: Find a man to stand behind.

He taught the Metabolism Review, which was meant to renew our understanding of knowledge that we'd supposedly brought with us from our undergraduate course work. That was the theory, so the pace through this complicated material was fast—Kreb's cycle, the complex multi-enzyme reaction that is the basis of cellular energy, took five minutes of class time. My college course work was far enough in the past, however, that most of this review was more like news to me. The names were familiar—succinyl-CoA, pyruvate, oxaloacetate—but the processes and reactions just weren't in my head anymore.

So, for me anyway, Gossett's competence as a teacher—his excellence, really—was critical, and because of it, I could overlook a lot. I could ignore his peacock posturing, the way he worked his tobacco and strutted while he lectured.

I doubted that he had deterred anyone from becoming a veterinarian. He might handicap a daughter, if he had one, and I couldn't see him actually *helping* a woman enter the profession, but neither would he be a very effective gatekeeper, turning away hordes of hopeful women. No, his bias was too blatant to be very damaging. His flaunting of his prejudice defused it.

If there was sexism hidden like a cancer in the apparently healthy body of the college, it was subtle. An individual woman might be told—as Elaine and at least one other of my classmates were told—that *she* didn't belong in veterinary medicine, that *she* had no aptitude for it, that *she* should pursue some other field, but on the surface and as a class, there was no bias against women. Ours was the first class in history to be over half women. The numbers proved, did they not, that the official policy endorsed us as capable and qualified, as equals?

There might have been a bit of residual sexism in some of our professors, but the really dangerous biases were those we carried deep inside, quiet, sneaky, and often hidden even from ourselves.

It is easy to think of male chauvinism as an evil force that men use against women, when of course it is a cultural presumption that infects women as well. It is a prejudice that we hold against ourselves, and most of us women in the class of 1989 worked, whether consciously or not, to eliminate from our professional repertoire any behavior that seemed too "feminine." We took on the veneer of male toughness. We were aware, of course, of the long-standing argument that we were too sentimental, too soft, too weak—physically as well as emotionally—to be vets, and we were quick to turn on any woman who showed traits that would brand us as such a group. When a man cried, which was rare enough, we admired him; when a woman cried, we had little tolerance.

Had I gone straight through college and straight into vet school, I would have been in the class of 1977, which was 16 percent women. Whether there was a gender bias in the admissions policy or simply not many women applicants, I don't know. However, now we were the majority, and our sheer numbers told us that it no longer required the *extraordinary* woman to become a doctor. Even women like me—smart but certainly not *extraordinary*—could do it.

There were no models of professional women in my family—nor professional men, either, for that matter. And so, although veterinary medicine had *occurred* to me as a possible career, I had had no will or plan to get there. I had vaguely *wanted* to be a vet, but I'd invariably attached myself to some man and become his helpmate. In the past, I'd defined myself by those relationships. It had felt like a privilege, not a sacrifice, to sit for hours watching my first boyfriend rope calves, to drop out of school to cook and clean for Stan, to throw everything in the back of Alan's truck and head for Alaska, and to do the hundreds of things I had done in exchange for the pleasure of some man's company. I'd watched football games I hadn't particularly wanted to watch, cooked meals I hadn't especially wanted to cook, listened to stories that I hadn't particularly wanted to hear. It had been safe and easy—in spite of the typical agonies of romance—to attach myself to somebody else and live his life.

But now, for the first time, I had my own, and I was too busy for men, anyway. When I left Christmas break behind, I figured I'd have to leave my new boyfriend with it.

Sam called often at the beginning of that second semester. He wrote me long letters, full of news and tenderness. I sent back postcards, the essence of which was that I didn't have much time to write.

He came up to Fort Collins to visit, just as he had said he would. I didn't tell him not to; I wanted him to come. I wanted to have fun again, to relax, to be just a woman and not a genderless ascetic. I wanted to feel as young as I had felt during Christmas break. I planned to squeeze the extra time out of sleep. The night before he arrived, I drank hot coffee and studied until 3:30 A.M. I had a full day of lecture and lab, and when I got home at five-thirty that afternoon, he was waiting.

The pleasure of the reunion lasted almost through dinner.

I was so tired—what was I doing spending two hours *on eating dinner?* I thought, This is crazy.

"I don't have time for this," I said. He thought I meant dessert.

Next day, we drove to Rocky Mountain National Park. The bare, snow-covered mountains were hauntingly beautiful. There were elk at the edge of the road. We held hands in the car. I loved this man, and he was beautiful. He seemed to love me, too. I should have been happy. I wasn't.

We sat in a coffee shop in Estes Park, and I told him that I wasn't whom I had pretended to be. I just wasn't like that woman he liked so much, that carefree, laughing person I'd been at Christmas. I wasn't like that at all.

"I can't do this," I said, vaguely indicating the day trip, as well as our relationship. "I'm feeling crazy. I can't just drive around and look at the scenery. I have work to do. I have to study." That sounded lame, but it was true.

He was quiet for a while. Then he said that he realized I was under a lot of stress. I should have told him that this wasn't a good weekend for me.

No, I said, he *didn't* understand at all. *None* of the weekends would be good for me. I had to study. All the time.

People had careers *and* relationships, he said.

It wouldn't work, I said, not while I was in school. I had to study.

He said he understood, but he didn't. He called a few weeks

later (Mama was right about playing hard to get, but you can't just *play* it, you have to *be* it). He had a business meeting in Denver the following Friday, he said, and he'd like to come on up to Fort Collins and spend the weekend with me.

I hesitated. "I could have dinner with you Friday, but I couldn't spend the weekend. I have too much to do."

He was silent for a couple of seconds. "I'd leave you alone. I'd let you work."

"No, you wouldn't."

He laughed. "Yes, I would."

I laughed, too. "Okay, I wouldn't study. You'd distract me."

"What about a compromise? Give me Saturday and I'll leave Sunday at the crack of dawn."

Now I was quiet. "Sam, Friday night *is* the compromise. It's all the time I can spare." He didn't say anything. "If I can't give you what you need, then maybe you should find somebody else," I said.

Men had said those words to me before, and they sounded strange from my mouth, not like me at all, at least not like the old me. I had thrown away a lot of things to go howling at the moon. This didn't even seem like a choice, but rather a natural law, a fact, like gravity. I couldn't separate *veterinarian* from my definition of myself, no more than I could have separated *woman*. It wasn't just a job I wanted; it was also the essence of the person I wanted to be. I couldn't risk losing it without risking my whole self. I seemed to have stumbled upon one of the big secrets of the world, the one the men have always known: You are what you *do* and not who you sleep with.

Not that Sam wanted me to quit school or give up my dream. He just didn't understand the risk and how terrified I was, how I had given up newspapers and magazines, television and movies. I didn't write to Laura or talk on the phone. I didn't see my family—not while I was in school. It was too scary to take time away from my work.

And he didn't understand, either, how much power men had had over me, how easy it had been for me to hitch my wagon to a man's star, how sexism was rooted in me, a cancer of selflessness in its most literal sense.

I was prepared to give up whatever I had to for the duration of these four years, and I could turn my back on this, too. You have to have courage; you have to cut deep. I would do whatever I had to do. I could give up friends, family, and romance. I cut my life to the bone.

CHAPTER 9

The Barbarians

THE wad of tobacco in Scott Gossett's mouth occasionally got in the way of what he was saying, but Professor Charles Eyskens was consistently original and fantastic in his pronunciation of the English language. He was the first in a string of foreign-born professors that cast fear into our xenophobic hearts, for their accents were one more barrier between us and the subject matter. We called them the Exotics.

Dr. Eyskens was the first Belgian I'd ever known who wasn't a horse. Slight and bearded, he deferred the introduction to bacteriology for most of the first class session in order to acquaint us with his country—and, incidentally, to his strange way with English vowels.

He drew a squiggly map on the board and lectured on the basic differences between French- and Flemish-speaking Belgians, a distinction that was new to me. He told the Belgian version of Aggie jokes, and the class relaxed, put down their pens, and laughed with him. But I could barely understand what he was saying, and *these* were words from the common vocabulary. He said *milk*, and I scribbled myself a note: *mellaick?* Then, as he talked on about the cow and dairy, it clicked. Aha!

I couldn't imagine what trouble I'd be in when he got into the scientific lexicon. I had a nightmare vision of a notebook full of phonetic approximations punctuated by question marks. Was I to spend my study time translating *his* English into *my* English?

Dr. Eyskens was to us a true foreigner—exotic, odd, and a bit mysterious. We were to him, I think, true yapping barbarians.

The day after the first exam, Dr. Eyskens could barely contain his anger. The test, on the morphology of bacteria, had been multiple-choice. On a question about the size of bacteria, he had offered as a possible response the throwaway option of .2–.3m. A sizable number of us had chosen it, and I think the man was stunned.

He began quietly, but his voice grew louder and louder as he discussed the results of the exam. He began to swear, making it harder than ever to understand what he was saying. Perhaps he had slipped into Flemish. We sat in silent wonder as he had what amounted to a fit across the breadth of the stage.

"What do you people think?" he shouted at us. "That bacteria are the size of bananas?" He threw up his arms. "You don't need antibiotics! Just use your sneaker and stomp on them!"

He stomped around the platform in an exaggerated demonstration, as though the room were filled with invisible cockroaches. We turned to look at one another in amazement, biting our lips to keep from laughing out loud at this temper tantrum. When his anger was spent, he looked at us forlornly and shook his head. Someone near the front offered an explanation.

"We're more familiar with American measurement, Dr. Eyskens."

He nodded thoughtfully, even mournfully, perhaps considering the wide gulf between him and his raw, rough, unlettered, and uncivilized students. "But you are scientists," he said at last, paused for that to register, and then repeated, "You are scientists."

He turned his attention to the lectern, where he had set his notes. He picked up the slide projector's remote control. *Click.* We opened our notebooks and he bent to retrieve the pointer from the floor, where he had thrown it. He looked at us again then for a long moment, with the dazed demeanor of someone who has just surfaced from a seizure.

"We will now take up the work of the folic-acid inhibitors," he said at last.

At the end of a Eyskens lecture, we would stumble from the lecture hall, flipping through our notes, madly scribbling and filling in blanks.

"Did he say *perfringens* type A causes food poisoning in humans, or was it type D?"

"Did he say a *sea rob* is at risk for *E. rhusiopathiae*? What the hell is a sea rob, anyway?"

"Could you make out what he was saying about enzymatic activity in the clostridial diseases?"

"Was he talking about feedlot *lambs*, or was he talking about *hams*?"

Clostridium novyi, Cl. chauvoei, Cl. septicum, Cl. haemolyticum, Cl. colinum, Cl. tetani, Cl. botulism—imagine these words in the mouth of a man who couldn't pronounce *milk*. At the beginning of each lecture, I was sore afraid. But you had to keep a sense of humor.

"Dalton, do you think he said *Erysipelothrix rhusiopathiae* is a *pig* pathogen, or a *big* pathogen?"

She turned around and grinned. "*Big*, I think it was. About a quarter of a meter long, about like a good-sized banana."

At least the exotics didn't chew Copenhagen.

"Don't worry," Dalton said. "We'll figure it out, we'll figure it out."

And so we banded together, a small troupe, to compare and decipher our notes. Soon our function grew to include the identification of what Dalton called the GTQ, or guaranteed test question. She, Elaine Davis, Eric Ferguson, Mae Daniels, and I shared our best guesses—which became increasingly accurate—about what information from the volumes of text and notes would show up on each exam.

I liked the game partly because it confirmed my judgment.

My GTQ guesses were as likely to show up on a test as anyone else's. I seemed to be honing my instincts for sorting the meaningful from the trivial, and I was beginning to believe that I would continue to pass my exams, that I would progress through this and the remaining six semesters just like everybody else.

The gnawing fear remained, however, that I was getting by on luck and luck alone. Whatever my grade on any given exam, I knew that a good part of my score came from guessing—*educated* guessing, yes, but rarely from certain knowledge. If I got 83 percent of the questions right, I was shaken by the conviction that I did not know 83 percent of the material—not dead-to-rights. If I was to take any given exam a month later, would I pass? What about a year, two years? But everyone in the GTQ gang was skimming along by guess and by golly. I took some comfort there.

The game was meant to help us spend our study time wisely, for it was an impossibly long semester filled with impossibly short days. It was easy to remember those facts that were obviously applicable to clinical practice; for instance, that sperm take approximately sixty days to mature in all species that I expected to see in future practice, so an insult that endangers sperm production shows up in about two months. But we needed tricks to sort the relevant but abstract from the trivial and merely esoteric.

The entire Perspectives in Veterinary Medicine course was a catchall of information, much of it maddeningly general and useless. I resented the hour spent listening to a local goat farmer talk about his business. I felt annoyance at the "breeds" tests over each species. I wondered how it was possible that I could remember the embryogenesis of the mammalian ductus deferens, the twelve toxins of *Clostridium perfringens*, the origin of Auerbach's plexus—and *still* have trouble keeping straight whether it's the Chester White or the Berkshire hog that has lopped ears, or whether the Pomeranian or the Pekingese has a tendency toward ectopic testicles.

And so we muddled and sorted the volumes of stuff that

came at us. Some GTQ were, in fact, *guaranteed* by our professors to show up on the exam. Others we deduced by whether they *seemed* fundamental or important. We knew still other material was vital because of the amount of time and energy given it in lecture and laboratory.

Classroom and laboratory time spent on the heart and the great vessels confirmed what every schoolchild knows—that it's a muscular pump of profound importance. Every fact and every iota of information was a keeper.

We spent six hours listening to Professor Rob Marron lecture on the subject. We spent many, many more than that dissecting the hearts of horses, dogs, cows, sheep, pigs, cats, and birds, until we could pick up a crimson muscle with its various arteries and veins spewing off and identify the species, the legamentum arteriosum, the moderator band, the conus arteriosus, and the chordae tendinae. We went back to our greyhound cadavers and dissected all the vessels supplied by this pump, until finally those arteries and veins began to make a certain beautiful sense. All this prepared us for the cardiac-shock lab.

We had the distinction of being the last class at CSU to conduct this lab, and the young dogs that were our subjects had the distinction of being the first we would actually kill in our veterinary training.

The dogs were anesthetized before we entered the lab, for we would be eased step by step into this killing business. There was nothing for the rational mind to rebel against. A recent rabies outbreak in Wyoming had forced a moratorium on adoptions from the pounds; these dogs had been shipped down from Cheyenne. Their lives were over, whether they were euthanized by animal-control officers or freshman vet students.

Our intubated dog lay motionless on the table. He was a yellow crossbreed, predominantly Labrador retriever. With his consciousness sedated, his life was only a technicality. His physiological responses to our manipulation of his circulatory system would illustrate what we had learned from books and lectures. The lab would illustrate that when an animal initially loses blood, the cardiac output, arterial pressure, and venous return to the heart all decrease. These factors then reverse as the body reacts: The adrenal gland releases epinephrine—adrenaline—to trigger the "fight or flight" response; the heart beats faster; the spleen contracts; the walls of arteries and veins tighten, constricting the flow of blood to the extremities and the less critical vascular beds, thereby increasing blood pressure and the blood supply to the heart and brain; and the mucous membranes therefore pale, losing their pink, well-oxygenated hue and turning ashen to white.

These are the signs of shock, which we were to induce and monitor.

My responsibilities on our team were to install a catheter into the jugular vein (a "jugular cut-down") and to suck blood from the dog with a 60 cc. syringe as we manipulated the variables and recorded the resulting data. We began, drawing from the dog small and measured amounts of blood and measuring and recording his vital signs every ten minutes—temperature, heart rate, and respiratory rate.

In conscious animals, blood loss can approach 40 to 45 percent before circulatory failure and shock occur, but anesthesia reduces the reflexes significantly, causing failure to occur much more quickly—which is why small blood losses during surgery are so dangerous. It was critical, then, to watch our subject closely and replace blood with saline solution to maintain the animal's circulatory volume until we had finished the experiment and gathered sufficient data to illustrate and confirm what we had earlier read and studied.

We continued manipulating blood volume and checking our dog's responses. Our equipment—hematocrit, manometer, thermometer, EKG—gave us a quantitative breakdown of how hard this unconscious animal was fighting for life, meeting our every action with a reaction. The battle waxed and waned as we bled the dog, then replaced fluid, and as his own mechanisms attempted to compensate.

Finally, our readings told us that the dog was losing his battle, that his mechanical and unconscious intelligence was dug into the trenches and making its best last stand to perfuse with its remaining blood, and thus preserve, its critical—or sacred—circulatory beds, the cerebral and the coronary. When these are lost, the body in question crosses that line where humans report seeing a bright or loving light, a host of angels, their mother, or Jesus Christ coming for them. We do not know what—if anything—the dog sees when the struggle is lost.

The *idea* of death may be hard, the idea of dying and, particularly, of killing. We had long grown accustomed to the pieces and piles of bodies that were a significant part of our daily existence, however. They were merely tissue samples in aggregate.

We disconnected the dog from our machinery and cleaned up the mess.

The Gross Anatomy lab final was Friday morning, the next-to-last exam of the year. We entered in staggered groups of twenty-five to look one last time at the dissection tables laid out with dead dogs and cats, chickens, parts of horses, cows, and goats. Each was tagged; each tag was numbered. We wandered through—some dazed with fatigue, some giddy with it—and identified each marked organ or tissue, wrote its name next to its number on our answer sheets.

The Anatomy faculty monitored as we rotated among the exhibits, but it seemed more a party than a final exam. There was no pretense of formality; we observed no rules of silence. Each student obeyed his or her internal honor code—or didn't. We talked among ourselves about our plans for the summer and joked with our professors as we jotted down our answers and moved on among the dead.

That afternoon, we settled in the cubes for the *final* final of the year. I weighed and reweighed each answer, finished, then went back to think again about the choices I'd made and the ones I'd rejected.

Voices were starting to ring out in the hall. Those who had finished freshman year had little patience with those of us who prolonged it. Dalton came into my cube, carrying a coffee urn. She raised it over my head.

"Open wide, Retta."

"Damn it, Dalton, I'm still working."

But she was having none of that. She opened the spigot and beer trickled onto my head and down my face. I gave up. Who was I to resist high times?

Dalton picked up my paper and looked it over. "I'm turning this puppy in right now," she said, and started down the hall.

I put down my pencil. They always told us that our first impulses are probably correct, anyway. It was over. I surrendered to it, slid my empty coffee mug under the spigot of the urn, and opened wide.

More than half of us were more than half drunk when we met a while later in the gross lab for one last chore. We donned our green lab coats one more time, pulled on rubber gloves, hauled out the carts and wastebaskets, and fell to work, throwing out the long-dead animals we had lived with this whole year. We loaded them—dozens of dogs, a few cats, horses, donkeys, cattle, llamas—onto carts and wheeled them outside to the Dumpster, tossing and heaving them unceremoniously into the huge metal bin. It was late afternoon at the end of May. It was paradise, it was nirvana, and we were its full citizens—125 green-clad and drunken students, whooping, laughing, and throwing dead animals.

A sober-looking professor in a gray suit came blinking out into the sunshine. He yelled at us to shut up. His undergraduate Anatomy class was taking their final at the other end of the building, he said, and we were so loud, they couldn't concentrate. What was the matter with us? Had we gone mad?

We stopped and looked at him. "Who's he?" someone asked. No one seemed to know; he wasn't one of ours. Several more vet students came laughing through the door, wheeling a cartful of greyhounds. They stopped at the sight of us, all stock-still and silent. "What's happening?" one of them asked. "He said we should be quiet," somebody answered. "Oh."

We *were* quiet, and then, as he turned to go inside, this anonymous professor said, "I think it's disgusting, the way you people are treating those animals. They deserve some respect."

We looked from him to the Dumpster, where the hacked-up and desiccated carcasses were stacked.

"Oh, fuck you!" somebody yelled. The professor stopped in his tracks and turned to glare and threaten, but he was too late. We'd started pitching more bodies into the pile. The party was on again. Nobody could touch us. We were one-quarter of the way to becoming doctors.

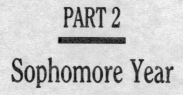

PART 2

Sophomore Year

CHAPTER 10

―――

Pilgrim's Progress

OUR class moved this year into the pathology building, across a grassy field from the anatomy building, where the new freshmen were settling into the gross lab, the lecture hall, and our cubes.

The cubes seemed a symbol for all we had left behind— innocence, youth, warmth, and love. Everyone seemed to have heard someone say that this year was not going to be the cakewalk that, apparently, last year had been. There would be no more coddling, no more professors holding our hands, no more Jake Wilder.

I hadn't felt all that safe. I hadn't felt truly pampered. But I had felt at home in the cubes, and now I missed that feeling. I missed having that base, that cozy place to stash my gear—we had only lockers now—to sit and study, to read, or just to shoot the breeze.

The cubes had broken a class of 125 into groups of eighteen, and in those groups, we had gone through the kind of stress, work, and worry that made true friends out of strangers. So strong was that bonding that a great many of the friendships that would endure over the course of the entire four years and beyond were made from within one's own cube, and thus were somewhat alphabetical. Because Dalton and I had sought each other out—over a can of Copenhagen—that first day of orientation, my closest friends included people from her cube, *D*'s, as well as the *G*'s and *F*'s from my own cube.

I'd left my other home, with Lloyd and Jennifer, this year, too. Dreading another hard winter, I'd moved to town.

It had been a good summer. Sam and I had spent a lot of time together, including a horseback camping trip to the Jemez Mountains. With Sam's help, I had bought a little white Honda, which I hoped would be more economical and more reliable than old Blue. And when I drove back to school, Sam came along, making even the trip an extension of the vacation.

Elaine Davis, who lived in Fort Collins year-round, had found an apartment for me and sent me the address and the key. We arrived after dark and let ourselves in. It was a roomy basement apartment, and we camped that night in the living room. By morning's light, I was pleased with the neighborhood and location, about a mile from school, an easy bike ride.

We began the job of moving me in, collecting my stuff from the garage of one of my classmates, where I had stored it over the summer, and taking it to the new place, trip after trip in the little car. We bought a secondhand kitchen table and hauled it home on Mighty Whitey's roof. The place still seemed empty. In the living room were only my red overstuffed reading chair and a table I'd borrowed from Elaine to hold my lamp. The spareness appealed to me. I planned again to live as ascetic a life as possible, for sophomore year was reputed to be the most academically challenging of the four, lecture after lecture, body system after body system, laying the foundation of knowledge we would carry into the final two years, when we would begin our clinical experience, and beyond.

I drove Sam to the airport shuttle and kissed him—and vacation—good-bye.

There was an official buddy system, in which sophomores acted as "big siblings" to freshmen. My assigned helper had gotten off easily, for Lloyd had been a real and constant "big brother" to me all year.

Now we were sophomores and required to serve, so I resigned

myself to it. I had picked Rick Calvin from the list of newly accepted freshmen posted the previous May, partly because he lived in Albuquerque (I'd figured we could talk during the summer) and partly because one of my classmates knew him and had told me he was older, married, and a graduate student, so I hoped he wouldn't be too insecure and needy. I needn't have worried.

Although my name and number were part of his introduction packet, he didn't call that summer, so I met him for the first time in Fort Collins at a get-acquainted picnic. He was concurrently enrolled in a master's program at the University of New Mexico, he had a small child as well as a wife, and he seemed to be handling the vet school transition with great aplomb. His participation in the Big-Little Sibling program was as perfunctory as my own.

To my surprise, I found myself resenting the fact that he didn't seem to need or want the benefit of my new wisdom and that he didn't need any reassurance. He planned a few trips back to Albuquerque during the year, he said, to wrap up his master's degree. I didn't like him one little bit.

Later in the year, he would tell me that he had never dreamed how demanding vet school would be and that he wouldn't be able to finish the master's until the next summer. I began to like him quite a lot more then, and sometimes I'd leave a plastic bag of frozen green chiles on his desk in his cube—one New Mexican looking out for another. And sometimes—after his trips home—I'd find a gift of blue-corn tortillas in my mailbox.

Our class of 125 was down to 124 now; as predicted, some of the cream had sunk. We had lost one woman to nerves and terror; she took a year's leave of absence and would join the next freshman class for a new start. Another had dropped out because of poor health, and one of the men had flunked out. We had gained two. Rita Marshall had had to drop out of the class ahead of ours after a horse carcass derailed in the gross lab and fell on her, damaging her face; she'd taken a year off for plastic surgery and recovery. And Jeff O'Neill, a quiet, earnest student, had transferred here from the vet school at Washington State.

There wasn't a lot of time for getting acquainted with our two new members, because we were carrying a twenty-four-credit-hour course load: Veterinary Jurisprudence, Agents of Disease III (a.k.a. Pharmacology), Agents of Disease IV, Introduction to Disease I, Population Medicine, and Diseases of the Endocrine-Metabolic System, our first "systems" course.

Jurisprudence was taught by a lawyer, and it seemed to me purely an annoyance. Although it touched on the issue of malpractice and liability (inherently interesting), its core was bookkeeping. There were set after set of accounting problems to work, and, in an apparently time-honored tradition, the completed problems were passed down from class to class and student to student. There was no guilt involved; the honor code obviously and logically didn't apply to this bull, which had nothing to do with medicine. There was too much real work to do to agonize over mere arithmetic. I started skipping classes. The issues of contracts, real estate, equipment purchases, staffing of a clinic, and investment planning were all fantasy to me. They had nothing to do with my life, at least not in any foreseeable future.

We were required to write a paper addressing some area of legal or moral consideration in the vet profession. I chose the issue of advertising, in large part because there was an abundance of material available and I wouldn't have to work too hard on it. In fact, I didn't give a tinker's damn how big some vet's Yellow Pages ad was, whether he put his picture on a highway billboard, or whether he mailed out fliers advertising that he could talk to animals.

I figured if I could just get through vet school, *then* I'd worry about contracts and how to spend my money. Looking forward to a starting salary of twenty thousand dollars a year—if I was lucky—and facing thirty thousand dollars in student-loan debt, I didn't anticipate setting up my own clinic or buying many stocks and bonds any time soon.

The real work of the semester promised to be overwhelming,

and I resolved to be relentless in meeting it. I didn't need this extra aggravation.

Dalton, who had worked in the Veterinary Teaching Hospital (VTH) barn before she was accepted into vet school, knew a way to whet our appetites and get a glimpse of what it would be like to be a doctor—or at least an upperclassman.

Rounds were held daily at 8:00 A.M. in the hospital barn. Clinicians and vet students moved from stall to stall, stopping for senior students to present their cases to the group—signalment (species, breed, sex, age, etc.), the CPC, or chief presenting complaint (i.e., diarrhea, anorexia, aborted fetus), findings of the physical and diagnostic tests ordered, differential diagnoses, treatments, response, and prognosis. At that point, any and all of those present—the students on that particular rotation, the clinical staff of that service, and any interested faculty or students—were welcome to question the presenter.

On Fridays, sophomore lectures didn't start until 10:00 A.M., so on that day we could jump ahead a year and attend rounds with the big boys. Dalton and I alone of our class attended; but for her, I would not have known this world existed. She was familiar with the hospital routine, however, and took her place as near the front as she could get.

I felt conspicuous and in the way when the fifteen or twenty people who had an official reason to be there crowded around the X ray view box or pressed forward to look at a pertinent tissue sample. I wasn't sure we were really welcome, but no one ever challenged us. In fact, the clinicians seemed to like our enthusiasm—the very fact that we were there—particularly as the term wore on and we stayed with it, Friday after Friday, when we could have been home in bed. The students on rotation changed every couple of weeks, but Dalton and I were as steady in our attendance as the staff.

We were quiet about how we spent our Friday mornings, jealous of this privilege we'd lucked into, a privilege that would no doubt be revoked if the other 122 sophomores—or even a higher percentage of them—started showing up.

We went for the fun of it, mostly, and it *was* fun. We understood more and more of what we were seeing and hearing as the term progressed. Isolated facts began to come together, and we would catch one another's eye and nod. These were breathing, belching, real live animals with real diseases, and it was a sneak preview of a time when we would know how to fix them.

It had a practical benefit, as well. Our Introduction to Disease (a.k.a. Pathology) lab consisted of necropsy tissues from those VTH cases that had some teaching value. We sat in the sophomore lecture hall and watched the video monitor, and often Dalton and I would recognize a case from our Friday-morning rounds. We would have seen the animal from which the tissue had come; we would have heard the history, diagnostics, and treatment. She'd catch my eye and I'd give her a wink.

After the video presentations, we went to the laboratory itself, just down the hall, where we examined the actual tissues, felt their texture, weight, and size, noted their shape and color. We moved in small groups from case to case and recorded our morphologic diagnosis (specific structure and anatomy and the general character of the disease process), our etiologic diagnosis (the specific cause of the pathology), and our definitive disease diagnosis (indicating a specific entity with self-defined signs and clinical manifestation, such as rabies or cholera).

We were being trained to discuss disease properly with anyone, anywhere. The main emphasis of the lab was on the proper gross description of the lesions we saw, and these descriptions were to be constructed in a rigid, codified, and time-honored manner.

The first word of the description would relay the time frame (i.e., acute, chronic, peracute); the second word, the distribution (i.e., focal, diffuse, disseminated); the third word, the nature of the exudate or process (i.e., catarrhal, serous, purulent, hemorrhagic); the fourth word, the etiology (i.e., viral, mycotic, mycoplasmal, parasitic, toxic); the prefix of the fifth word, the organ or part affected (i.e., hepato-, nephro-, myo-, pneumo-, encephalo-, dermato-, entero-); and its suffix, the nature of the process (i.e., -itis, for inflammation; -oma, for tumor; -opathy, for disease).

The language was beginning to make sense. Repetition would make us fluent.

Population Medicine was my introduction to epidemiologists. They were clearly a different breed, occupied with statistics, epidemic curves, measurements of disease rates and ratios, and the sensitivity of tests, predictive values, attack-rate tables, case-control studies, and clinical trials. I was resistant to this material; I wanted to concentrate on the diseases that came up in the study of these tools and methods. I was a clinician (would-be clinician, anyway) to the core, and I was eager to get on with it. I wanted to know about the individual, the disease, its effects on the body, the treatments. But these guys seemed to regard the diseases only as a means to put their analyses into action.

Of course, we would study these animal plagues again in the detail and with the focus I wanted as we moved through our systems courses. Their brief introduction here (for many of them were completely new to me) served to whet my appetite and also to make me impatient with the subject at hand.

The course introduced us to APHIS (Animal Plant Health Inspection Service), the feds in charge of preserving our livestock and protecting it from FAD (Foreign Animal Disease). These *federales* spring into action, like G-men, whenever there is a threat to the U.S. animal—and, by extension, human—population.

The lecture hall's lights were dimmed and we were shown an unintentionally funny government film of federal vets wiping out disease and pestilence. The subject wasn't humorous—the avian influenza epidemic of 1983, which killed 4 million broilers and 287 million laying hens, was declared a national emergency and cost the government $65 million. But the film, with its highly serious tone and implied moral correctness, was hilarious.

This course was our first look at Lyme disease and other tick-borne diseases; anthrax; psittacosis, or parrot disease; undulant fever; tuberculosis; and other occupational or food-borne zooneses (diseases that can spread to humans from vertebrate animals). It was also our first, and most compelling, look at rabies.

Dr. Sullo, a tall, distinguished-looking man, showed us a scratched black-and-white film of a Russian peasant dying of the disease. Although the film was old, its impact was strong and immediate, for the stages of dying and death were gruesome and terrifying. The man's suffering made believers of us budding vets. It made automatic the correct response to an unvaccinated animal that has bitten someone—recommend euthanasia. We were to chop off the head of such an animal for immediate microscopic examination of the brain for the rabies virus, because speed is of the essence in preventative treatment. I will remember always the anguished death of that man a half century ago on the other side of the world. The memory made it possible, three years later, for me to hack off the head of Nada, our cat of eighteen years, and ship it to the lab. In her death struggle, Nada, whose vaccination was not current, had bitten my mother. I didn't hesitate. I remembered the Russian, and so I chopped off the head of our dear old pet as if she were so much meat. Thankfully, and expectedly, she tested negative.

As Dr. Sullo drilled home how respectful and fearful we must always be of rabies, he made another point, one with legal and economic ramifications: Veterinary malpractice insurance does not protect against human loss, so it was prudent to make sure there was none. Any haste we lost in killing and examining a potential rabies carrier could make us liable, at least in theory, for the suffering and/or death of anyone it had bitten.

We were taught how "smart" the rabies virus is. Before it kills its host, it ensures its own propogation by lodging in the brain of that host and making it mad, a crazed, biting animal, spreading the virus in its saliva.

We saw films of rabid animals and studied the variety of signs the virus can produce. Rabid cows have a change in the character of their voice and can be aggressive. Rabid horses can become extremely agitated, to the point of walking right through fences, oblivious to pain. An animal afflicted with the "dumb" manifestation of rabies is confused, disoriented, uncoordinated, and lethargic. With "furious" rabies, the animal is hypersensitive, restless, and biting. The most consistent sign of the disease is an ascending motor paralysis. The other major sign is a change in an animal's behavior. And because animals can show all or none of the signs, rabies must be on every differential diagnosis list for a neurological problem.

At first, it seemed that the course spent an inordinate amount of time on this disease, which we tend to think of as almost eradicated. Rabies is more or less controlled in the U.S. pet population (although there were 180 documented cases of canine rabies in the United States in 1973—180 cases too many). It is not uncommon among wildlife, however; once contracted, it is almost always fatal. Our teachers meant to convert us, to make our response to the disease or its threat automatic and decisive, to make us into evangelists in the cause of rabies vaccination.

After they indoctrinated us fully in the horrors of rabies, we willingly submitted to being vaccinated ourselves, three shots of an inactivated rabies virus over the course of a month. Our arms swelled visibly, and the vaccine was expensive (although we got a discount), but no one complained. The virulence of the disease was driven home by the fact that even the series of innoculations would not eliminate the need for additional therapy if we were bitten by a rabid animal, although it would simplify the treatment and help ensure a favorable outcome; that is, we'd have a better chance of living through it.

Pharmacology naturally required an understanding of chemistry and mathematics, as well as some skill in problem solving.

Professor Don Hendrix joked that his introduction to Pharmacology had been as a student at Berkeley in the seventies, where there had been ample opportunity to observe the effects of various drugs, including smoked banana peel. I'd been in the vicinity myself and could imagine how he looked fifteen years earlier with his thick black hair down to his waist.

His area of expertise was the absorption and bioavailability of drugs and the dreaded pharmacokinetics, the science of how and how quickly drugs move through the body and take effect. His exam consisted mostly of problems, equations involving dosage, concentration, volume of distribution, IV infusion, and elimination halftime.

Professor Caputi started with autonomic pharmacology, material most of us had had at least fleeting exposure to in the long ago far away. We studied the drugs that either mimic or block the effects of the autonomic nervous system, which maintains homeostasis. The material was intriguing, and the more I studied it, the more logical it became.

Adrenergic drugs are described as sympathomimetic (mimicking the action of the natural hormones epinephrine, which stimulates the heart and other muscles, and norephinephrine, which assists in transmitting nerve impulses). It was epinephrine, I remembered, that had saved that guinea pig last year in Professor Kearns's video, and I was beginning to understand why. Many of these drugs are used in emergency situations where an increase in cardiac output is desired.

The deeper we ventured into the workings of the nervous system, the more fascinated I became. And yet it was frustrating, too, for we passed quickly from subject to subject, and it seemed that no sooner were we into autonomic pharmacology than we moved on to the antiarrhythmic agents and vasodilators, then diuretics, followed by sedatives, hypnotics, tranquilizers, and anticonvulsants.

Then we took up the study of steroids. These anti-inflammatory agents are the center of a long-standing controversy in veterinary medicine, and one that seems to have no end in sight. On the one hand, they can be—or seem—almost miracle workers, fixing almost instantaneously a myriad of ills, from relieving an itching dog to their emergency use in reducing swelling around the bone-encased central nervous system. On the other, they suppress the immune system and also mask symptoms. Steroids can be seen as a quick fix, shortcutting a thorough diagnostic workup and discovery of the true cause of a complaint. One needs to consider their positive side, however, when realizing a client often won't opt for lab work, radiographs, and other diagnostic measures that can be expensive and offer no guarantee of success. I could see virtue on both sides of the issue, and I'd worked for vets who swore by steroids and those who scorned their use. No matter which camp I ended up in, I was going to have to know these compounds cold.

We approached the end of the course with the study of antibiotics—ninety-three of them at that time. This class of drug accounts for 80 percent of veterinary prescriptions written and are the bread and butter of practice. These included antibacterials, antifungals, and antivirals, each with a description, mechanism of action, pharmacokinetic pattern, adverse effects and toxicity precautions, indications, distribution, and spectrum of activity. Once again, there was an avalanche of information, and all of it relevant. Almost as a single organism, the class grew weary, nervous, and unhappy.

Concurrently, of course, we had our first systems course, the Diseases of the Endocrine-Metabolic System, coordinated by Pam Purcell, who led a real hit parade of clinician lecturers from the VTH. Dr. Purcell was kind, encouraging, and supportive, as well as a gifted lecturer. Freshman year, in physiology lectures and during dissection of the adrenal medulla, we had had some instruction in hormones, and Dr. Purcell began the course with a quiz concerning that material:

1. List 6 steroid hormones.
2. List 6 protein hormones.
3. List 6 hormones produced in the adenohypophysis.
4. Which hormone has the lowest molecular weight?
5. Where is estradiol produced?
6. Chemically define the thyroid hormone thyroxine.

I had known these answers last year, but that was about all I knew for sure. This course was obviously going to take everything I could give it.

We began with the mechanism of hormone action, the pituitary gland, the parathyroid, and the thyroid. Dr. Sarkis, a confident young fellow, lectured on the pituitary and diseases manifesting as water abberations (psychogenic water drinkers); the antidiuretic hormone (ADH); calcium and phosphorous metabolism; and diabetes insipidous (insufficient ADH, a disease of the pituitary gland). On this material, Sarkis wrote some of the toughest exam questions I would see during the entire four years.

Dr. Woodford was a Canadian who headed up the Dermatology department at the VTH. He came to teach us the thyroid hormone, the disorders of which cause many abberations in an animal. Woody, as we called him, was young, tall, and thin, and could have been a stand-up comic. He was a great hockey fan and Wayne Gretsky was his main man. In addition to everything we could learn and remember about the signs, diagnosis, and treatment of hyperthyroidism and hypothyroidism, we would do well to know that Gretsky played for the Edmonton Oilers, wore jersey number 99, and was born January 26, 1961, as Woody joked that this was pertinent and testable information and that he might offer extra credit points for knowing it.

Purcell returned for a couple of weeks to lecture on her specialty, reproductive disorders in small animals. She had spent time and effort applying educational theory to her teaching, and the notes she handed out were basically outlines that we were to fill in, the theory being that participation in note taking gets better results than passive listening, something I had found to be true during freshman year. I couldn't quite keep up with her clear and rich presentations, so I resurrected my practice of taping and transcribing lectures.

Dr. Owen Colson covered the use of steroids in large-animal medicine, an overlap and partial repetition from Pharmacology that was welcome and reinforcing. He made his own position clear on the controversy regarding steroid use. According to him, although corticosteroids are commonly used in large animals for a wide variety of conditions, there are relatively few instances in which these drugs are genuinely indicated.

Dr. Glaser, a gray-haired fatherly type, delivered seven lectures on diabetes mellitus, and then it was on to liver disease in small animals with Dr. Joseph Fortel.

In rapid succession, Dr. Cochran (who had conducted my admissions interview) covered equine liver disease, Dr. Lester covered metabolic disorders in food animals, and Dr. Tom Purcell, Pam's husband (whom she called "the mean Dr. Purcell," though he wasn't) presented more information on metabolic function in cattle.

This course, along with Introduction to Disease and Pharmacology, and to a lesser degree Population Medicine, was a killer—too much material, too little time, and everything too important.

Sam called and wrote letters, and at first I tried to write him back. Surely, I thought, it must be possible to have a life *and* be in vet school—other people seemed to do it. But it wasn't long before I gave up letter writing, then gave up postcards; the phone was quicker. And then, as time inevitably collapsed under me, I began to make my calls shorter and less frequent. Sam didn't pressure me, but he said I wasn't any fun.

Dalton said the same. And surely, I wasn't. Fun seemed an incredible luxury, one I couldn't afford. I felt tired, but then everybody was tired. What I felt was *old*.

I ran into Dave Ramo, the other "old" person in our class, older even than I, and I more or less whined to him about my insecurities. I told him about the nagging conviction that I didn't have quite the brainpower I had had a decade before and that handicap made me feel that if I didn't devote every hour, every scrap of energy, every move and every thought to my studies, I'd fall short and flunk out. That may have sounded ludicrous, since I was comfortably in the top half of the class, but it seemed to me that I was there partly through luck and partly through superhuman dedication. I felt that if I relaxed even a bit, I'd lose ground I could never recover; I'd lose my grip on the ladder and fall off completely.

Dave listened sympathetically, but then he shook his head. With a bemused smile, he said he didn't really understand. He couldn't identify with my lack of confidence. Yes, he said, it was hard, and he knew he had to compensate for some loss of memory power (he was in his late forties), but he never doubted that he'd finish and earn his D.V.M.

I felt like a freak. It was hard to know whether my insecurity was well founded or paranoid. I kept thinking of the classmates we had lost after freshman year, however—the one to poor grades and the other to an anxiety that must have been greater and more freakish than my own. These two casualties were real evidence that there was something here of which to be afraid.

Besides, it didn't really matter whether I was justly single-minded and maniacal in my studies or whether I was crazy, because it simply was the way I was. For better or worse, I was stuck with it.

CHAPTER 11

———

Mean Spirits

THE groups that had formed freshman year around cube assignments or special interests were solid, none more solid or more visible than the Meat Inspectors, a self-styled group of hard-core and hard-ass cowboys. Rowdy, loud, self-centered, intolerant, contemptuous of almost everybody, they fancied themselves outlaws.

Freshman year, they had had spitting competitions with the llamas in the gross lab pens. They talked to one another whenever it suited them, at whatever volume they liked. They were bright enough that they could lean against the back wall—where they'd staked out a row of seats—and sleep through lectures. They were clever, young, and full of themselves. This year, they wore billed caps with their club name emblazoned across the front and held the exclusive Meat Inspectors Golf Classic and the Meat Inspectors Fishing Tournament. They were scornful of authority, and that indifference to convention gave them a certain charisma. They weren't bound by rules, they seemed to say. They weren't bound by any inner terror. They weren't bound at all. But they seemed to be having fun, something I had given up for the duration.

During freshman orientation, Dr. Tennant had said, basically, look to your left, look to your right, some of you ain't going to be here when it's all over. Three already were gone, and we had come back after Christmas break to find another of our mates missing in action.

This latest casualty had been a cube mate of mine freshman year, and I'd known he was having trouble even then. Everybody in Cube D had known. I felt a mix of guilt and empathy. I wondered now whether I could have helped him somehow. But feeling as I did that I was barely staying afloat myself, I wouldn't have known how. At least that's what I told myself.

I supposed that I would never see him again; when they disappeared, they seemed to be gone for good. I knew that if it happened to me, I wouldn't be able to face my former classmates ever again. It was too horrible a prospect even to contemplate.

A chill settled over us and we closed ranks and began our sophomore second semester.

Introduction to Disease (Pathology) would continue this term. We would have three more systems courses—cardiovascular, respiratory, and urinary, plus the short (eight weeks) Principles of Surgery, Veterinary Ethics, and our first choice of an elective—either Non-Domestic Animal Medicine (a.k.a. Exotic Animals) or Food Animal Management and Herd Health.

In Principles of Surgery, we were taught the philosophy of the surgeon, written by the fourteenth-century Guy de Chauliac: "Let him be modest, dignified, gentle, pitiful and merciful, not covetous nor an extortionist of money; but rather let his reward be according to his work, to the means of the patient, to the quality of the issue, and to his own dignity."

Sometimes we may have appeared short on dignity, but the course was what we all craved—steps toward becoming a clinician. We were to learn the terminology of surgery, the instruments, suture materials and patterns, sterilization techniques, the difference between Crile and Kelly hemostats, Doyen versus Kocher intestinal forceps, which suture was suitable to use in an infected abdomen, how long it takes catgut suture to lose its tensile strength, and which suture has the best knot security.

A knowledge of surgical asepsis involved studying the chemical and physical properties of ethylene oxide, the principles of chlorine disinfection, the preparation of the surgical suite, and prep of the team—the gowning, gloving, and scrubbing. We studied electrosurgery principles, the use of drains in wounds, the four stages of wound healing, what cells arrive when, how long each stage lasts, what each cell contributes to healing, wound contraction, when to bandage, and when to use a skin graft.

This was playing doctor, a glimpse into the future, and it fed our egos and our imaginations. We would have every bit of this again in other contexts—as Lloyd had said, the important stuff gets repeated—but this first taste made it real, made us hungry.

Pathology began with a study of toxins—how they produce damage, how organs react to this damage, the body's defenses against toxic damage, and the numerous toxicants relevant to veterinary medicine, including various plants, pesticides, gasses, and drugs with harmful effects.

This was followed by a unit on Development and Disease, which concerned congenital defects, abnormal development in organ systems in the embryo and fetus, whether caused by genetic error, nutritional deprivation, or environmental factors. The material was fascinating, and, as always, the pace through it much too fast.

The first exam was scheduled for March 24. The material had me spooked, so I stayed in town during spring break, which was right before the test. Sam came up from Albuquerque and we took a couple of day trips that week, but I paid more attention to my Pathology notes than to him, adding stress to a relationship that was growing weaker all the time. I pressed him to quiz me over my notes, then got impatient when he didn't ask the right questions, failing to pick out what was relevant and important.

I missed but one question on the exam, savored the relief and pleasure for a moment, and plunged into the second half of the course, the "Basics of Immunology."

The lecturer, Dr. McAllister, was a researcher, and most of the class had a deep bias in favor of clinicians. Of course research was important; it was the source of some of the knowledge we were so relentlessly cramming in order to make ourselves practitioners. But that didn't change the fact that we felt generally antagonistic toward researchers. They were the "ivory tower" guys. Researchers were generally thought to be an egocentric and greedy lot, hoarding their findings as they competed to make breakthroughs that would bring them individual glory and wealth.

Perhaps the most important factor in this distrust and dislike of researchers, though, was that we were, by and large, not researchers ourselves and not planning to be. As always, we were biased toward material that seemed clinically relevant and directly useful, and researchers had a tendency to digress into the intricacies of their own specialized interests and, assuming an interest and knowledge base we often didn't have, to talk above our heads. We had no appetite for the esoteric.

McAllister could go off into flights of pure science, but since a firm foundation in the theory and practice of the immune system is critical to understanding disease, the course was vital. The material was complicated and compelling, particularly because of its relevance to the AIDS virus. Many of us were just then becoming aware of the nature and ramifications of that human plague.

The immune system's primary function is biologically to identify and establish the individual and to destroy any invading tissue, material, or organism it identifies as "nonself." A complex of genes, the major histocompatability complex (MHC) does this work. MHC is found in the same chromosome (seventeenth) in all mammals and consists of three classes of molecules that serve as markers of an individual animal's "self," each class being "read" or recognized by different kinds of lymphocytes, or white blood cells, the invasion-fighting cells of the immune system. These lymphocytes originate in the bone marrow; B-cell lymphocytes are "educated" to be immunocompetent in the spleen and lymph nodes, while T-cell lymphocytes are "trained" in the thymus.

This material read like a good story, and I was astounded to learn that the thymus, the "college" to which these baby

T-cells are sent, seems to chew them up for the sheer pleasure of it—in a normal healthy animal, a whopping 90 percent of the new T-cells die. There are theories, but it is not yet understood why the thymus eliminates such massive numbers. (Because of the advent and threat of AIDS, there has been increased funding for research in this area, and the question may soon be answered.)

As the surviving T-cells "graduate," they become specialized, becoming either cytotoxic, or cell-killing, cells (a.k.a. killer T's); T-suppressor cells; or T-helpers. They then go to the lymph centers of the body, where they do their complex and somewhat confusing work.

The etiology of tumors, too, was amazing to me—the common and frequent occurrence of cells that for some reason go crazy. Most of the time, the immune system recognizes the nascent tumors as foreign bodies because their malfunctioning usually alters the MHC on their surfaces; killer T-cells routinely wipe them out. The tumors that do grow and threaten the host organism have escaped immune surveillance by modifying their surface molecules, making them virtually invisible.

I moved to a front seat early in the presentation of this material, not wanting to miss any of it. I began to see how someone could be led off into the rarefied air of pure research. I began to be more sympathetic to Dr. McAllister and even to feel a bit responsible for his growth and development as a teacher. I thought that with a little interest and enthusiasm on our parts, he could actually blossom into a fine lecturer. He was a soft-spoken man and seemed a bit shy. The classroom was not his natural arena, but he did respond to the mood of the class. It seemed that if we grew restless or began to tune him out, his energy fell off. Sometimes, though, he seemed almost high on the mystery and beauty of the immune system. I suppose it was that high that carried him away on occasion into places the class did not want to follow.

One day after we had been through most of the function of the immune system, Dr. McAllister was lecturing on the difference between mammals and birds in the production of B-cells. In birds, these cells are produced not in the bone marrow but in a lympho center called the bursa of Fabricius, located in the butt of the bird. McAllister was expounding upon these B-cells and the immune responses of chickens (our primary avian species of study). The class was tired, and the points McAllister was making seemed rather minor in the context of everything we had to assimilate about this complicated system.

Suddenly, one of the Meat Inspectors apparently couldn't take any more. He snapped his notebook shut, stood up from his back-row seat, and walked out, but not without making a loud editorial comment. "I've got better things to do than to sit here listening to his bullshit. Fucking chicken B-cells, what next?" He shook his head as if he simply couldn't believe what he was being asked to endure.

McAllister stopped his lecture as if stunned. I was stunned, and embarrassed for him, too. He checked his watch and then seemed to regain a measure of poise. "Why don't we break it off a little early," he said. "I think I've kind of overloaded you with information today."

He didn't seem angry, just weary. I imagine he was eager to get back to the laboratory and away from the philistines. And very soon he was able to do just that.

Professor Francis, who coordinated the course, presented the last eight lectures, which covered immunopathology, specific immunologic diseases. This, of course, was material more firmly grounded in the world in which most of us lived, more relevant to clinical practice, and the class was generally more responsive to this section than to the one before.

Among these diseases, naturally, were some that didn't seem pertinent enough for more than a mention, although these always did seem to take a disproportionate amount of lecture time. Perhaps their very quirkiness made them fascinating to the lecturers.

Chediak Higashi syndrome, for example, in which certain white blood cells are unable to dump their lysosomes (a particle containing digestive enzymes) and thus are ineffective in killing microbes, affects a bizarre and memorable list of animals: killer whales, Aleutian mink, Hereford cattle, beige mice, white tigers, Persian cats, and humans.

We studied an ugly new cat virus, feline T-lymphotrophic virus (FTLV), which is morphologically similar to HIV, the AIDS virus.

There were more lists to memorize, putting names together with function, origin, and structure. The mediators of inflammation—histamine, platelet aggregation factors, serotonin, heparin, SRS-A, prostaglandins, and bradykinins. Autoimmune diseases—lupus, rheumatoid arthritis, autoimmune hemolytic anemia, Hashimoto's thyroiditis (a.k.a. struma lymphomatosa), pemphigus vulgaris. Memorizing lists was a task always at hand if we had a free moment.

Diseases of the Cardiovascular System was filled with diagnostic techniques and tools, beginning with the physical exam.

A terrific many-hearted machine was brought over from the VTH to teach us what it was we were hearing through our stethoscopes. A phonocardiogram with an electrocardiograph display (more correctly called a phonoelectrocardioscope), it allowed us to hear the workings of a variety of hearts (different species, normal and with various murmurs and arrhythmias) while we watched the corresponding EKG. The speed and volume were adjustable so that you could pinpoint just exactly where in the cycle an aberration was occurring. If you just couldn't seem to pick up that third heart sound, or if you couldn't quite tell whether a murmur was systolic or diastolic, you could slow the machine until you could hear just when the ventricles contracted or when the aortic and pulmonic valves snapped shut and thus just exactly when the aberrant sound occurred. The machine was a wonderful training tool and something of a toy. They let us keep it in the pathology building for a few weeks, and we all took turns listening to its various hearts when we had the chance.

Dr. Dayton, a South African with a musical accent, taught the diagnostic technique of cardiac catheterization. Then Dr. Bleven, who looked like a younger version of actor Ben Johnson, lectured on normal radiography of the thoracic organs; he would show up for a lecture or two in each systems course we took, giving us the diagnostic tool of X ray and making it specific to each body system.

Dr. Caputi, autonomic nervous system expert, made an appearance with a review of that system's workings and its relevance to the cardiovascular system, its neurotransmitters and receptors, the autonomic control of the heart, drugs that altered this control, the mechanism of different arrhythmias. Brandon Brown, head of the VTH Critical Care Unit, lectured on the electrocardiogram and cardiac ultrasound and how to read them. He was so soft-spoken as to be barely audible, and he clearly considered these trips to the main campus a chore. He assigned homework to hone our skills through the old reliable method of repetition—more than two hundred EKG cases for us to decipher, measure, and diagnose.

There was a lot to remember, and not all of the lecturers were gifted, but as we practiced these techniques and sharpened our eyes and ears for reading them, we could feel ourselves becoming veterinarians, listening to the actual patient hearts that were surely in our futures. We were learning to ask automatically, every time we put stethoscope to chest, "Is the heart rate normal or abnormal? Is the rhythm regular or irregular? If it's irregular, is it regularly irregular or irregularly irregular? Is each heartbeat accompanied by a pulse palpated in the femoral artery? Is it full, weak, or thready? Is there a murmur? What's its timing, its location, its intensity? Is there a cardiac 'thrill' [vibration] palpatable on the thorax?" We moved on to cardiac arrest.

And then we progressed to the diagnostic tool of echocardiography, in which ultrasonic waves of energy are bounced from a transducer held on the outside of the chest to the heart and back again. The monitor displays a pie-shaped image of the heart in "real time"; that is, it is not a frozen image, and you can watch the valves moving. By moving the ice pick–width scanner, you can isolate areas that show the mitral valve, the left ventricular wall's width, the aorta and its valve, and the right ventricular chamber's size.

Dalton was my best study buddy, and we made lists of GTQs on which to drill each other. What's the most common cardiovascular defect in the canine? Patent ductus arteriosis. In the bovine? Ventricular septal defect. What size dog usually is afflicted with hemaningoscarcoma? Large to giant. What kind of EKG pattern do you expect to see with a pericardial effusion? Alternating high, low, high, low. What is the most common dysrhythmia in trauma patients? Premature ventricular contractions.

We made a game of writing exams for each other, trying to make them as difficult as we could. We'd take the other's exam and then review the answers together. It was fun, and it worked.

There were two lectures on echocardiography, and on the exam there would be projected slides of echocardiographs for our interpretation. Recognizing the structures of the heart in these displays takes some skill, which, in turn, requires some practice, due to the many different planes you can dissect the heart into with this tool, and thus the many different images you can create. So Dalton and I took a trip to the VTH library for some echo pictures to review. These made all the difference, and several classmates asked us for copies. In a gesture of the cooperative spirit we were *supposed* to feel, we complied, but grudgingly. Cooperation came easily with friends, although we were competitive against one another, too. It wasn't easy to be as openhanded with the people I wasn't particularly close to, however. I wanted to feel differently about sharing information, but it was hard not to be possessive of my notes and materials. They cost me such a lot of time, and I resented it when people who hadn't invested that time and made that effort wanted to profit from my work. It would happen again at the end of the semester in Diseases of the Urinary System, and again my mean spirit would show itself.

CHAPTER 12

The Sin-Eaters

OUR sophomore course in Veterinary Ethics seemed rather beside the point. Like the videotape of the tormented guinea pigs, it could only rekindle feelings that we worked constantly to snuff out—not that we were all of a cloth or all of one mind.

At one extreme was Elaine Davis, whose heart often seemed to control her head, who still wept openly six weeks after her very old Labrador retriever, Goldie, had been put to sleep because of acute kidney failure. At the other extreme were the Meat Inspectors, who thought that mice were for feeding to snakes, snakes were to make belts and hatbands out of, and rabbits were for target practice. Animals were to use. These guys hadn't come to CSU and plunked down their dollars to be scolded and told that animals have rights, as if they were Americans or something.

The rest of us fell somewhere in between crippling compassion and calloused insensitivity, but the truth was that we were all hardening and that we *wanted* to harden. We envied the toughness and detachment of the Meat Inspectors. We consciously sought to disengage our feelings—by ignoring them, by reasoning, by overload. Feelings were debilitating; feelings were a hindrance. They hurt, and they served little purpose, given the tasks we must perform. So the Vet Ethics course was an annoyance to those hard-hearts who needed it, and an anguish to the softies who didn't. I myself had had to come a long way to get this far. I didn't need anybody peeling away any half-formed calluses from my heart.

I had been as soft as anybody. I'd had sentimental episodes concerning all manner of animal life my whole life long.

Nancy and I were well into adulthood the day her Siamese cat, Ping, jumped onto the window ledge with a baby bird hanging from her mouth. We yelled and ran outside; Ping dropped the bird and darted away.

We both knew immediately that we'd made a mistake. We should have turned our heads and, as they say, let nature take its course. Ah, but nature's course is so unkind and so very hard to watch.

Nancy picked up the featherless bird. It was conscious and alert. Its big-eyed head swiveled on its skinny neck as it stared back at us. It appeared unhurt, except that its right leg stuck out from its body at an unnatural angle, and there were four bloodless punctures in its smooth breast. It's not easy to keep even an uninjured nestling alive for long, and the bite of a cat is ugly, filled with bacteria. The bird had a slim chance, if any. We both knew it. The easiest thing would have been to give it back to the cat, which had circled back to demand its prey. That was unthinkable.

We made a tissue-lined nest of a soup bowl and set it on the table between us. We regarded the solemn creature and it regarded us. We wished it would keel over, gasp, and die of its wounds, die of fright, die of shock. It didn't. We ran through all the options we could imagine.

To wring its neck. We'd seen our grandfather kill chickens by holding their heads in his big hand and snapping his wrist until the body fell free. We'd seen the body flop and flap, and run, too.

To cut off its head. Even the paring knife would do, one quick slice.

To bash it with a rock.

To take it to the vet and have it "put to sleep."

To drown it in the toilet.

To put it in a paper sack, put the sack behind the rear wheel of the truck, and back over it quickly. The ghoulish height of our brainstorming, this caused us both to shudder and turn away.

To put it in the oven, extinguish the pilot light, and turn on the gas, as Sylvia Plath had done. This option was passive enough that we decided to try it. But the safety feature on Nancy's range cut off the gas when we blew the pilot out. Still, we thought, we might be able to gas the bird on top of the stove, by blowing out the pilot lights, putting the nest on one of the burners, and fitting a larger bowl over the top to seal in the gas. The bird was tiny; surely, we reasoned, just the gas escaping from the unlit pilot would kill it.

We sat at the kitchen table. Minutes crept by. It seemed like a long time, and we figured that mere minutes should be enough to kill such a small and injured baby. Like a cook peeking at a baking pie, I lifted the edge of the larger bowl, bent down, and peered under. The bird peeped. We abandoned the experiment. We didn't have the stomach for it.

The bird died two days later, two days of hearty worm-eating vigor, just when we were getting our hopes up that we and this bird would defy the odds. We wondered whether it had suffered much.

"Death is not the worst thing," Mama had said again and again all through our lives, whenever the occasion arose to offer this cold comfort. *Her* mother's life was evidence enough of that. Our grandmother suffered the deaths of her two sons in separate auto accidents, suffered a loveless marriage to an alcoholic bully, and then finally suffered a slow death from a cancer that, by the end, had eaten away most of her abdominal organs.

Mama's second daughter, Kay Lynn, born between Nancy and me, had hydrocephalus, and her death, five months later, was, to Mama, a blessing and a mercy.

But "Death is not the worst thing" was something you said

after the fact. It was, like surrendering to God's mysterious will, a way to survive, accept, and move on from loss. It was her credo, but it was useful only in the aftermath. Death might not be the worst thing, but it was not for mere mortals to decide what it was better than.

Daddy was suffering one of the final crises of his sixteen-year stay in the Fort Lyon Veterans Administration Hospital, and Mama was trying to tell the doctor that his suffering had gone on too long. She clutched a crumpled wet tissue in her brown and work-worn hand as she said that she wanted no heroic measures, no extraordinary procedures to save her husband. As if with its own life, that hand shook back and forth. What she wanted was to put the matter in the doctor's hands; she wanted him to decide what a "heroic measure" was; she wanted him to deal with the specifics. He should be the one to play God; he was the doctor.

She couldn't escape, however. The doctor listened, nodded, and then explained that Daddy's veins were so overused, worn out, and broken down that it was impossible to find one through which to administer antibiotics, vital fluids, and nutrition. He needed her consent to perform a jejunostomy—to implant a tube in Daddy's jejunum, a portion of the small intestine, through which to deliver those life-sustaining substances. It was, of course, a surgical procedure; he needed Mama's signature.

She regretted doing it, but she signed, for it was one thing to say no heroics and quite another to be the one to stand and say that no, this particular procedure, without which he would die, would not be done. She would not take his life into her own hands and extinguish it. She could not.

Killing is hard. It does not come easily or naturally. To learn to kill is work; it takes effort and practice.

I was practicing.

Death is the inescapable conclusion of all life, sooner or later, and sometimes it is sooner. And sometimes it would be by my hand. I had delivered death; I could do it. I would do it time and again before I graduated, after I graduated, on unto the end of my practice.

• • •

And the last thing I needed was Morris Kahn and his course. What was the point, I wondered, of persuading us to a position that would make it difficult or impossible to do our work? But no one had asked me whether I wanted this course, just as no one had asked whether I wanted to memorize the rules of veterinary nomenclature or the names of 173 viruses. Whether or not I *wanted* to enter into abstract discussions of a dog's right to procreate or a cat's right to its claws or a steer's right not to be eaten, it was a hoop through which I was obviously going to have to jump. I gritted my teeth and prepared to jump.

I attended class. I did the reading, which included works by Kant and Descartes, decidedly *not* medical texts. I wrote one unspectacular paper. I spoke up in class what I hoped was enough to earn my "participation" points. But I didn't like it. It made me uncomfortable, as it was meant to.

Morris maintained that the bulk of the vet school program was a nonthinking curriculum, a pile of facts and a set of tasks that demanded compliance rather than questioning. Of course, that was what most of us wanted.

The Meat Inspectors despised Morris, with his beard, his potbelly, and his bleeding heart. The course was beneath their contempt. And the topics he demanded we discuss— such as whether it was moral for veterinarians to be hunters— incited them to gut ugliness. Some of the Meat Inspectors could be plenty nasty. You couldn't help feeling sorry for Morris.

From there, it was just a step from genuinely sympathizing to actually liking. Eventually, Morris and I got to be friends of sorts. After the course was long over, he confided to me that a couple of the Meat Inspectors had been baldly honest on the final exam, stating flatly that they hadn't read "one fucking word" of the assigned work and that they thought the class was bullshit.

I was stunned. How could he have passed them after they had admitted to not doing the work, after they'd insulted him?

Morris shrugged. They would have had to repeat the course, he said, and he wasn't up to wrestling them again through the issue of animal rights. Our moral leader had taken the expedient route. I couldn't hide my shock.

"You pick your fights," he said. His work made him privy to a lot of cruelty and misery and, you might even say, evil. His code of right and wrong had absolute parameters—it is inexcusable to alter an animals' physiology, to deny or compromise its *telos* (an Aristotelian term meaning the nature or function intrinsic to a living being). As the Vet Ethics professor and a member of the Animal Care Committee, he had to rule on every question concerning animal welfare, and his position had to be defined by his strict code. But, of course, the very nature of veterinary medicine is in violation of that code, which, at its extreme dictates that one has no right to own, cage, or confine even the best-loved pet.

There were lots of fights, lots of situations in which his job was to defend the animals' position, usually in the face of busy and pragmatic professors and administrators. His job was a constant lesson in compromise. It wore on him.

He had brought one such issue before the class for discussion, the motion to "debark" the blood-donor dogs at the Veterinary Teaching Hospital; that is, to surgically remove tissue from their pharynx, which renders them unable to howl or bark, though they can still utter a low uncaninelike sound. Morris called this operation a "mutilation."

He asked us to consider also the larger issue, the morality of caging these twenty-some dogs for several years, to use their blood for transfusing client dogs at the hospital. The defense, of course, was that if these dogs did not serve this function, they would have to be destroyed. There were not enough homes out there for all our extra dogs. We were confronted with the ideal versus the real.

And it was more bearable, too, knowing that after a dog had served for a few years it was put up for adoption. And, too, their lives at the VTH were not horrible—they were cared for by students, taken on walks, fed well, kept in a warm building, caged with other dogs. However, Morris asked us again and again to consider what quality of life is to a dog.

Morris's position, of course, was that "debarking" is inexcusable and unacceptable.

The reality, however, was that these twenty to twenty-five dogs were caged directly beneath faculty offices, and the dogs were bored and would bark whenever anyone passed through their area, whenever they saw a shadow, whenever they heard a noise, whenever another of them barked—in other words, all the time. The constant barking was like Chinese water torture to the men and women working upstairs.

While we could not know what significance it had to a dog to have his bark altered, somehow we needed to imagine and then weigh that against the bombardment of the people who had to work, study, and think in the same building.

We in veterinary medicine are not, on the whole, philosophers. We don't enjoy grappling with insolvable moral questions. And there is no end to them, in school or in practice. Reality dictates that most new vets work in someone else's practice; and as hired guns, they must do what they are paid to do, which is usually whatever the client wants done. Not only must they debark dogs and declaw cats but they are also asked to euthanize healthy animals that have developed bad habits or become inconvenient, as well as curable animals whose owners cannot afford, or choose not to afford, the treatment.

That was the real world, and I had been there already.

I was a technician in a small-animal practice a few years before I worked for Jill Henderson. A small black-and-white terrier was brought in to be put to death. My boss "let" me do it, although it is not legal for a technician to euthanize animals (what would constitute malpractice in a euthanasia case, I do not know).

I remember Domino because he was my first and because he was sweet and obedient, because he wanted only to please.

It was a test of strength and will, a moment that I was only too aware could separate the sheep from the goats and determine my future. I talked to the little dog, patted him, carried him down the hall, and put him on the stainless-steel table. I asked him to shake, and he raised his paw, pleased to do his trick, pleased to please me. I slipped a tourniquet around his leg, and when the vein stood out, I inserted the needle, released the tourniquet, and pushed the plunger. The dog slumped dead on the table.

For a moment, I stood there in horror at my power—and in greater horror that I had been able to wield it. In the privacy of that small exam room, I cried. And then I picked up Domino's body and put him in the freezer for Animal Control's weekly pickup.

Domino's owners were moving away; they'd said they couldn't take him. They left him, alive, in my arms, did not see him die so trustingly. I wish I could talk to them today, ten years later, and tell them that I still see that room, the reflection of the bright lamp off the shiny table, the black-and-white dog. I would tell them that it hurt. I hope that they still think of him, and I hope that they hurt, too, for that is as it should be.

We veterinarians are the sin-eaters. We are the butchers. We do the dirty work and keep quiet about it. We make it all too easy.

In the real world, our meat appears ground or sliced and wrapped in plastic. It comes from Safeway or Piggly Wiggly and not from the shoulder of a pig or the rump of a steer. I don't think about it, either, as I eat my bacon.

Our next-door neighbor Beverly raises a pig every summer. Every spring, there is a new piglet; every fall, a freezer full of pork. She teaches the piglet to sit, stay, and come on command. The pig is smart and eager, and this training makes Beverly's life easier when it's time to clean the pen. She pulls his favorite weeds for him and feeds him through the rails while she scratches his back and he grunts with pleasure. She turns the hose on him when the days get hot, and he jumps and twists in the cool spray, squealing with obvious delight, for he's just a baby, just a growing boy, full of young life and energy.

Those pigs—one each year—that live in Beverly's backyard and are killed there with a single shot in the head are the lucky ones. Their lives are short, but they are real lives, with mud and water and good food and space to romp and root and sunshine and shade and an occasional shower and back rub. Their lives would be even better if they had the company of another pig, but Beverly has room for only one pig at a time in the freezer and one pig at a time in the backyard.

If we had the courage, we would buy a litter mate of next year's pig and would build a bigger pen to straddle our properties. We would eat honest pork from pigs that never knew the terror, the sounds, the smells, the sights of the slaughterhouse, nor the misery of the feedlot.

I love ham, pork chops, and *carne adovada*. The contradictions were not new to me, nor to any of us. I did not welcome this ethics course that asked me to consider absolute right, that rubbed my nose in the enormity of the gulf between what I might feel or believe and what I had to do. *Had to do*, or not become a veterinarian. *Had to do*, or not work.

During this course, a speaker from the VTH Oncology unit's grief-counseling service told us that it's okay to cry with our clients. But I wanted not to cry; I wanted to feel less, not more. How easy and therapeutic it must be, I thought, to grieve with clients in the purity of the cancer unit, where beloved pets die only after a good, fierce struggle. These patients are brought to CSU at great expense after their illnesses have exhausted the resources and training of their local vets, and when death comes, when death is *delivered*, it is a final kindness. It is the last ministration of the warrior doctors who have battled until the end for *life*.

But in the pathology building, where we sophomores tested and dissected, or in the typical veterinary practice, where the bottom line is the bottom line, who comforts *us*, the sin-eaters, the dealers of death?

You tell yourself that to pay for these sins, you will some-day alleviate pain, save life, and heal. But you will also crop ears, cut tails, amputate kittens' knuckles, eliminate dogs' voices, and kill dozens, hundreds, whole litters at a time because a dog's or cat's owner just didn't get around to spaying the animal or because she wanted her kids to see the miracle of birth. At first, you'll be working for someone else, and perhaps you'll tell yourself that it will be different when you're the boss. But when you get your own practice, you'll have so many bills to pay, you'll have employees—a technician or two, a bookkeeper, a receptionist—and insurance, rent, utilities, your student loan, equipment to pay off, drugs and supplies to buy. And you will have grown accustomed to compromise. And you might kill the dog that is brought to you for killing, because you need the money, you need the client, and because you don't have a better option for the animal that has for some reason lost its value to the one person in the world who had been willing to be its advocate in this crowded, hostile world.

Animals are property—closer to an automobile than to a human being—in the eyes of the law. And so we veterinarians—though trained as physicians—are, in fact, more like mechanics in many ways. Our patients are repaired only as long as their value exceeds the cost of upkeep, though often, it is true, that value is defined by emotion and love. Very often, however, the owner opts to junk the animal and get a new one.

When I think of the emotional beating we take in school—and in the real world—I wonder why more veterinarians are not psychopathic murderers, rampaging through the streets. The fact that, by and large, we don't go mad attests to how much the human heart can take.

Morris Kahn's goal was no less than to change a generation of veterinarians from the society-dictated role they play—with its view of animals as mere property—to the advocates of these fellow travelers. He had to weigh the value of every fight he chose to fight, every cause that he took up. I hadn't thought through as carefully or articulated as clearly my own moral code, but I had one. We each had one. And I ducked under it when I had to. Faced with two evils, I picked one every time. We were all trying to stay upright on slippery slopes. There was no self-righteous place to stand and blame Morris for choosing not to spend his energy trying to convert the Meat Inspectors, the ossified hard-asses, in whose stony hearts sympathy found no purchase.

CHAPTER 13

▬

Food Animal Medicine

SOPHOMORE year, we took our first elective, a choice between Exotic Animals and Food Animal Management and Herd Health. This was the first branch in the road, the first in a series of choices to be made during the next three years that would separate the large-animal from the small-animal practitioners. Many of us would want it both ways, but as veterinary medicine becomes increasingly specialized, fewer and fewer can actually *have* it both ways. (Future vets will no doubt have to specialize in one species, or even in a particular system of one species, as human physicians do.) Still, in my vision of the ideal future, I was a dog, cat, and horse doctor, and in this perfect practice, I thought I'd be more likely to see the occasional cow than the occasional ferret. So I signed up for Food Animal Management.

It was the wrong choice for a couple of reasons. I naïvely thought of the course as Farm Animal rather than Food Animal, and I completely overlooked the Management. There was truth in advertising; I just chose to ignore it. I had no one but myself to blame when the course turned out to have little to do with medicine—and everything to do with business. For that occasional cow I would see in practice, the core curriculum of systems courses would hold me in good stead. The exotic pets I would often see had marked physiological differences from the

135

standard domestic species that we studied, however, and I would have to educate myself case by case, wishing I had a broader base from which to begin.

It didn't take too long for me to realize I was in the wrong course. (I'm not a slow learner, but it was too late, anyway.)

Economics—the market value of an animal—is the essential concept for the food animal vet; I soon realized it was one I'd never master. The animal that I thought of as a patient was essentially a machine that took hay, grain, and water and converted them to meat, wool, milk, or eggs. The goal was to minimize maintenance and make these "machines" work more efficiently. The issues were species variations in feed-conversion rates, hybrid-vigor potential in crossbreeding programs, carcass yield, shipping losses due to stress or disease, cost effectiveness of vaccination programs, and how to manipulate the variables to increase profit.

It would be fair to say that I couldn't connect with the basic message, nor with some of the speakers, either. We got the "real life" perspective from an assortment of hard-nosed and rednecked guest speakers, officials from the Cattlemen's Organization, a fellow from a sheep feedlot, a panel of dairymen.

I was furiously scribbling notes about the ratio of the fall in milk production to the incidence of mastitis, screw claw, hoof rot, and muscle spasms when one of the speakers broke in to impart a gem of wisdom. "It is true that the profitability of any dairy operation does depend upon milking equipment and the herdman's efficiency and nutrition and mastitis rates, but the essential factor," he said, "is this . . ."

He paused for dramatic effect. I looked up from my notebook, my pencil at the ready. As a group, we leaned slightly forward, lured by the confidential tone of his voice.

He grinned. ". . . how much money your wife spends."

The Meat Inspectors hooted. The panel erupted in laughter.

I looked at Dalton, she looked at me, and I could read her face: We're paying money for this? We're sitting here listening to this bullshit when we've got real work to do? She sat back in her chair and shook her head. I closed my notebook and slipped my mechanical pencil into my backpack.

We had to do a group project for the course, to visit a food animal facility and assess its ventilation system. I'd never considered the complexities of ventilation before; the subject had never crossed my mind. The project was pleasant, however, a field trip with my buddies, Dalton, Eric Ferguson, and Mae Daniels. We chose the American Breeder's Service, about ten miles north of Fort Collins. This facility housed bulls and assessed their genetic traits and their success or failure in passing these traits to their offspring.

We dutifully sketched the ventilation system and asked pertinent questions, but our real interest was not in the air flow in the barns but in the work that was done there.

Cows were artificially inseminated with the bulls' collected semen; then the calves were studied for each of a series of desired characteristics: birth weight, weaning weight, yearling weight, ease of giving birth, and, in dairy cattle, udder width, height, and depth, percentage of fat and protein in milk, and pounds of milk given daily. It took about five years for a bull calf to "prove" himself as a superior breeder; otherwise, he would be culled for slaughter. The semen was available for sale, sold in "straws," ranging in price from under ten dollars to many hundreds of dollars. A catalog listed the offerings, including a breakdown of each bull's scores on the list of desirable traits, so a cattleman could shop for those traits that his herd lacked. The scores were also posted on a board hanging above each bull's stall.

The animals themselves were beautiful and huge, all with rings in their noses. Although the facility specialized in dairy cattle (its home office was in Wisconsin), there was a great variety of breeds, including beef cattle. The most exotic looking was the Belgian Blue, a double-muscled beef animal with a beautiful pearly gray coat and a massive build, the bulk of a sumo wrestler. We stood and admired their amazing bodies. Still, I couldn't help but think of Morris Kahn and what he must think of such genetic manipulation.

Course coordinator Marvin Anderson surprised me by also assigning a paper on "animal welfare." I thought about the Belgian Blue bulls and genetic manipulation, but for all their unnaturalness, these exotics were well tended. I simply couldn't work up much anger on their behalf. Instead, I kept thinking of veal calves.

In the food animal industry, the concern for animal welfare is in direct relation to its impact on profit. When overcrowding increases mortality, these pragmatic business people will address overcrowding. When stress decreases carcass yield, they will work to reduce stress. When unsanitary conditions increase disease and mortality, cleanliness will become their concern. They would *prefer* to treat the animals humanely, as a rule, but only up to the point where kindness begins to cut into their earnings.

This particular course was concerned with the economic health of the rancher, and I considered how to walk that line. I didn't know Anderson, and I didn't want to brand myself as an emotional, weak-minded bleeding heart. Every time I sat down to write the paper, though, I found myself confronting the horrors of the modern factory farm. There didn't seem to be a way to avoid the subject, so I took a deep breath and poured out my opinions.

It is up to veterinarians, I wrote, to work for the changes that would make the lives of food animals bearable. There had to be alternatives to sows bearing their young in farrowing crates twenty-two inches by seven feet, to denying veal calves the opportunity to turn around, feel the sunlight, run and buck. I talked about the five freedoms that animal-rights activists demand: to turn around; to groom; to stand up; to lie down; and to stretch their limbs freely. The activists were radicals, and some considered them destructive lunatics, but I wrote that I found these demands moderate in the extreme. I would add two more: freedom of access to others of their own kind and freedom of access to the outdoors. I turned it in, thinking that I had probably exposed myself once again as an idiot with a fourth-grade sentimentality.

The paper came back with stick-on stars on the top. Anderson had written that it was a good paper and that he liked my proposals, though he noted that paying for improved (and thus more expensive) animal care was the hitch. I felt just a little bit better about Food Animal Management; Morris Kahn had more allies than it sometimes seemed.

I was glad to see the end of that course and its business orientation, however. We would take up the *diseases* of food animals in our systems courses.

Hardware disease was covered in the cardiovascular course, because the organ at risk is the heart, but it is also covered as an eating disorder in the course on the digestive system. My notes called it traumatic reticulosis, the most common cause of pericarditis—inflammation of the sac surrounding the heart—in cattle.

Whether by accident or intent, cows apparently have a tendency to eat metal—baling wire, nails, bits of fencing, nuts and bolts. These pieces travel from the rumen (or first stomach) to the reticulum (second stomach), where they are separated from the heart and its surrounding sac (the pericardium) by mere inches of tissue. Any number of things—the normal contractions of the cow's four stomachs, a change in posture, lying down, getting up, being mounted by another cow—can cause the wire to penetrate the reticular wall and the diaphragm, move into the thorax, and puncture the pericardial sac. When this happens and the disease progresses undetected, the prognosis is poor, the treatment uneconomical (the bottom line, the bottom line), and a bit of a horror show, as well.

The pericardial sac fills with pus, causing a pressure upon the heart that decreases the return of blood through the veins. Cardiac action whips the fluid, creating fibrous threads that attach to the heart, a condition called "shaggy heart." Blood isn't moving where it should be moving, and the cow is in pain. She doesn't want to move, she grunts and moans, and her milk production falls off sharply. When detected early, the disease can be treated with antibiotics. For advanced cases, however, the treatment is radical.

Cattle have a complete mediastinum; that is, the chest is divided by a membrane into two separate compartments. So if a pneumothorax (air in the chest cavity, but outside the lung, which inhibits breathing) develops on one side, the cow can still breathe via her other side, which is still functional. This gives her a nominal chance of living through this surgical remedy: removing that portion of the cow's ribs that lie over the heart, piercing the pericardial sac, draining the fluid, perhaps removing that troublesome little bit of wire, treating the cow with systemic antibiotics, and sometimes cutting away the sac itself. The success rate of this invasive procedure is not high, and cattle with advanced cases of hardware disease are usually culled for slaughter.

The prevention, however, is cheap and easy—feeding each cow a magnet. The cost is about seven dollars, and the magnet tends to lodge in the reticulum and gather the loose wire the animal eats over the course of her life, keeping it safely away from the heart. Once or twice a year, it's prudent to check the herd with a compass to make sure that none of the cows has passed the magnet through her digestive tract and out into the pasture, embedded in a cowpie.

Respiratory ailments are the number-one medical problems in feedlots, so in the respiratory course, fourteen lectures were devoted to the diseases of cattle. In the high-speed turnover of course topics, this was a major block.

Unit instructor Owen Colson handed out 112 pages of single-spaced notes that listed each disease; its numerous synonymous names; its definition; a short summary of its effects; etiologies or theorized causes; pathogenesis—how it did what it did when it did it; history; clinical signs; any age, breed, or sex predilections; season most prevalent; how it presents; histopathy; differential diagnosis lists; and treatments. It was a daunting document, but as Lloyd had assured me *again and again*, the most common and most important ones would be covered *again and again*. That was the good news.

The bad news was that the most common diseases, such as infectious bovine rhiotracheitis (IBR), have evolved zillions of names; it is also known as red nose, vesicular exanthema, Blaschenausschlag, necrotic rhinitis, and on and on. Caused by a herpes virus, it also occurs in many different forms: abortion (we would cover it in Reproductive Diseases), conjunctivitis (we'd have it in Ophthalmology), encephalomyelitis (Neurology), enteritis (the Gastrointestinal System), and vaginitis-genital form (we'd see it yet again in Reproduction).

At the end of Colson's fourteen lectures, he arranged a lab session in a pen near the anatomy building. Monford's Feedlot had donated a sick steer, and we were to auscultate—listen to—the length of his trachea and his lungs, note his behavior and attitude, and decide what kind of pathology we expected to find. Once the entire class had examined him—we would stagger our departures from the lecture hall so that the poor beast would not be overwhelmed by all of us at one time—we would euthanize him and confirm or disprove our theories.

That day had been fairly mild, but a storm system was moving in. The sky was heavy and dark. The snow that began to fall was very wet; the huge flakes fell hard as rain.

Anyone could see that the steer, a Hereford, was dying. He was very thin, and he held his head and neck low and as straight from his body as he could, in his weakened condition, to straighten the airway. He breathed openmouthed; his tongue lolled out. His eyes were shut against the snow and the crowd of students around him. Every breath shook his sides as he used his abdominal muscles to draw in oxygen. He made a very slight grunting noise as he worked at staying alive, and a ropy strand of green snot hung from his left nostril. The right nostril was crusted, and where the scabs had broken away, the mucosa was red and cracked. He coughed occasionally, but the effort was so great that he seemed to suppress the urge. He tensed his small frame against the effort, and after a cough, he panted. Only a few of us heard both lungs, for early on in the session, he collapsed on his left side.

The heat of his body and the footsteps of 123 vet students turned the snow to mud, but the temperature was dropping and the snow continued. Left alone, he would have soon disappeared under a white mantle and the storm would have taken him in its quiet, wet way.

But our stethoscopes brushed the snow away and our constant prodding of his poor body soaked the hair through and through. With our hands pressing on him, his coat could not hold the water away from his skin. He didn't shiver; I don't think he had the strength. By the time I reached him, he seemed in a stupor, his body suffering mightily but his consciousness already gone.

I placed my stethoscope on his cold, wet red coat. Lungs meant to be airy, buoyant, and springy were now filled with a thick exudate that rattled with his every breath. Parts of the lungs had collapsed; the walls stuck together with the thick junk that filled them. When he inhaled, the air popped them open with a crackling sound.

Crouching next to the dying animal in the falling wet snow, my right hand holding the diaphragm of my stethoscope against his side, my left hand resting on his chest, I suddenly thought of another steer, another time, twenty-two years before, when most of my classmates were still in diapers, and a fourteen-year-old girl first decided that she would be a vet.

Chama, a small town in northern New Mexico, didn't have a vet, but it had a lot of livestock, and I made it a point to hang around wherever there was a chance that I could ride. In the summers and on weekends, I'd walk down the highway six miles to John Perry's ranch, where I'd do any chores they asked me to, or just hang around and get in the way until somebody let me ride a horse.

The summer I was fourteen, a vet whose name I've forgotten, whom I'll call Dr. Jones, came up from Santa Fe to write and sign health papers for the Jicarilla Apache livestock sale in Dulce, on the reservation about twenty-five miles northwest of Chama. He needed somebody to record numbers and pertinent facts about each animal as it passed through the sales barn; John Perry recommended me. And so I got my first job in vet medicine.

We worked outside, checking each steer or cow as it came down the narrow alley to the auction ring. From inside the barn, I could hear the hypnotic cadence of the auctioneer's chant as Dr. Jones examined each animal for overt signs of illness. Most of the cattle had diarrhea, and the constant swishing of their tails spattered them—and us—with flecks of cow shit, but it seemed no cause for alarm. He read off the number on the ear tag and flipped down the lower lip to check the animal's age. "Number seven ten," Dr. Jones would say, then he'd run a gloved arm up the cow's rectum. "Open," he'd call, which meant she wasn't pregnant, and thus wasn't worth as much, might have a uterine infection, and would probably be sold to slaughter. Then he'd mark her side with a crayon so the bidders inside would know. I would write her number and *open* on my list. I hated it when they were open.

When we broke for lunch, everybody crowded into a big room in the back of the auction barn. There was a huge coffee urn and long tables with plastic cloths where the men sat to eat and laugh about their shrewd dealings of the morning. Two Jicarilla women were selling hot dogs and tamales from two big trays covered with foil. They talked to one another and joked with the men in Apache. They wore velvet blouses and long skirts, which covered their ample laps and fell in folds to the floor around the legs of their gray metal folding chairs. The room was hot with summer and the press of bodies and the coffee and food, but they seemed not to notice.

I took a foam cup and filled it with hot black coffee. I didn't see any sugar or cream, and I wouldn't ask. The Indian women pulled back the foil from the two trays. I took a paper napkin and a hot dog, fished out the $2 that Mama had given me that morning for lunch and paid them the $1.25 they asked for.

Dr. Jones was sitting with some other men, so I ducked back out the door, away from the voices and the heat, walked down the long cattle chutes, found a shady spot, and sat down to eat. Flies buzzed around me, the cattle bawled, and the muffled sound of laughter and talk drifted to me from the lunchroom.

Two Apache cowboys opened a pen above the chute and started the cattle down toward the sales ring, not pushing them but just getting them going, and then they went back inside.

I sat there in the New Mexico heat and dust, alone with these slow-moving, slow-witted cows, which were coming toward me as if by habit or lack of any thought to stop. The first in line was a Brahma steer, a beautiful animal, with a

143

pearly gray coat and huge brown eyes, the enormous hump above his shoulders making him an exotic creature among the Herefords and Angus crosses. His loose skin hung in heavy dewlaps from his neck and his large ears drooped like those of a hound.

I had spent some time trying to draw these wonderful animals—from pictures in books and from memory of those I'd seen at rodeos—and I leaned forward to admire him. I wanted to be an artist, I thought. I wanted to capture this beauty, but I wasn't nearly good enough yet. Every time I put pencil to paper, the mystery eluded me.

As he drew up almost even with me, the steer groaned and went down on his knees. Breathing heavily but not struggling to rise, he knelt there, his butt high in the air. I sat very still and looked into his large brown eyes. After a moment, he groaned again and his whole body shuddered to the ground. His enormous weight seemed to shake the earth. He lay there, his chest wall heaving. The cattle behind him stopped.

I got slowly to my feet and walked to the fence, bent under the bottom rail, and slid into the alley with the cattle. I knelt beside the steer, but he gave me no notice. Tentatively, I touched him, ran my hand along his soft gray neck, his big jaw, his enormous round cheek. He did not protest, and so I petted him gently. I liked the sweaty sweet smell of his coat. There were bubbles coming from each nostril and a pool of spit flecked with blood made a damp ring around his leathery nose in the dirt. His eyelashes were thick and long, stuck together with tears and spiked with dirt.

I don't know how long I sat there watching his quiet struggle, absorbed in looking at this huge animal. But suddenly, Dr. Jones was outside the chute.

"What's going on here?" His alarm sounded in his voice.

"He's sick, Dr. Jones. He just fell down here."

"Get out of there. Are you trying to get hurt, or what?"

I stood up. "What about him?"

He ignored the question. "Get your clipboard and let's get back to work. They're ready to start." He had already turned from me and was walking down the alley.

"But what about him?" I called after him.

He turned around and looked at me. "He's dying, Loretta. He's got tuberculosis."

"Oh," I said. I looked back down at the pretty gray steer. "Are they going to move him, so the other cows can get by?"

Dr. Jones was obviously losing patience with his emotional girl helper. "They'll just go over him."

"Oh, no, please, can't we move him, so they won't step on him? He's sick, Dr. Jones. He feels awful."

"No." His voice was stern. "Now get out of there and let's get to work."

I hesitated only another moment before I slid back under the rail and got my clipboard and pen, readied myself to record numbers and data on the cattle lined up in the chute. All afternoon, I did my work, wrote down what Dr. Jones called out, efficient and obedient as a machine.

I tried not to look at the steer, getting stepped on, getting crapped on, getting covered with dirt. His damp nose was crusted with dust now, and sometimes he would cough and try to stand, but he never struggled long before he collapsed again. He was still there, lying alone in the chute when the auction was over and we headed back to Chama. Maybe he never got up. Maybe he died there. Or maybe somebody finally came and shot him.

By the end of the day, I didn't want to be an artist anymore. Mama was probably right—I couldn't draw well enough, anyway. I would be a veterinarian. And I wouldn't be like Dr. Jones. I'd be as kind as I could be. I'd be able to help the next down-in-the-dirt steer I came across, even if it was only to help him out of this world. But I wouldn't run cattle over other sick cattle.

As we drove back into the growing darkness, I didn't talk. I didn't have anything to say, and neither did Dr. Jones. I just sat quietly, resolved to be a better veterinarian than he was. I didn't tell anybody about this plan of mine. Maybe it seemed too farfetched, and maybe I didn't want holes shot through it. I'd just surprise them, Mama and Daddy, Dr. Jones, John Perry, all of them.

• • •

It had been a long, circuitous road from that dying steer to the one before me in the snow.

I shut my eyes and listened to the sounds inside the dying Hereford being trampled not by cattle but by students.

"Excuse me," one of my classmates said, interrupting my thoughts, squeezing next to me, in a tone that let me know that I was the one who needed excusing. I had hogged this particular spot long enough. "I'd like to be able to auscultate his entire lung field," she said. She was angry, and I was angry, too. We were cold and wet. This wasn't fun.

"Sorry," I said, and stood up.

I walked past Dr. Colson to the fence. "Did you hear the fluid in his lungs?" he asked.

"Yes, thank you, I sure did." I leaned against the fence and jammed my hands deep in my pockets. We were just about finished examining the steer, and he was just about finished with his struggle, as well.

When the last student was satisfied, Dr. Colson knelt and injected the steer with euthanasia solution, thus ending his life quietly and quickly. Colson's stocking cap was pulled tightly down, his coveralls were blotched with mud and manure, and his jutting beard was collecting a layer of snow. He sharpened his knife on a whetstone while he asked in a rhetorical way what we thought we'd heard; he wasn't expecting answers from the 123 of us lined up along the fence and crowded around the pen.

Two students pulled the steer's legs up and out of the way, and Dr. Colson made an easy incision into the chest. He cut quickly through hide and muscle, and one of the students handed him the rib cutters. As he broke through the bone, the crunching sound filled the quiet afternoon. Steam rose from the steer's chest cavity, like his spirit unleashed.

Dr. Colson reached inside and with a couple of quick slashes freed the lungs and pulled them out, dripping with fresh, hot red blood. He held them aloft like a trophy and slowly turned so that each of us could get a good look at the tissues. They were the wrong color, the wrong texture, the wrong weight.

146

They were bluish and mottled with deep red, streaked with creamy yellow pus, when they should have been pink and light and filled with air.

Night was falling fast, and a couple of students volunteered to help get the carcass winched into the back of the CSU pickup to take it to the VTH, where it would be picked up by a rendering company.

I walked away, snugging my jacket closer, chilled to the bone. I had to study tonight, should review bovine respiratory disease and get it firmly fixed in my mind. I wasn't exactly in the mood, but I'd do it, anyway. I'd feel better once I got warm. There was no point in getting depressed about a steer that was bred, born, and raised to be a piece of meat. I reminded myself that I wasn't a little girl anymore.

CHAPTER 14

Gunner

DR. Charlie Goodman was the star and leader of Diseases of the Urinary System, a.k.a. Urology. He had gone to Cornell University vet school with my friend and former boss, Jill Henderson, who confirmed his reputed genius. He had completed a rapid Ph.D. immediately after his seemingly effortless D.V.M.

He had an urban look that I normally didn't find attractive—shiny black hair combed straight back, Italian boots with pointy toes. He was short and flashy; he drove a brand new Corvette. He put me in mind of a young Mafia don. And yet he *was* attractive, with his boyish grin and teasing manner. He started every lecture with "Good morning, class," to which we answered, "Good morning, teacher."

I liked him, too, because he was good to his research cats, and committed to them as well. His work in feline leukemia has implications for human medicine, because this disease, like AIDS, is caused by a retrovirus, and its victims often succumb to secondary infections. The animals he experimented upon were not subordinated to the importance of the research, however. He never destroyed them, sent them to the pound, or recycled them to CSU for surgery students to practice upon. He found homes for those that could be safely adopted (those free of the feleuk virus, which is contagious to other cats). The virus-free cats that he couldn't place in individual homes went (after being neutered or spayed) to the large country place—and barn—of Scott Gossett, who had been our Biochemistry instructor freshman year. I figured that Gossett, too, must have a heart if he took in those homeless cats. Goodman's research cats were reputed to be affectionate and social because of the care and attention they got in Goodman's project. They were cats that had been loved, and they returned that love. This was a remarkable level of commitment, and I admired him and liked him all the more because of it. He was a stand-up guy.

His subject was the electrolytes of the body, minerals, salts, and ions that could be thrown out of balance by disease, and that, once out of whack, caused changes in nerve conduction, muscle contraction, heartbeat rhythm and strength, blood volume, and the volume of urine produced and excreted. He seemed the master of the body's salts and their balances.

His presentation was impressive. He lectured from his head, without notes, and he didn't use slides, although almost every other lecturer depended upon them. (The typical systems course lecture began with the professor setting his notes on the podium, going to the back of the hall to load his carousel of slides into the projector, walking back to the podium, dimming the lights—whereupon the weariest among us began to doze—and then beginning to teach, laser pointer in one hand, projector control in the other.) Goodman occasionally used the blackboard to make a point or to calculate a fluid or electrolyte deficit, but usually he simply stood in front of us and delivered.

His lectures were fast-paced, so I taped them all. I think it stroked his ego. He teased me once when he happened to see me recording another professor's presentation. "Oh," he said, a hurt tone in his voice, "I thought you recorded only *me*."

Goodman's presentations were case-oriented, which we liked. It was clinical thinking, and we were eager to practice thinking this way.

His colleague in the course, Dr. Elder, gave us some experience in preparing cases. He gave us paper animals; that is, a written case history—signalment, presenting complaint, some physical-exam findings, and maybe another clue or two. Then he sent us home to work them up. We searched back and forth among notes and textbooks, looking for differential diagnoses, tests to order, interpretations of lab findings, possible treatments, and prognoses. These puzzles took hours to prepare, and everybody *did* prepare, for the clinicians selected students to present at random. No one would risk the humiliation and embarrassment that fell upon the unprepared. Besides, this was fun—simulated vet med.

But when we assembled in the lecture hall, prepared or not, it was raw nerves. Dr. Elder would look up from his list of our names, gaze around the hall, and, after we had squirmed for a moment, call one of us under fire.

When I heard him say, "Loretta Gage," my mouth went dry and my heart began to pound against my rib cage. I waited to see whether he was going to say something more. He looked around the room. "Loretta, where are you seated?"

"Here, Dr. Elder." I knew I was smiling nervously. I hoped it didn't look to him like a smirk or a grimace, like a cowering dog pulling back her lips in submission. He followed my voice, and our eyes met.

"Oh, good, Loretta. You're representing the back-row faction?"

I felt myself flush. He already had me pegged as some kind of ne'er-do-well because I was in back with the Meat Inspectors.

"Yes, sir, you bet," I said, hearing my own nervous words, which I hoped didn't sound as smart-ass to him as they did to me. Just answer the question, Retta, I told myself. Don't elaborate.

"Well, Loretta, I'm sure you're familiar with the fact that in our first case we have a male standard poodle with a recent history of vomiting, and that this dog was seen three weeks ago by another veterinarian, who performed an exploratory celiotomy and removed a rubber ball from the proximal duodenum. Two days post-op, the dog spiked a fever, and the referring veterinarian started him on a course of gentamicin injections, one hundred milligrams intramuscularly twice a day for two weeks. He referred the case to you, an expert gastroenterologist, after the dog started vomiting four days ago. He feared an intussusception and would rather you perform a second surgery. You *are* familiar with this case?"

"Yes, Dr. Elder, I am."

"Good. You have reviewed the diagnostic tests and their results, as well?"

"Yes."

"Excellent." He paused as though for effect. "Would you please share your interpretations with us?"

"Yes, sir." I referred briefly to my notes, although I knew the case thoroughly. I looked back at Dr. Elder. I was terrified. I took a deep breath and began.

"The packed cell volume is moderately elevated, and, when taken into consideration along with the fact that the total protein is elevated and given the physical signs, the indication is that this is a true dehydration. The serum chemistry values for blood urea nitrogen, creatinine and phosphorus are interpreted as an azotemic state. The azotemia could be due to either prerenal, renal, or postrenal causes. When you consider the history and urinalysis results, it seems the most likely cause of the azotemia is renal."

"I agree. But that's elementary. Would you please explain what you feel to be the cause of the renal compromise in this dog's history and just exactly what sort of pathology you'd expect to find in his kidneys? What in the urinalysis supports this?"

I was okay. I knew this stuff. "The dog was in a compromised state as far as absorbing adequate liquid from his gastrointestinal tract post-operatively, and therefore, unless diuresed by the referring veterinarian, was at risk for antibody disposition in the glomeruli. The dog then suffered another insult to his kidneys when the vet put him on an aminoglycoside antibiotic, which is both nephro- and ototoxic. The fact that there were casts in the sediment exam of the urinalysis supports a primary renal problem." I finished, amazed that all that had come from my mouth in a more or less seamless piece. I heard my classmates murmuring, but I held Dr. Elder's eyes. I couldn't be distracted. I waited for his pronouncement.

151

"Very good, Loretta. Your assessment is correct. The back row can be proud of you." He smiled now and I felt relief flood through me.

One of the Meat Inspectors, Johnny Henckel, leaned forward and looked down the row at me. "Way to go, Mom!" he yelled.

I smiled. I had done fine. I had done just fine. But I made a mental note to think about a front-row seat.

I shouldn't have been surprised that my performance was good; I didn't stint on my effort in Urology. In addition to preparing cases, every night I transcribed each lecture meticulously in longhand, writing out every word. It took hours, but it was enormously effective, a daily, minute review of the material. I was proud of my effort and of the notes it produced—every word Master Goodman and his colleagues uttered made visible and permanent.

One day toward the end of the term, Joanne Kramer asked whether she could borrow those notes. She was struggling, she said, and her own notes weren't very complete or very clear, and everything depended upon the final. Her whole veterinary career depended upon it, and, she implied, upon my willingness to help her.

I was not exactly sympathetic. She and I were not actually friends. I thought she was silly. I knew she cut class sometimes. I hesitated. She pleaded.

Please, she said, she would run to Kinkos and copy them right then and return them just as fast as she could. She'd be so careful, she'd have them back in my hands within the hour.

I was jealous of my notes. They represented hours of work, hours I had stolen from sleep and from other courses and from my meager social life. I was jealous of them, just as I was jealous of the GTQs my buddies and I ferreted out, just as I was jealous of attending rounds with Dalton. There was something else, too: As I transcribed the tapes each night, I often made personal notes to myself, asides that amounted to diary entries, half a page here, a sentence or two there. They were in the margins or boxed off at the top of the page, scattered throughout the whole notebook.

But she stood before me, desperate, and we were supposed to be colleagues. I was supposed to be a compassionate person.

I needed them back right away, I said.

Of course. She wouldn't keep them a minute longer than she had to.

I told her about my personal notes throughout. They were very private. Would she please not read them?

Of course she wouldn't. She'd ignore them completely.

Reluctantly, I broke open my loose-leaf and handed over more than one hundred pages. I worried incessantly while she was gone. She'd lose them somehow, I just knew it. She'd drop them and the wind would carry them off. She'd leave them in her car and the car would be stolen. She'd stop for a sandwich and leave them on the café table. I didn't see how I could pass the final without them. I should have gone to the copy shop with her.

But then she was back, notes in hand. She thanked me over and over again. It was nothing, I said. When I was alone, I leafed through the pages; everything was in order. She'd been prompt and careful. I felt like an ass for being so selfish and distrustful.

Several days later, I sat in the lounge at the large oval table that was, as usual, laden with debris—newspapers, handouts from class, napkins, coupons, foam cups, *People* magazine. There in the mess was a scattering of my Urology notes. They were not in a neat stack, as if Joanne had been studying and stepped away for a moment. Rather, here was page 23, there was page 47, messages scrawled on the backs, coffee rings, just miscellaneous pages, used as scratch paper.

I gathered them up and stuck them into my notebook. I thought about the notes among the notes, notes about a fight with Sam, notes about whether I'd ever have a normal life and children and marriage, notes about how cute Master Goodman was. Trembling with anger, I tracked Joanne down in the hall.

"My notes," I said. I was sputtering. "They were scattered all over the lounge."

She looked at me as if I had lost my mind. She shrugged. "I didn't think you'd mind. There were a couple of people who wanted a copy. They needed a little boning up, and your notes are pretty thorough."

"You should have checked with me first."

"Sorry." She didn't seem sorry. She seemed to think I was very strange.

"Okay." I nodded. "It's okay." There was nothing to do about it. It was a done deal. She thought my notes were "*pretty thorough*"? I wanted to grab her arms and shake her; I wanted to shout in her placid round face. Goodman hadn't sneezed that I hadn't noted it. *Pretty thorough,* indeed.

I tried to shrug it off. I forced a smile. Somehow, I ended up apologizing, which made me feel even worse.

I had always believed in karma—what goes around, comes around. But karma doesn't count if your attitude is wrong; I believed that, too. It does no good to do good or be good if you feel mean and nasty about it. I'd screwed this whole thing up, and I couldn't even enjoy any self-righteous anger.

At year's end, I was invited to the Awards and Scholarship ceremony, which meant I was to receive an honor of some kind—me, of the fourth-grade mentality.

My prize was one of three Chiron Circle Awards. Chiron, centaur and wise teacher of Achilles, Hercules, and Asclepius, was now *my* benefactor as well, in the amount of one thousand dollars. The criteria for the award were listed in the evening's program: It was given to a professional veterinary student with financial need who demonstrates great effort to succeed but is not necessarily academically outstanding. It was not exactly the commendation I craved.

I was grateful for the money. God knows, I could use it. Before these four years were over, I would take on thirty thousand dollars in debt, and my only assets were my secondhand Honda and all the miscellaneous crap that fit into it. Yes, I'd take the money, and happily, too.

I was used to being razzed about my grade anxiety. I'd learned to take my classmates' kidding when I lined up to check my score on this test or that, always sweating the outcome. I'd walk away from the grade board scowling, maybe doing some mental arithmetic as I computed this latest score into my average and tried to figure how close or far I was from the cumulative total I needed to pass this particular course. Someone would always say, "What's wrong, Retta? Did you only get a ninety-three this time?" That someone would laugh, but I tried to laugh, too. It was never funny, though. I didn't understand why they didn't understand.

Now they teased me about the award, the "scholarship," someone called it. But no, I made a point of saying, it wasn't a *scholarship*; it had nothing to do with scholarship. It was given to me *not* because I was smart, *not* because I was outstanding, *not* because I was achieving anything noteworthy, but simply because I was poor.

I was glad for the money and I accepted congratulations, but in my heart I was disappointed. I had wanted to win because I was smart, because I was the best, because I was at the top of my class, and not because I was poverty-stricken.

Without meaning to, and certainly without noticing it myself, I guess I had done it—turned into that most scorned and humorless animal, that tedious bore, the gunner.

PART 3

Junior Year

CHAPTER 15

————

Basic Skills

JUNIOR year, we moved to the Veterinary Teaching Hospital, two miles south of the main campus. The hospital was a world unto itself. We shared it, not with undergraduates but with senior vet students, faculty, clinicians, researchers, clients, and client-owned animals.

Built in 1979, the VTH was a massive two-story building, a maze of hallways, offices, clinics, kennels, treatment rooms, and classrooms. Directly to the east was its huge barn, with four aisles of horse stalls, two aisles of stalls for food animals, loading chutes, neonatal equine intensive-care ward, rounding rooms, a bay for ambulance trucks, two horse-treatment areas, an isolation pen for "bad" bulls, llama chute, cattle chutes—another big maze.

It was a *teaching* facility, but first of all a hospital, a hospital that housed the best minds, the best equipment, the newest technology. Veterinarians from all over the Rocky Mountain region relied on its resources when they were stumped by a particular medical problem; they referred clients to it when they reached the limit of their own facility or expertise. It was where we would gradually—this year primarily as observers and glorified technicians and next year as beginning clinicians—take the steps from student to veterinarian.

The hospital had a 332-page user's manual. As juniors, we

were the lowest form of life at the VTH, and the manual told us everything we needed to know—and then some: what to do about what; where to go when; whom to tell what, and when; how to submit samples to the lab; how to make requests of the secretaries; how to speak to clients; how to keep our noses clean; how to stay on the friendly side of management; how to use the photocopier and for what; how to evacuate the building; where, when, and how to check out surgical instruments from central supply; where to park; what to wear; what clinical rotations we would be on every morning; what was expected of us at every turn. We were to step and fetch for the seniors; we were to bathe animals; we were, basically, to be seen and not heard. We had a lot to learn from everybody, they let us know. And that meant, to some extent, becoming glorified technicians, doing the grunt work in exchange for the opportunity to watch and listen.

Orientation seemed meant to puncture whatever ego we had managed to hang on to for the last two years. Brian Tennant, who had two years before delivered the prediction that some of us would fail, was hospital director, and he had a few remarks for us. We may have made it this far, he seemed to imply, but that didn't mean we were worth a damn.

"When you walk down these halls and pass someone scrubbing the floor, I want you to smile and speak to them," he said, in case our mothers had neglected to teach us simple manners. "We're a team here, all working together to make this place function smoothly. I want you to adopt the attitude that every job—from scrubbing the toilet to performing orthopedic surgery—is equally important. You will treat the workers in this hospital with the respect they are due, or you will answer to me. You're not the hotshots you think you are."

We were the children of the hospital. We were to be quiet, nice, well behaved, to say please and thank you, clean up after ourselves, flush the toilet when we finished, and never, ever practice veterinary medicine except under the direct supervision of a faculty member.

The last rule implied the presence of actual animals and the opportunity to practice, resist it though we must.

At last, lectures would be balanced by practicum rotations. We would spend only half our time meeting as a class for lectures, continuing to build our basic knowledge. The other half, mornings, we would be scattered here, there, and everywhere for our clinical rotations and preparatory labs (Small Animal Medicine, Neurology, Radiology, Clinical Pathology, Parasitology, Necropsy, Small and Large Animal Surgery, Anesthesia, Equine Medicine, Food Animal Medicine, and Reproduction), a different one each week. Our role in these clinics and labs would be something like that of a vet tech in the real world—to serve, but also to watch and listen.

"Now," Tennant said, "veterinary school will be more like what you expected when you arrived here two years ago."

The initial group of rotations involved preparatory labs, for we had a lot to learn and a lot of work to do before we would be ready to be seen in public on the clinic floor.

We had plenty of opportunity to do the practical procedures that we would eventually need to perform as if they were second nature: to clip nails, draw blood, express anal sacs, restrain an unruly animal, muzzle a dog, administer pills and drops, apply splints and bandages, aspirate bone marrow, intubate an animal, place an intravenous catheter, and catheterize a bladder.

Some of these practical tasks called for more manual dexterity and common sense than intellectual brilliance. Some might seem more the practices of a nurse than a doctor, but a veterinary practitioner is, in fact, a nurse as well as a doctor. These skills would be vital to our ultimate performance.

All of our understanding of the workings of the body and its systems, of the chemical actions of drugs, and of the technology of modern medicine would be useless if we couldn't do the grunt work, and if we couldn't do it smoothly, cleanly, and easily. All our professional lives, we would perform these functions over and over again, often in the presence of a client. That client's faith in us would derive in no small measure from how well we did the little things, for he or she would have very little way to evaluate us on the more complex and demanding work we did as vets.

We would soon be coming in contact with real clients possessing real animals who had real medical problems, all of which had been theoretical to us until now. In the clinics, we would be working closely with clinicians, senior vet students, and clients. It was natural that we wanted to get the most from each rotation by being prepared for the cases before us. We wanted to impress, and we certainly didn't want to embarrass ourselves. Thus, it was easy and natural to spend an inordinate amount of time preparing for the clinical rotations and not enough time reading and reviewing the systems course material. It was a trap unto which most of us fell. Time, always an enemy, seemed to keep shrinking.

We had a new vocabulary to master, the jargon of the insider, acronyms that were meant not only as shorthand but also as secret code. Much of the language we were learning was meant to save time in keeping charts; they were abbreviations meant to be written, to cut down on the record keeping that was to take up so much of our time. C/S meant either *culture and sensitivity* or *coughing and sneezing*; AMA didn't mean the American Medical Association but rather *against medical advice*; PTA meant *prior to admission*; QNS was *quantity not sufficient*; RACL was *ruptured anterior cruciate ligament*; TNTC was *too numerous to count*. In addition, we relied on slightly less-medical acronyms: ADR meant *ain't doin' right*; WYA was *watch your ass*; CYL was *call your lawyer*. By paying attention to our elders and betters, we were to learn the knack of knowing when to switch from our in-crowd lingo to layman's terms.

This year, we would become proficient in administering anesthesia. We began in September, with lectures on the principles, the machinery, the vaporizers, the workings of the different anesthetic agents, the pre-anesthetic drugs, the evaluation of patients prior to anesthesia, the assessment of anesthetic depth, and the differences in canine breeds and different species with regard to anesthetics. Then we would run anesthesia for one another during junior surgeries. Finally, we would run anesthesia for the senior vet students as they operated upon Humane Society or client animals.

Australian anesthesiologist Justin Harper had a broad smile and a charming accent. I liked him right away, though some found him too demanding. Under his direction, we were responsible for assessing an animal's particular needs and problems prior to surgery and preparing an anesthesia plan. Harper spent a few minutes with each student, evaluating the plan, either okaying it or suggesting changes to improve it. He questioned continually and challenged us whether we were right or wrong, testing to see how deep our knowledge and conviction went.

He could make you think hell wasn't twenty feet away, too, when the occasion was right, as it was one early morning during junior lab. We were to be at the hospital and preparing our patients by 6:00 A.M.; not everyone was. And when nearly everybody had trickled in, it was clear that many hadn't bothered to do a pre-anesthetic workup.

Harper stood at the end of the long, narrow prep room and began to yell. We were a worthless bunch of lazy, unmotivated, undeserving spoiled brats. We didn't deserve the sacrifice of these animals' lives. We weren't worthy of becoming veterinarians, and he was willing to see to it that we didn't.

When he finished, there were pouts on some faces, some jaws set in anger, and some eyes shining with tears. I knew he was yelling at all of us for the sake of a few, but it still terrified me. I wondered whether we truly were the worst class ever to darken the doors of the VTH, or whether we were typical—a few goof-offs, a fair number of egotistical assholes, and the rest of us.

It was also time now to practice and perfect the surgical techniques that we would be using our whole careers. We rotated in small groups back to the anatomy building, into one of the side rooms off the gross anatomy lab, to begin our surgical apprenticeship by reviewing the pertinent anatomy and operating on dead dogs. I remembered vividly being a freshman working in the huge lab and seeing Lloyd and other juniors working in the adjoining room. Now I looked the other way through the open door, at the new class of freshmen. Silently, I wished them well.

We spayed and castrated as many dead dogs as we found time for, in preparation for doing the same procedures on live but "nonsurvival" dogs—dogs that would be euthanized at the end of the surgery—and then later on Humane Society dogs that would be placed for adoption, and still later on client animals.

We checked out a "knot box" with its pamphlet of instructions and practiced in earnest the surgical knots that would secure our sutures. At night, I would break from my more serious studying to sew my pillows with dental floss, trying to find the manual dexterity to make the motions natural, trying to get to the point of muscle memory, where my fingers would perform without my conscious bidding a continuous cruciate, a Lembert, a Connell.

We were tested on our knots in groups of ten or twelve. We sat on raised stools at stainless-steel surgical tables as the surgeons circulated among us. They watched our hands, seldom raising their eyes to our faces, which were drawn tight in concentration, lips pursed, brows knit. Our hands worked to be swift, steady, and accurate. They needed to be hands capable of ligating a major artery during surgery, if need be—to calmly but quickly end any sudden hemorrhage.

As the surgeons passed among us, their own hands folded behind their backs, I could hear echoing in my head the high-blown commandments of surgery that we had been taught.

A surgeon must first be a veterinarian in the most complete sense of the term. In the most complete sense of the term meant a veterinarian, a doctor, a healer, a minister to animals. It must be all one.

From student to student, the surgeons made their deliberate way, stopping to request a particular task, as surgeons had always rotated among their apprentices, their disciples.

Surgical technique is the sum of the surgeon's relationship to tissue. As they called for first this knot, then another, then yet

164

another, I thought of this commandment. What was my relationship to tissue? What did that all mean?

Dr. Andy Bartell paused at my side. "Let me see a single-handed tie." My hands became his instruments—what he requested, they would fly to do. "A miller's knot." Done. "An instrument tie." Done.

The degree to which surgical skill can be developed is limited only by muscular coordination, manual dexterity, and total integration of the student as an individual. To be totally integrated, a goal devoutly to be wished, and to be pursued for an entire lifetime, it seemed.

"That's fine, thank you." He moved on to the next student.

The knots, the anatomy, the instruments, the judgment, the relationship to tissue, the conscience, the "total integration of the student as an individual." I could master the knots and felt I had a fair shot at the anatomy, but the rest of it was an elusive goal, one I wasn't even certain I fully understood. I trusted that I would come to understand. For now, keep throwing those knots, manipulating those instruments, taking it in, working toward that mastery, knowing we would all be, always and forever, apprentices in this art.

And so we passed little tests of competence, advancing us ever nearer to the nonsurvival surgeries, in which we would use all we had learned and practiced to perform a surgical procedure on a dog from an animal-control facility in Fort Collins, Denver, or Wyoming. The sheer surplus of animals afforded us this "luxury," and we understood that it *was* a luxury, of having patients to practice on without fear of mistake or fatal miscalculation. We could learn from our errors with far less penalty than the student surgeon whose patients are human, and we would be certified to practice in far less time. The luxury tax, of course, was the deaths of the animals and our pain.

The afternoon before the nonsurvival surgeries, we crossed the parking lot behind the VTH and entered the building that housed the dogs. Each dog wore several tags—federal, state, city, and university identification—for the school was very sensitive to charges from animal-rights groups that dogs may have come from pet-stealing rings. Each animal was thus fully documented—its place of origin, movement, and fate.

They were a random assortment. Perhaps they had killed chickens or bitten someone. Perhaps their families had moved and not wanted to take them along. Perhaps somebody in the family had developed an allergy to dogs, or maybe they shed too much hair or gnawed a hole in the couch. Some were old, discarded pets. Some were pups, whole litters of them. Their mothers were tired-looking bitches with teats hanging, sometimes almost to the floor. They shared a common destiny—to die for our education. And a common ability—to break our still-too-tender hearts.

Choosing is a grim task, even when one knows they will all be chosen before too long.

The din inside is deafening as the dogs bark and crowd to the front of their cages for your attention, a kind word. You enter the building and choose as quickly and randomly as you can. You slip your leash around the neck of the dog you have picked, slip the dog through the kennel door, pushing back the others that are rushing to get out. You walk back across the parking lot to the hospital with your dog, which is perhaps prancing a bit, happy to be outside, happy to be with you. And you take him into the prep room and clip the hair from the surgical site—abdomen, leg, throat, wherever.

In the prep room, the clippers hum. The dogs sometimes roll on their backs, asking to have their bellies scratched. And we do scratch them, pat them, talk quietly, reassuring them, praising them. You're a pretty boy, yes, you are. We don't talk loudly and we don't talk to one another. Are you a nice girl? Does that feel good? Some of us cry, but quietly, to ourselves, tears slipping down our faces as we confront and determinedly move past yet another ugly reality, over another nasty hurdle on this path we have chosen and so relentlessly pursued.

We put our clipped dogs back into their cages, pat their heads, bid them good night, and go home, where we forbid ourselves to think of the dogs. Instead, we think of the surgery, reviewing our notes, studying the anatomy, the suture patterns, the likely complications. We lose ourselves in the science and in the pursuit of our skill. Tomorrow we will anesthetize the dog quickly, and work on it a long time, at our beginner's pace, and by the time we inject the fatal drug into the IV line, we will be a few paces further down the road to being surgeons, to being practitioners, to being veterinarians. Not one of us will cry.

CHAPTER 16

The Third and Fourth of the Critters—Milo and Kris Kringle

THERE was a lucky little goat at the VTH. He lived there.

Milo was small, maybe thirty pounds, but his personality was big. The VTH was his home, and his home was his castle. He had free run of the place, and it seemed to be his mission to fill the building with his spunky presence. He raced down the corridors and to the top of stacked bales of hay, where he reared on his hind legs, arching his neck, king of the mountain. He liked to chase the two gray barn cats, Rodent and Control, and scamper in and out of pens, looking for fun and trouble, which may have been the same thing to Milo. Apparently, he never met a species he didn't like or at least consider a potential play-mate. He would give a friendly butt to whomever he met—vet student or professor, cow, horse, llama, or pig. The human population of the barn patted him, fed him, scratched his ears or his little black rump. The three standard-sized goat does and their kids tolerated Milo, but many of the patients were too sick to take much notice of him. A fair number of those in better health didn't take too well to the mad scampering visits of the impish goat, however. It seemed that almost everyone had seen the little daredevil narrowly escape the horns of a grouchy bull or the flying hooves of an irritable horse at one time or other. Milo was fast, agile, and just plain lucky, but it began to seem inevitable that he would someday have his cute but thick little head bashed in.

And the little guy had already had more than his fair share of medical problems.

Milo was a pygmy goat, but he had giant-sized problems with his urinary tract. When he first came to CSU, he was unable to urinate because his urethra was blocked with crystals, a condition called urolithiasis, which is common in castrated ruminants. Females also develop urinary calculi, but because their urethras are wider than those of the male, the condition is generally not life-threatening. In male goats and sheep, however, the calculi tend to lodge in the vermiform, or wormlike, appendage that dangles off the end of the penis and houses the terminal urethra. It is a narrow structure with no apparent function; it serves only to accumulate urinary crystals, easily plugging and poisoning the poor beast with its own waste.

This was Milo's condition when his owners first brought him to the VTH clinic. He was one sick little goat, but the surgery he needed was minor, requiring only a local anesthetic. The vermiform appendage—with its trapped sediment—was amputated, and Milo was able to pee again. His health was so compromised, however, that he now required intensive medical therapy. Urine had leaked, or seeped, from the blocked urethra into the surrounding connective tissue, creating a significant inflammation, or cellulitis. Unable to eliminate liquid, he had stopped drinking, so he was dehydrated, and the fluid circulating in his small body was highly toxic. Therefore, he needed intravenous fluids and electrolyte replacement before he could go back home. Finally, though, home he went.

Before too long, though, he was back at the hospital, blocked again, higher up, at the sigmoid flexure, another feature of the ruminant anatomy that makes the male goat prey to urinary problems.

The sigmoid flexure is where the urinary canal and penile musculature make a sharp S-shaped curve. In most species, the penis is a rather small organ that becomes enlarged when the animal is sexually aroused. In the ruminant, however, the penis enlarges only slightly; for all practical purposes, the penis is erect all the time. To get it out of the way when it's not needed, nature arranged for it to fold up and tuck away, and

169

the sigmoid flexure is where the unit folds back on itself, creating another narrow constriction of the works, another place where junk accumulates and clogs the plumbing.

The treatment goal in most ruminants is to salvage them for slaughter, using a procedure known as high and low heifer surgeries, which are done under an epidural. The urethra is opened above the blockage and sewn to the outside of the abdomen. This is called a heifer surgery because the animal is basically reconstructed so that his urinary equipment resembles that of the female; the *high* or *low* refers to where the new urethral opening is positioned in relationship to the scrotum and anus. These surgeries are performed frequently in feedlots when the steer in question is not up to slaughter weight and needs more time in the lot. In extreme cases in which the urinary bladder has ruptured from the pressure of the blockage, the animal is merely slashed open, through the belly into the abdominal cavity, so that the pooling urine can drain; for these unfortunate animals, slaughter is not far off.

Milo wouldn't have made much of a goat roast, though. He was blessed with a collector's item body style and an engaging personality, so instead of being cut open in the mire of a feedlot, he was operated on in a sterile OR under general anesthetic, and he had an analgesic for post-op pain. He was turned into a low heifer and again returned to his owners.

His healthy and hearty stream of urine gradually narrowed to a trickle, then to a fine mist. Fibrous scar tissue had filled his urethra. He needed another operation, an operation his owners decided they could not afford.

And so Milo became the property of the state of Colorado, and the state of Colorado lost no time in making him a "high heifer," excising the scarred-down urethra, cutting it back to a wide, healthy pink tube. Milo was peeing again, strong, vigorous, bountiful jets of urine, and it became the unofficial duty of everybody to take note of his peeing and to report immediately to Dr. Owen Colson, head of Food Animal Medicine, if the stream was ever less than the size of a pencil. Whenever Milo stopped his spinning, romping, and frisking to urinate, there was usually somebody there, bending a bit to peer under his low belly at the yellow jet of fluid.

All of Milo's medical problems had been solved by the time I first saw him, during sophomore year when Dalton and I were making our Friday visits to the barn for rounds, and he was still the little prince of the barn when we arrived to take up our own residence there junior year. But by this time, the concern was growing that soon Milo might be on the table again, to repair a fractured skull—if it was repairable, which seemed unlikely, given the size and the force of the animals that were trying to kill him.

Early that year, the decision was made to put Milo into protective custody. Confined to a pen adjacent to the Goat Club's does and kids, the little guy seemed to grow smaller and smaller. He was allowed out of his pen only during rounds or under somebody's watchful supervision. We were all sworn to lock him up immediately if he started flirting with death—or, from his point of view, if he started having any fun at all.

He sulked. He lost his spark. He seemed listless and withdrew more and more into his own little head, where it must have been pretty lonely. Morris Kahn might well have raised the philosophical question of what constitutes quality of life for a goat, but whatever *did*, this clearly did not.

His unhappiness was clear enough that the powers that be took notice and made another decision: Milo was to have his own "pet," his own companion animal. The next suitable animal donated to the Food Animal Service was to be Milo's very own.

A bull with reproductive problems came and went—too mean. A llama with neurologic disease came and went—too sick. A dairy cow with a fractured hip came and went—not repairable. And so it went, animals in, animals out, during the long autumn semester, and none of them right for Milo, who grew sadder and sadder and sadder. It looked as if the little goat was never going to find a friend.

And then a crippled brown Swiss calf was born at the dairy. He had an angular limb deformity. The metacarpal bone—what the layman might call the calf's "shin"—veered off sharply.

The fetlock, or metacarpal/phangeal joint, was misaligned. As the calf grew, his weight would either break the bones or he would be walking on the inside of his hoof. His helter-skelter, pick-up-sticks legs could barely support him now, and he hobbled along, a true cripple, misfortune's child.

Except that, for this calf, his deformity was his fortune. Most male calves are sold to slaughter. This calf was at birth clearly a teaching case, however, and so he was delivered to the VTH.

The deformity was ugly, but it was fixable, and a student surgeon did the work. It was actually a relatively simple procedure, based on the premise that one side of the bone was growing faster than the other, creating a concave surface that lagged behind the convex side, an imbalance that would grow only worse with time. The surgical manipulation was done on the concave side; the periosteum, the connective tissue that covers the bone, was cut open, which released the growth plates from what was thought to be a girdlelike binding. The slow side then began to catch up with the other side, and once the leg was straight, the two sides of the bone continued growing at a regular, matched rate. No overcorrection had ever been reported. It is a procedure that works only as long as the growth plate is "open"; that is, still actively growing. The brown Swiss calf had all of its growing ahead of it; its prognosis was excellent.

The calf's deformity was Milo's good luck, as well, for the baby was to be his pet, his friend, his Christmas gift, for the semester was almost over and the holiday was upon us. In honor of the season, the calf was named Kris Kringle.

Kris was grayish-brown, and his coat was soft as velvet. His deep brown eyes were shaded with long, thick lashes. His nose was covered with moist, tender black skin. He was as beautiful a creature as God ever made.

Small as Kris was, he was already more than twice as big as Milo, and he had none of the goat's coordination. His baby nervous system—like that of every infant—was not yet myelinated; it would be many months before the white fatty substance had grown to sheathe all his never fibers and thus allow him to move his body as he directed. For now, he was prone to "spaz" attacks, when he seemed touched by a charge beyond his control. He would shift into overdrive and a power boost would send him careening around at the breakneck speed, veering this way and that, only to reverse himself midcourse and come to a screeching stop, balanced for a moment on two legs, or toppling into a heap, only to scramble up and bolt off again, wild and reckless. The surgery slowed him down only briefly.

Goat and calf fell in love at first sight, or soon thereafter.

The resident barn cow was named Pin Cushion, in reference to her primary duty as a just-for-practice patient. We used her to perfect our techniques of giving injections, drawing blood, auscultating lungs and hearts and gut sounds, trimming hooves, intubating, cattle handling and restraining, and incidentally, milking. This sturdy holstein produced fifty to sixty pounds of milk morning and night, a fair amount of which fed the rapacious Kris Kringle. He bawled for the vet students who appeared at regular intervals with his big bottle. He would butt the bottle vigorously as though it were the udder of his mother, so you had to brace yourself against the enthusiasm of his nursing.

To occupy his roommate, we would pour a bit of milk into a rubber tub, but Milo never seemed to relish it. He'd drink a tiny bit, or sometimes only touch his lips to it, and then bounce around the pen as though it were kerosene or rocket fuel. Kris would watch his careening buddy through half-closed eyes, but until the bottle was dry, Milo would just have to entertain himself. Kris was not to be distracted.

And so he grew quickly from a seventy-pound baby we could cuddle in our laps while he nursed to a larger and larger calf headed to adulthood. We could lean across the broad back and chat with a classmate, for he was a complete pet, bonded to people, used to a variety of us, and always gentle. He soon grew so large that the barn pen was scarcely big enough for their romping, and so they were turned out during the day into the field that adjoined the barn.

When one of us hankered for a little critter love, we had only to call and Milo and Kris came trotting in to have their ears scratched and their jaws rubbed. Kris was soon a monster beside his little buddy—seven hundred pounds—but he stood with his neck outstretched, his eyes closed, his lower lip flapping limp in ecstasy as one of us massaged that magic spot behind his ears.

Milo could easily stand under Kris's belly, and he seemed to delight in darting between the big guy's legs like a goat possessed, inspiring the giant calf to tear off in the opposite direction. You could usually find somebody leaning on the fence or watching out the barn door at the antics of our two clowns.

This was a vet school and not a petting zoo, though, so there came a time when Kris had to pay his way by teaching. We castrated him before he could turn into a turbocharged young bull. We practiced passing the stomach tube on him, drawing blood, and giving shots. Though we transgressed on his body again and again, he remained steadfast in his affection for us, stolid and stoic as cattle are.

Each day of junior year was divided down the middle: Mornings we spent in the clinical setting, rotating through the various hospital services at weekly intervals; afternoons we were back in the classroom for the lectures and exams that would finish our systems courses. Since all our tests were in the afternoon, a decided change from our first two years, the lunch hour of those days seemed set for last-minute cramming and drilling back and forth.

I hated the last-minute quizzing that my classmates did. It had more than a little bit of one-upmanship to it, and I soon discovered that it put me in a blind terror if somebody threw out a question I'd never heard of. I'd get confused, alarmed, and frantic.

I remembered that a nursing instructor at the University of Albuquerque has told our class that it was best not to think of your studies on the day of an exam, so I decided to get clear of my classmates on those particular lunch hours. I took to strolling through the barn, looking at the animals, emptying my head. Most of the animals were strangers to me, and many of them were very sick, so I'd just look, not touch, not crawl in beside them. But then there were Milo and Kris.

One day before an exam, I was feeling more than usually

anxious because I was more than usually unprepared for the test I was about to sit. As I walked the barn corridor, I discovered the little goat and his big calf inside, lying side by side in the straw. As I approached, Milo scampered to his feet and came over to have his ears rubbed. I climbed over the pipe railing and sat down beside Kris, who swung his big head into my lap and half-closed his eyes as I stroked his jaw. Milo nestled up against my other hip, and with a hand on each, I sat there, talking softly to them and enjoying the peace and stillness of their warm bodies. I pushed all thoughts of the coming test from my mind. With "Good boys, pretty boys" as my mantra, I emptied my head in a kind of informal meditation.

As 1:00 P.M. approached, I reluctantly got up, gave them one last pat, and went back across the driveway to the hospital to take the test. A week later, the results were posted. Incredibly, I had scored 97 percent, the third highest in the class. I knew I would never take another exam without a "test blessing" from the goat and the calf. Even if it was only a brief hug, I placed my hands on those two critters before every test for the rest of junior year, for all of senior year, for the federal accreditation exam, no matter what. If it was storming and they were in the far corner of the field, I hiked across to touch their woolly bodies.

Sometimes, when the rigors of vet school got to be almost more than I could take—and it still did get that way sometimes—I entertained the brief but wonderful fantasy of kidnapping Milo and Kris and joining the rodeo circuit, a rodeo clown plus critters. They had such charm, were such people-pleasing cutups, our act was sure to be a winner.

CHAPTER 17

Systems

AT the end of sophomore year, Lloyd had asked me whether I would move back to Douglas Road, into the upstairs apartment that had been Jennifer's, to keep an eye on the property for him. He had just taken a job in Kentucky and would be leaving the house unfinished and unrented, although a carpenter friend of his was going to be working on it, finishing up the remodeling that had somehow never gotten done while Lloyd was in school. I'd hesitated. It could be a long seven miles into town in the winter. My car was a bit cantankerous. The snow could get deep. But he had offered me rent so cheap that I hadn't been able to say no.

When he handed over his house, Lloyd also gave me his old surgery gowns and towels, some final words of encouragement, and his notes for the dreaded Diseases of the Hemic-Lymphatic System.

This course was infamous. It had broken many a junior, the story went. I, of course, had taken the warning to heart. Over the summer, I'd kept Lloyd's notes close at hand and learned what I could from them about red blood cells, white blood cells, anemia, clotting mechanisms, neoplasia (cancer) of the lymph system, feline leukemia infection, and the response of white blood cells to infection.

When the course began, with Dr. Lyon at the podium, my tape recorder was rolling. We learned how to read lab reports (that is, blood counts), how to identify abnormalities, interpret these into processes, and then to rule in or rule out particular diseases. We studied the different responses of different species, and, as a matter of course, the particularities of our instructors.

Dr. Lyon had a special interest in Ehrlichiosis, a disease that first showed up in Germany shepherd military dogs in Vietnam and that is now most prevalent in the southern United States. This infection is carried by ticks and proliferates in mononuclear cells, trashing a dog's bone marrow, causing death within six to twenty-eight weeks if not treated with a weeks-long, or even months-long, course of antibiotics.

Course coordinator Judith Givens was friendly and helpful. If we were unsure of a correct response on an exam question, she said, and if it was Dr. Lyon's question, we should always put Ehrlichiosis. If it was her question, the best guess would be feline infection peritonitis.

She emphasized that, intrigued as we might be by the bizarre and unusual, we should drill ourselves on the most common (MC) causes of various syndromes, symptoms, and diseases. This was the first diagnostic question that we should ask ourselves once we were in practice, as well. We had been warned already that our impulse as new graduates would be always to think of the most exotic rather than the most common cause of any given symptom. As Paul Warner, equine surgery professor, would remind us, "When you hear hoofbeats, you should expect to see a horse, not a zebra."

Dr. Givens supplied what seemed like thousands of questions for us. "Most common cause of hemolysis in the dog?" Immune medicated hemolytic anemia. "Most common cause of microcytic anemia?" Iron deficiency. "Most common manifestation of systemic lupus erythromatous?" Polyarthrisis. "Most common cause of heinz body formation (injured hemoglobin)" Acetaminophen, or Tylenol.

In the same way that we had once learned our multiplication tables, we ran one another and ourselves through an ever-growing list of MCs. Some of us made flash cards. We hunkered down and got serious.

I settled well into the apartment on Douglas Road. It was cozy, one small bedroom and a larger room that served as kitchen, living room, and study. I rummaged through the junk Lloyd had piled out beyond the backyard fence and found an old door that was straight and strong enough to serve as a desktop; then I splurged on two two-drawer file cabinets to set it on. Jennifer had left her swivel desk chair (she'd gone into practice in her native Arizona).

So I was well outfitted for studying, and the studying went well at first. The carpenter was laid-back and in no rush, and the downstairs was quiet.

In October, a family moved in, however, a young couple with two small children, two cats, and two large dogs. The husband, Ken, was a truck driver/cowboy, his wife, Suzi, hardly more than a girl. The kids were ragamuffins. There was plenty of foot traffic, lots of cowboys friends, and loud good times.

Loud bad times, too—arguments and kids crying. I was to become more and more of a recluse in the country farmhouse that had once been a home to me. I began to wear earplugs in the evening when I worked—the rubber kind that loggers wear. You wet them and twist them down into the ear canal. They didn't completely block the sounds from below, but they did turn my ears into warm, wet, unaerated bacteria-culture media. I would fight off earaches all year long.

That fall, we also began Diseases of the Digestive System, a course that would continue into the second term. It was perhaps the least glamorous of the systems, and our contact with it would usually be when a patient presented with diarrhea. This symptom could mean anything from a fatal illness to a bit of stress. It had different meaning at different life stages. It was caused by viruses, bacteria, cancer, pancreatic enzyme deficiency, stress, eating sand, protozoa, helminths and amebas, and by factors as yet unknown. We would face a lifetime of trying to figure out how to cure it.

178

Dr. Teller, a professor we'd had in freshman Anatomy, had begun teaching at CSU vet school with a Ph.D in Anatomy, and then went through the program himself and earned his D.V.M. When he'd been asked to criticize the program, he'd answered, "Diarrhea, diarrhea, diarrhea." And now it did seem that this abundant subject was the core and root of the curriculum. What drugs would tighten, decrease peristalsis (contractions), relax cramping, kill the parasites? What electrolyte losses occurred with the use of each drug? Did the diarrhea originate in the small intestine or the large? What kinds of cells were in it? Bacteria? Undigested food particles? Blood? Foreign matter? Viral particles? Worms?

Our leader in this area was Dr. Sargent, an astronaut and physiologist. He dealt with the motility (spontaneous motion) of the different areas of the digestive tract—the regulators, the hormones, neurotensin, cholecystokinin, gastrin, secretin, motilin, insulin. Where were these made? Where were they sent? What caused an increase or decrease in their manufacture? He explained how the intestine seemed to have a mind of its own, responding to two plexi of nerves, which acted seemingly without higher input.

Dr. Joseph Fortel, a gastroenterologist, introduced the companion to diarrhea—vomiting. Fortel, impeccably dressed, coiffed, and groomed, called our attention to the different processes that a client might call vomiting—regurgitation, which was a more passive expulsion of matter from the stomach; food falling from the mouth right after entry, a problem with swallowing; food exiting passively in the form of a bolus, or a small round lump, which formed in the esophagus. True vomiting, Fortel said—and then demonstrated—involved abdominal muscle contraction. He stood center stage, his shoulders humped, his body shaking, heaving and making throaty grunts and moans to drive home the violent spasmodic nature of vomiting. We were riveted at the sight. What a layperson called vomiting, he said, could be a swallowing problem, an esophageal problem, a stomach problem, or a problem at one of the vomiting "centers"—the pancreas, duodenum, small intestine, peritoneum, liver, gallbladder. Even the uterus, heart, pharynx, ears, and cerebral cortex—all can send impulses to the central vomiting center, which is in the medulla.

Vomiting is a common and complex mechanism, which we would use to our advantage in poisoning cases. All our professional lives we would be trying to induce it or quiet it, understand and cure it.

Dr. Jack Langford was another Australian, the star neurosurgeon at the VTH and the coordinator of Diseases of the Nervous System. About my age, he was an energetic and gifted lecturer. His enthusiasm for his subject was infectious, but he was a perfectionist as well, and intolerant of imperfect attention or interest from his students.

I remembered as a freshman loving Ted Miller's presentation of neuroanatomy, and Lloyd's saying that I could look forward to Langford. When you finished his course, Lloyd had said, you knew you'd been somewhere. It was true.

As part of the junior practicum, we attended a neurology lab in small groups. Here we examined animals and attempted to answer the questions: Does a neurologic deficit exist? What is your neuroanatomical diagnosis? Can you localize the lesion? What is the nature of the disease? Is it treatable, nontreatable, transient?

We studied specific neurologic disorders, such as that caused by the toxin in locoweed and the ammoniated feed syndrome, a.k.a. bovine bonkers.

Langford presented an overview of the nervous system, the brain, spinal cord, and peripheral nerves. In veterinary medicine, it is abnormalities in movement and posture that sometimes signal a malfunctioning cerebrum, even though this structure is the seat of cognitive function and consciousness.

Langford favored a "thinking man's exam," one requiring essay answers as well as multiple-choice ones. He reinstituted the must-pass comprehensive final, which annoyed some students. However, he maintained that he didn't want anyone to go on if they couldn't pass an exam over the whole of the course material; it was too important, he said.

Another major factor in the course was Roger Robinson, a

very tall and balding older man who had one lazy eye that wandered. He wasn't very communicative with students; a standing joke was that when you were on clinics with him, you spent half your time trying to find him. He moved quickly and didn't bother to tell students where or why he was going, so it became typical that those on clinic with him (four to six students) would follow him everywhere, like a string of ducklings trailing their mother. Legend had it that once a string of students followed him into the men's room and that another time a group followed him out the back door of the hospital, across the parking lot, and to his car, where he got in, waved, and drove away. He rarely showed emotion, but he was said to have smiled on those two occasions.

I myself saw him cry that year. Over a horse.

This particular horse had come into the VTH with neurologic signs. First, a physical exam was done; then cerebrospinal fluid was tapped and analyzed. There was still no diagnosis so Robinson performed a myelogram, which is basically an X ray of the spinal cord, with dye first injected into the subarachnoid space (that space between the arachnoid and pia mater, the vascular membrane enveloping the cord). This is no simple procedure and requires that the animal be anesthetized.

When the horse recovered from the anesthetic, it had lost the use of its hindquarters. Robinson waited for function to return, sedating the horse as much as was prudent, while hoping to bring it tranquilly back to full consciousness. Whenever the sedative wore off, however, the animal struggled to stand, thrashing around the stall, falling into the wall, hitting its head again and again as its panic grew. The senior students on the rotation called Robinson, who had gone on with his other duties.

Robinson didn't want to give up on the animal, probably in large part because his exam was responsible for its worsened condition. He wanted to give it sufficient time to turn the corner, for some healing to take place, and he ordered more sedation. Finally, he ordered the horse into a sling to support its hindquarters and hopefully to reduce its terror at being unable to rise.

We sedated the horse, got the sling under and around it, and lofted its massive weight. But again as the drug wore off and the animal became more alert, it became more and more frantic, lurching from one concrete wall to the other, pounding its one-thousand-plus pounds into the walls with its forebody, its lifeless hind end serving only to unbalance it. He had become a crazed battering ram. His eyes were swollen shut, his face bloodied. By this time, it was late evening. We called Robinson again. He said to put a helmet on the animal to protect its head from further damage. But there was no getting near the animal now in its present craze. One of the seniors again called Robinson back and asked him to please come in and look at the hopelessness of the animal's situation.

He came, looked at the horse for a long, silent time, then called its owners for their authorization to end the animal's suffering. With the help of the student team, Robinson euthanized the horse.

Robinson stopped just outside the dead horse's stall, sat down on the cold concrete, his knees drawn up to his chest, his hands cradling his head, and bawled like a baby. He cried for a while as we students stood by helpless, not knowing whether to offer comfort or to respect his privacy. Finally, he stood up, and without a word to anyone, he walked away and out of the building. He was a strange man, closed off from students and impossible to read.

Langford was easier; he said what was on his mind. As we neared the end of each semester, we wrote evaluations in each of our courses. Langford set aside fifteen minutes at the beginning of one class for that purpose. He made a little speech as he handed out the forms.

"People," he said, "I've tried hard to make Clinical Neurology a course you could sink your teeth into. Every year, the course improves a little bit, thanks to my students and their comments. I read every evaluation and take them to heart. So I ask you to take some time with these and think about what you'd like to see added or deleted, what could have been better or clearer."

As we finished and a designated student collected the forms, which were to be sealed in an envelope and delivered to the dean (professors didn't see the forms until after they'd turned in final grades), Langford stood at the front of the hall, his head bowed as if he was deep in thought. He was always moving, always talking, always drilling material and bemoaning the lack of time, and so it was uncomfortable now to watch him stand so still for so long. The class began to mutter and whisper, and he raised his head and looked at us.

"Excuse me," he said, "but I still have the floor." The room grew quiet. "I'm disappointed in you," he said. "Not all of you, of course, but some, a group of you fellows sitting back there at the top." And then he raised his voice. "Yes, you! I don't care if you get mad—I'm mad, too."

I could hear their voices behind me—the Meat Inspectors, predictably.

Langford continued. "I've spent several months now trying to make you the best clinical neurologists that I can, and you couldn't be bothered to give back fifteen minutes. You would rather BS with your pals up there than give me the courtesy of evaluating me and my course."

I heard more noise behind me and turned to look. One of the Meat Inspectors had risen and was walking out. One by one, the pack—or most of it, anyway—followed. They reminded me of dogs, stiff-legged, their testosterone—and their hackles—up. It wouldn't have surprised me much if they had lifted their legs and peed on the doorjamb as they went.

Langford watched them go and then apologized for the loss of time and began the day's lecture.

Diseases of the Musculoskeletal System required not one but two three-inch black binders to house its notes; it also required the reading of *The Handbook of Small Animal Orthopedic Surgery and Fracture Treatment.* There was an abundance of videotapes to watch in the AV Center. The material was overwhelming in its sheer volume.

The first part of the course covered bone development, the mineralization process (cartilage changing to bone and diseases affecting this process), metabolic disease, the biomechanics of bone, and the radiology of bone. This was followed by pathobiology and histology of fracture repair, then the fractures in the dog and horse, methods of repair, joint disease and the radiology and treatment thereof. There were several radiology lectures—what degenerative joint disease looks like on a radiograph, what infection looks like, dead bone, what was and what was not repairable in the horse.

It wasn't until the first exam (and there were only two, plus the final) that we found out what trouble we were in in this course. It was the one that most of us let slide a bit. We had initially spent an inordinate amount of time on our junior practicum rotations. Diseases of the Nervous System had that damned mandatory-pass comprehensive final. We were afraid of Hemic-Lymphatic. And so we'd neglected bones and muscles until it, too, was dangerous.

Several people failed the first exam, but Charles Church, course coordinator, held special office hours, counseled students, and held review sessions (just as if we were freshmen). At the end of the term, when the dust finally cleared, we all had passed on the first attempt. He'd pulled everybody through.

Diseases of the Nervous System proved to be the bear. Seven people failed and had to resit the final, and one of those failed the second exam and flunked out of the program.

Amazingly, everybody had done well in Hemic-Lymphatic. I asked Dr. Givens how that could be, given the course was such a bitch. She told me it was cyclic: We'd been too well warned to risk neglecting the material, but word would get to the next class that Hemic-Lymphatic wasn't so bad after all. They'd have a difficult time, some would flunk, and they'd warn the class behind them. The grades were predictable from year to year—good, then bad, then good, then bad.

It made sense to me. Terror had always helped my academic performance.

CHAPTER 18

Petrified Wood

WHEN I was a child, Daddy drilled into the earth looking for uranium. I found my treasures above ground. The high desert was full of petrified wood, shiny and brilliant as jewels. These pieces were wood and yet they were stone. They had the contours, the rings, the rugged and living appearance of the trees they had once been, but they glinted in my hand as I turned them in the sun. Surely, I thought, these were trees that had been struck by lightning and transformed in one hard, brilliant flash from branches, twigs, and bark to cold, shining stone.

Eventually, science robbed me of my lightning theory. These trees had lived 200 million years ago, at the very beginning of the Age of Reptiles, the Triassic period, and had been buried under volcanic debris. It was not magic hurled like a lightning bolt, but delivered so slowly, so gradually—like the pressing of diamonds from dinosaurs—that the mind couldn't grasp it. Infinitesimally slowly, slowly as the movement of continents and the evolution of species, immeasurably small bits of mineral replaced the organic cells of wood.

It takes a long, long time for living tissue to petrify, so long that change is incomprehensible, for a tree to turn to rock. It is not one change but a multitude, millions, billions of changes as first this cell, then that one is petrified. And what results, the beautiful gemlike wood, is not an object that was once alive; it is merely a replica of it.

It takes a long time, too, for a heart to turn to stone. It's a process you barely notice. And I was three years into it.

Sometimes it was hard to remember just why it was I wanted to do this. It seemed it would never end, and there was no way to quit. I couldn't quit, didn't want to quit. I told myself it would get better. It *would* get better. And it *would* end, someday, too.

I told myself it was just the combination of things. I felt under seige at home. Our surgeries were all nonsurvivals, and we would each kill many animals before the year was over. The course work was as tough as ever, or tougher. My relationship with Sam had come to smash. Our practicum labs were always hard, often tedious, and, just as often, miserable.

The lab in large-animal production was five days long, none of them pretty.

We began with palpating—or examining by touch—the uterus of the cow. This is a heavy organ, and if the cow is pregnant, the uterus tends to fall low in the cow's belly. To examine it, you must retract it, your hand inside the rectum, pull it up and ever up until you can probe its surface.

The rectal wall of the cow is sturdy, tougher than the mare's, but it is usually possible to feel the ovaries and cervix straight away. You grasp the cervix, which feels like a very thick cigar through the wall of the rectum, and you work toward the body of the uterus itself, pinning the cervix, advancing the hand, pinning the gain against the pelvic canal, advancing the hand again, pinning, advancing, pinning, until you have retrieved a palpable portion of the uterus from the deep recesses of the animal. But if your pinning is weak, or your hand slips, or you lose your concentration, the uterus will slip back down inside that cow just like a big, lazy old carp that has surfaced in a murky pond and then settled back to the dark and muddy bottom, where she rests. The principle is simple, just like reeling in anything, but the execution is not.

Although many of my classmates in the bovine palpation lab hoped they'd never again be shoulder-deep in a cow's rectum, I figured I'd probably have the odd cow or two to minister to once I got into practice. While I didn't expect to become a bovine expert, finding and feeling the uterus is pretty basic stuff. I'd never be as quick as Dr. Jones had been, two decades before in the Dulce sales barn, at running through a herd of cows and determining whether they were bred or open, but I'd probably also never have a whole herd to work through. However, I needed, and knew that I needed, this basic training.

Our group—which included a number of Meat Inspectors—met Dr. Swinson, the reproduction clinician, in the palpation shed behind the VTH, where a small herd of holsteins was penned and waiting. The Inspectors were eager to play cowboy, round them up and drive them into the pipe headcatches that lined each side of the shed. But these old girls were so used to the routine of the milking barn that they simply filed in and took their places, waiting for us to secure their heads and lock them in place. When the lot of us had palpated each of these cows, we'd turn them loose, corral the next bunch, and do it again and again for the rest of the morning.

Dr. Swinson had recently been slowed down by a total hip replacement, and he walked with a cane and a major limp. He was still an imposing figure, however, tall and weathered, with big, ropy, muscular arms. He directed his remarks to the Meat Inspectors, which is no doubt as it should have been, for surely at least some of them would end up in predominantly bovine practices whether they became ranch vets or the slaughterhouse workers they seemed almost pathologically bent on becoming. Perhaps in their rough, rude energy, he saw a younger version of himself.

A table at one end of the shed held our equipment—palpation sleeves, lubricant, and tape. We were in our regulation coveralls and knee-high rubber boots to protect us from the loose cow shit that was everywhere. The cows' tails were crusty with dried shit, their rumps caked, as well. We each pulled on a sleeve, which covered our arm to the shoulder. We would use just the one sleeve for the whole morning's work, so we taped it to the armpit and shoulder of our coveralls to keep it on. We squeezed a liberal amount of lubricant along its length, but for relubing we would soon be scooping up handfuls of the warm, loose, brown cow shit that covered the floor of the shed.

Dr. Swinson laid the ground rules and turned us loose on the cattle.

Ron Hadley, a freshman-year cube mate, was just ahead of me in the line. He had a loud voice and seemed pleasant enough, though I didn't really know him. I'd heard that he and his wife were divorcing, but he seemed like an upbeat guy.

When he pulled his hand free of the first cow, there was a splash of bright red blood on the fingers of his glove. We exchanged a look, and he grinned kind of sheepishly, shrugged, and moved down the row to the next cow.

Apparently, he had torn the rectal mucosa, or lining. It is possible to tear *through* the mucosa and submucosa and into the abdomen (very possibly a fatal injury), but a small rent in the tissue will typically bleed a bit and stop, the wound healing with little problem. I knew that. I told myself that it was so and just to carry on.

I stuck my lubricated and gloved hand inside the animal. Fingers together, I went deeper into her, wondering where the tear was and how bad. I probed gently, too gently. I could feel no structures, no ovary, no cervix, just the warm mush of the rectum. Well, I thought, she's the first cow of many. I'd skip her and move on.

The next cow had a bit of blood splashed through the loose fecal matter that dripped from her rectum. I hesitated, then pushed my hand inside her. Again, I was too cautious. Again, I felt only warm mush.

How fragile was a cow's rectum? I wondered. Not very, I told myself. Just how rough was Ron being? I told myself it didn't matter. I needed to do what I needed to do, no matter what the guy ahead of me had done.

I turned my attention to the next cow in line just as Ron withdrew his arm, streaked with blood. He laughed. "I can't find her ovaries, but maybe I found her ovarian artery."

That wasn't very likely, but it wasn't a very funny joke either. I took a deep breath and made a decision.

"Dr. Swinson, we're got some blood here," I called. Ron turned and looked back at me, narrowed his eyes, and shook his head, as if I was unbelievably petty, and a snitch besides.

"I'll be right there," Dr. Swinson called.

Ron looked at me. "A little bit of blood comes with the territory, Loretta. You'd better toughen up."

I waited while Dr. Swinson assessed the damage. It was a tear in the mucosa, nothing serious. But as he turned away, he said, "Be more careful, Miss Gage," apparently reading my name, which was embroidered on the pocket of my coveralls.

"Yes, sir," I said.

Ron grinned at me. The hand he pulled from the next cow was bloody as well. We stared at each other for a brief moment.

"I'm going ahead of you," I said, and walked past him to the next black-and-white cow.

He bowed slightly. "Be my guest."

I turned my back and resumed my work.

For the rest of the morning, I practiced fishing up the uterus from its subterranean depths and probing its secrets. I didn't get expert at it, but I made some progress. It was a little easier, knowing the cow wasn't already torn and bleeding inside.

The bovine udder-repair lab followed the next day. Severed udders—enormous, heavy, wet, and leaking sour milk—hung from metal stands meant to simulate the true anatomical height of a dairy cow. Technicians had slashed the udders open randomly. The wounds were severe, great slices and gashes.

Our charge was to fix 'em up, patch the leaky tits, salvage the animal, put the tissue back together, and save another one from the slaughterhouse. We sat on milking stools, one student per teat, four per udder, and assessed the damage.

"Mad titty ripper on the loose around here," Dwayne Lytle called out to no one in particular.

"Must have run the whole goddamned herd through a mowing machine," someone called back.

Dr. Lester, the clinician in charge, was young and straight-arrow, definitely not one of the good ol' boys. He paced the room with his hands clasped behind his back and stopped behind Dwayne.

"Mr. Lytle, did you read the handout on today's lab?"

Lester's formality only egged him on. "Sure 'nuff, Dr. Lester, sir." He had a smirk in his voice and a mock-Marine manner.

"Good. Then please tell us what course of action you would follow if you were called out on the case you see before you now."

One of his buddies called to him with effeminate affection. "What type suture pattern would you recommend, Mr. Lytle?" Contempt for the assignment was palpable.

"Mr. Lytle," Lester repeated, "your course of action?"

Dwayne rocked back on his stool and gave the udder a long, thoughtful look. He shifted the tobacco from his left jaw to the right, then he looked back up at the professor. "Well, sir . . ." He paused for effect. "I believe I'd tank the old girl."

That is, he would "give her wheels," ship her to slaughter, cull her from the herd, cut his losses. His running buddies hooted at his insolence, and a grin spread across his face.

When Dwayne's audience had quieted down, Lester tried again. "This particular dairyman says she's his best cow, she leads his herd in production, and he's very keen that you try to save her."

"Well, sir, if she's all *that* valuable, he's got a hunk of insurance on her. I'd have to point that out to him, take him aside and give him my heartfelt, honest medical opinion—tank her and buy a new pickup truck with the settlement." He spit toward a floor drain and the dark brown tobacco swirled into the milk and blood pooling on the floor.

Lester's face went red and he stiffened his posture. He turned and walked to the front of the room, backing down from the battle he was unlikely to win. "The type of injury you see before you is all too common in the dairy industry," he began, then launched into his pedantic lecture, trying to regain some authority. It was essential, he said, that the damage be repaired and the cow returned to full productivity. "Now, a few reminders and guidelines before you begin suturing the wounds . . ."

Lester's presentations tended only to repeat what we had

studied prior to the lab, and I only half-listened. The tension in the room was uncomfortable. The odor of sour milk was worse. The job ahead would be unpleasant. I just wanted to get it over with and get out of there.

Next day, bright and early, we learned the technique of electroejaculation of sheep and bulls. There weren't enough animals to go around, which suited me fine. I was quite content to watch the demonstration and forgo actual practice. It was enough just to watch it done to a ram who somehow had had the bad luck to end up in a teaching hospital. The Meat Inspectors volunteered to hold the animal down while the electric prod was jammed up his rectum. The ram bucked and struggled until he ejaculated. The cowboys hooted and crowed, their own testosterone apparently stimulated by the experience. I just didn't understand.

The grand finale of the week was the bovine dystocia (difficulty in birthing) lab, a simulation of what can go wrong in the birth process and what to do about it. Mostly what goes wrong is that the fetus is too big to fit through the birth canal, or the cow goes into labor when the fetus is in the wrong position to be safely and easily born. Mostly what you do about it is get the fetus out any way you can.

First, you try brute force—pulling the calf out of the cow.

In the mock-up calf pulling, the "cows" were again metal stands, each with a hole representing the pelvic canal. The calves, however, were real, and they were *real dead*, as in dead a long time, necrotic and putrifying, some of them worse than others. Our job was to load a dead calf into a metal cow, inside a plastic "uterus," and then to deliver it as best we could.

The plastic air-filled uterus was supposed to make the maneuvering and repositioning of the fetus more difficult and more lifelike, but, in fact, it didn't quite do the job. Some of these plastic sacs had leaks and didn't hold air, so that the simulated uteri were sloppy and had no tone. And, as I would discover in practice, nothing could quite simulate the arm-numbing effect of a contracting, pushing uterus pinning your arm hard against a bony pelvis.

Still, there was a degree of difficulty in the exercise, for the dead calves weighed between seventy-five and ninety pounds each. And they stank.

Dr. Swinson was again our instructor, and he was amused by our complaints. "When you go pull a calf out of a range cow, it's likely going to have been dead a while, too," he said. "It'll stink plenty good."

How swell, I thought, that they could provide the stench of rotting flesh for us, even though they couldn't quite simulate the experience itself.

We could, for the most part, reposition and pull the calves through the metal birth canals using only gravity and the strength in our own arms, but we were also to practice pulling with obstetrical chains.

Most often, in life, when the calf is stuck, it is something more than mere size that's hanging it up. The calf is usually positioned wrong, upside down or backward, its limbs or its neck bent strangely. Then the vet must reach inside the blackness of the laboring cow and, through the sense of her fingers, determine which part of the calf is which, find the pasterns (just above the hoof) of the calf's forelegs, pull them as straight and as far into the birth canal as she can, and slip the chains around them. And so in this lab, to ready ourselves for these emergencies, we chained the pasterns of those long-dead calves and pulled them out. Dead necrotic hide peeled away under the metal.

There was no pleasure in delivering long-dead calves from metal cows.

Sometimes your own strength is enough to pull a calf free. Sometimes you have to attach the chains to a mechanical calf-puller, or pulley. (The rule is never to exert more pressure than could be supplied by three strong men, but gauging that is something of an art, one more thing that experience, and nothing else, can teach.) Sometimes the pulley can't do the job. For those times, we learned to perform a fetotomy.

A fetotomy is, literally, the surgical removal of a fetus. It is a last-resort technique to save a cow when her dead calf cannot be delivered whole. In the small, crowded, and contracting dark space that is a pregnant cow's womb, you must section the fetus into smaller parts—decapitate it, saw off its limbs, sever the chest from the abdomen. (When the fetus is alive and cannot be delivered vaginally, of course, a cesarean is performed, but if the fetus is dead, the fetotomy is safer for the dam than opening the abdomen.)

The main surgical instrument used is specific to this procedure; called a fetotome, it is basically a long, narrow tube threaded with sharp wire. The fetotome is introduced into the uterus and the loop of wire slipped over the body part to be severed, usually first the head. At the other end of the fetotome, the ends of the wire are attached to wire saw handles, so the surgeon can manipulate the wire and saw through the hide, muscle, and bone of the fetus. The procedure also requires a Krey's hook, a sharp clamping hook with chain attached. Used with the fetotome, this hook is secured to the spinal column of the fetus to provide counterpressure against the force of the saw. Also useful is a hoe-blade knife, which has a guarded cutting edge.

What limbs or body parts the veterinarian severs in what order depends upon how the fetus is positioned inside the cow (and a fetus can be contorted in any imaginable way). If a dead calf is presented in the normal way (anterior, dorsosacral; that is, front first, right side up), the head is removed first, then the forelimbs, the viscera from the thorax, and then the hindquarters.

Every possible variation in fetus presentation or uterine condition means the procedure is done is a slightly different way. Fetotomy is best done with the cow standing, although that's not always possible. A successful fetotomy, of course, saves the life of the dam, although the success isn't properly complete until the animal again conceives, carries to term, and delivers another calf normally. In reality, most cows aren't so tested; rather, they are sent quickly to slaughter, not considered good candidates for breeding, both because the physiological problems that caused the first dystocia are feared likely to cause another and because the dystocia and fetotomy have likely complicated the problems of the reproductive organs. So this procedure was not only grisly and sad but doubly sad, for the cow would probably not long survive her dead baby. It was a procedure we needed to know, however, and one that large-animal practitioners would no doubt use in practice.

On sunny days, the lab students dragged the iron cows outside into the air. But it was raining the day of our scheduled lab, so we worked inside, the doors closed on us and the odors of the putrid calves.

Although it didn't involve living animals, this lab was as horrible as anything we had done. The work was physically hard, requiring strong hands and stamina. It was gory and grotesque. Something in the gruesome, nightmare nature of the job brought out high energy and macabre humor in my lab partners. It only made me grim and melancholy. It didn't offer even the glimmer of hope of a happy ending.

I had assisted in a calf pulling. I thought of it more than once during this ghastly week. I remembered it as difficult, scary, and as exciting as anything I'd ever done.

It was five or six years before, when I was working as Jill Henderson's technician. We had stopped for lunch at Sadie's, a popular Mexican restaurant in Albuquerque's north valley. The dining room was crowded and noisy. A jukebox in the corner played a country-western song. The noise almost—but not quite—drowned out the *beep-beep-beep* from the pager clipped to Jill's belt. We hadn't even ordered yet. She sighed, slid out of the booth, fished a quarter from her pocket, and headed to the pay phone to find out who needed her so urgently that it couldn't wait until after lunch.

I ate warm tortilla chips and salsa from the basket on the table; this would probably be all the lunch we had time for. Very few calls were settled over the phone. Within a few minutes, Jill was back. She put a couple of bills on the table to cover our chips and iced tea.

"What is it?"

"A cow trying to calf and can't get it done. The guy says the calf's dead."

It was a first for me, and for the cow, a heifer, a backyard cow not far from Sadie's. Her owner, a Mr. Apodaca, met us at the street. He seemed relieved to see us, and if he had a problem with the vet and her helper being women, he didn't show it.

The cow, a Hereford, lay in the backyard. She wasn't flat out on her side—a good sign—but, rather, on her chest, sternal, her head crooked around as though she was trying to see what was happening to her south end. She'd been laboring for over eight hours, Mr. Apodaca said, a good long time for a cow, which didn't make the picture any rosier.

Extruding from the cow's vagina were the two forefeet of a big black calf, its muzzle right between its big knobby knees.

"It's presented right, Doc," Mr. Apodaca said, "but I guess it's just too damned big to come out."

That seemed to be the case, all right. The calf's brow and eyes were still inside, but its mouth was open enough to show the bright white incisors on its lower jaw and its black tongue.

"Can you save the heifer, Doc?" Mr. Apodaca asked.

"We'll do our best," Jill replied.

I handed her the obstetrical sleeve and the bottle of lubricant I had brought from the truck. She pulled on the sleeve and squirted it liberally with the tube. She squatted beside the heifer and ran her hand around the vaginal opening, testing for space around the calf. She turned to me.

"Retta, we're going to need the puller. He's wedged in here pretty tight. It's gonna take more than I've got."

I ran to the truck, and when I got back, Jill was on her feet. She discarded the sleeve, made an assessment of the yard, and determined what stumps and posts we had to work with. She barked her orders at me, and I tried to obey as quickly and efficiently as a part of her own body.

"Run the come-along around that post. It'll reach. Good. Let's lube her up, and I'll get the little bugger hooked up."

Jill hooked the come-along, or calf-puller, to the obstetrical chains she had laced around the calf's pasterns. She lay down by the heifer, pulled on a clean sleeve, and began to lubricate every part of the heifer's vagina that she could reach. In a minute, she turned to me. "Okay, Ret, start crankin' him out, slowly now."

She slipped her arm as far inside the heifer as she could, along the calf's body, to check out its movement. The procedure had to be done ever so slowly and carefully, with just the right amount of force, or the birth canal could be traumatized, nerves injured, arteries ruptured, the pelvis broken, ending the animal's reproductive, or even her actual, life instantly.

Too much force can seriously damage the calf's joints, as well, and although the farmer thought the calf was dead, I wasn't sure Jill did.

"Okay, nice and easy."

I used the ratchet to move the levering device to the next setting and cranked slowly, meeting the resistance of the stuck calf with the steady force of the pulley, until the calf's wet black face came into view. A little more force, a little more cranking, and its massive chest cleared the birth canal. The rest of the calf followed in one smooth slide, like an otter down a mossy bank. The cow bawled, and the big bull calf lay virtually in Jill's lap, still and wet. She worked her hands over him, rubbing off the membrane.

"Shake him, Ret," she said. "Get his hind legs and shake the water out of him." I disconnected the OB chains from his forelegs and grabbed his hind legs just above the hocks. I strained and tried to hoist him up. He was greased with lube and wet from birth, and he slipped from my grip just as his hips cleared the ground. Instantly, Mr. Apodaca took off his shirt and handed it to me. I wrapped it around the calf's legs and tried again. Jill pushed his butt upward.

"Step on that stump," she directed me, and I stepped backward, feeling for the cottonwood stump that I knew was there. Up went the calf as Jill and Mr. Apodaca hoisted from below, and I shook him as hard as I could. He weighed ninety-two pounds—which Mr. Apodaca would tell us later—all deadweight, but I shook him like a rug, I was so pumped with adrenaline.

The black tongue lolled out and he uttered his first bawl, weak at first, then stronger. His mama bawled in return, turning toward her baby and clambering weakly to her feet.

"Okay," Jill said, and I set the calf down. He flicked his ears and struggled to stand, first getting his shaky hind legs under him, his butt high in the air, his little rope of a tail twitching. He struggled to hoist his front end, as well, placing first one small black hoof and then the other firmly on the ground and pushing with all his might. He stood then, his four legs stiff and braced, blinking in the sun. He bawled again. The cow sniffed him from one end to the other and gave him a lick with her big pink tongue. He wobbled under the force of the licking as she worked her way down his neck, but he did not fall.

We three stood silent in the hot New Mexico midday sun and watched as cow and calf nuzzled each other. Jill's expertise and my work had saved them both. I couldn't imagine two more beautiful animals. I was in awe of our power.

"I thought that calf was dead," Mr. Apodaca said finally, his voice as hushed as if he had just witnessed something even more amazing than the everyday miracle of birth. "His tongue was black."

"The bull was a Black Angus, Mr. Apodaca?"

"That's right, and he looks like his daddy, too."

"They've got black tongues, just like chow dogs."

"I'll be damned." He nodded. "I didn't think of that."

We watched the red cow and her black baby a few moments longer before we gathered our gear and headed to the truck. To me, just then, miracle making seemed all in a day's work for the veterinarian I was determined to become.

Back then, there were lots of moments when I'd take a breath and say something like a prayer that I'd get into vet school, that I would someday be the one with the power and the knowledge to save the calf, to save the cow, to save the whole damned day. Please, God, let this year be the one, I'd think.

Prayers had been heard, dreams had come true. Here I was, in the middle of it. I had to stop sometimes and remind myself of that—that this rough week, the disgusting dystocia lab, the brutal electroejaculation demonstration, and the nightmare fetotomy were part of the blessing, part of the road back to real work in New Mexico. I just had to keep hanging in there.

• • •

The night of December 3, the Douglas Road house was still, and I was grateful. It was just two weeks until finals and I was making every quiet minute count. The domestic war downstairs had raged and ebbed all semester; Suzi had moved out regularly, and had just left again a few days before. If the pattern held, Ken would have a big blowout party soon. But for now, everything was calm.

Then the phone rang. I sighed. Maybe it was just Dalton or Mae with a quick question about Diseases of the Nervous System or Hemic-Lymphatic. I wished I could ignore it, but I wasn't any good at that. I answered. When I heard the girlish voice on the line, my heart sank.

It was Nicole, the seventeen-year-old daughter of my old friend Laura. This friendship with Nicole was just a little newer, for she had been an infant when Laura and I met back in the early seventies, when I was giving up on college and getting wild.

Nicole and I had always been close, and recently she'd been calling just to talk. She wore a brittle veneer of pseudosophistication, and she mimicked Laura's relationship with me, as if we were running buddies instead of something more like aunt and niece. She'd been saying lately that she, too, wanted to be a veterinarian, although she wasn't putting in many regular hours at high school.

I didn't have time to chat right then, but I didn't want to rebuff her.

"What's up?" I asked, hoping there was a point to the call and that she'd get to it.

"I've got something to tell you, darling," she said. Although Laura always called me darling, it sounded funny from Nicole.

"Okay. What is it?"

"You'd better sit down."

"I'm sitting down." I had the sudden fear that she had run away and come to live with me, a fantasy I knew she sometimes had. "Are you in Fort Collins?"

"No, I'm in Albuquerque." I heard her drag on her cigarette and I could imagine her raising her hand to her forehead and

198

flicking back her hair in one fluid movement, one of Laura's trademark mannerisms. I waited for her to continue. "You're going to find this hard to believe."

"What?" I wanted to shake her.

"It's about Laura." She paused. She'd learned dramatic timing, along with a thousand other things, from her mother. She clearly was going to tell this at her own pace and in her own way.

"Yes?"

"She went into the hospital on Sunday. She didn't tell you because she didn't want to worry you."

"What's wrong with her?"

"What's wrong with her?" Nicole repeated. "Nothing. There's nothing with her. Not anymore. She's dead."

"What?" I said stupidly.

"She's dead, Loretta. Laura's dead." Nicole started to cry then, and I sat frozen, listening to her sobs. I could think of nothing to say.

Suddenly, someone took the phone from Nicole and introduced herself to me as April McCurdy, a nurse who had worked with Laura and become a close friend. She explained the medical facts of what had happened. Several days before, Laura had had excruciating abdominal pain and called an ambulance. She had an intussusception; that is, her bowel had telescoped, one piece inside another. She'd had surgery, had seemed fine, and then developed peritonitis. As they were taking her back into surgery to flush her abdomen, she had arrested, and they couldn't revive her. That had been this very morning.

I listened, understanding the medical explanation, knowing what had happened, what anatomical and bacterial processes had caused her death, but I couldn't comprehend that she was gone.

Nicole had been staying with April while Laura was in the hospital and would now stay on for a while, she said. It was all so sudden. She said that Laura had often talked about me. Laura had missed me. I could hear that April was crying now, too. "I'm sorry," she said, "but Laura was my best friend in the whole world."

Mine, too, I thought, but I didn't say it.

Nicole wanted to talk to me again, so April said good-bye.

"When are you coming?" Nicole asked. She sounded like a little girl now.

"Oh, I can't come, honey, not right now," I said. "Not until after finals. Nicole . . ." I groped for something else to say, but I didn't know what.

"When are finals?"

"They'll be over on the twentieth."

Nicole didn't say anything for a moment. Then she said quietly, "We're going to have her cremated, but I wanted you to see her first."

"I'm sorry. I just can't."

"She still looks beautiful." Nicole sounded as if she was trying to talk me into coming, trying to convince me.

"Of course she does," I said. I could think of nothing of my own to say. I was supposed to be the grown-up. I was supposed to be able to think.

Nicole asked me again to come "say good-bye" to Laura. I was struck by how alone Nicole was now. Her father had long been gone from their lives. Laura's parents were both dead, and Laura had been in a bitter fight with her only sister over their mother's estate.

I explained as best I could about my exams. She said she understood. I said I'd see her as soon as I got home. She said okay, then we said good-bye.

I sat for a long time. Then I got up and crossed the room, looked at my notes, closed my notebook. I picked up the phone again and dialed Laura's number, a number I hadn't dialed in a long time. It rang four times, the machine picked up, and Laura's taped voice was in my ear, "I'm tied up right now, darling, but I'll call you as soon as I get loose. Ta-ta."

Ta-ta, Laura.

I got a bottle of Jim Beam out of the cupboard and poured myself a shot. I toasted Laura and then I poured another shot. I thought about her and the crazy things we'd done over the years. I thought about the way she looked—"still beautiful," Nicole had said. And she was beautiful; she always had been.

I sat in my red chair, my head back, the bottle in one hand, my glass in the other, and I drank until I was good and drunk. There was no euphoria, the wonderful high Laura and I had loved after two margaritas. My mind just got cloudier and cloudier, and at some point, I went to bed.

The alarm went off at 6:45 and I clawed myself up out of sleep, hit the snooze button to give myself ten more minutes. I remembered then that Laura was dead. I closed my eyes. I couldn't imagine Laura's body lifeless. Maybe she'd faked it, I thought, and had gone away somewhere, somewhere warm. I could imagine her on a bench but not dead. Maybe she would call me soon. She'd send for Nicole. Maybe Nicole was in on it. They had both always been dramatic. Then I remembered the hospital, the telescoped bowel, the surgery. No, Laura could have faked an accident but not abdominal surgery. She really was dead.

The alarm went off again and I got up. My head ached a little. I went into the kitchen, filled the coffeepot, and plugged it in. I thought about peritonitis, a septic abdomen, microorganisms, bacteriology, Dr. Eyskens, Diseases of the Digestive System, the exams coming up.

I realized as if for the first time that Laura wouldn't be there when I went home for Christmas. She'd always been there, but now she wouldn't be.

I got ready for school, going through the motions of my morning routine one after the other, more slowly this morning, until it was time to go.

I stepped out onto my small porch. It was bitingly cold. The whole world looked dead. How could I go to school, I thought, with Laura dead? But how could I not? Would they cremate her today? I wondered. Would she be naked going into the fire, or dressed in some white robe? My thoughts were jumbled. I wasn't thinking quite straight.

Suddenly, it seemed like my fault that she was dead, that I hadn't paid enough attention, that I hadn't valued her, that I hadn't valued my own life, either, my *life* itself, but put it all into cold storage while I took these four years to do this crazy thing, to go to this horrid school, and do these dreadful things, to become a vet. No. I shook off that thought. That was crazy.

Laura had died, but it didn't have anything to do with me or with vet school. It had just happened.

I drove to school, but the feeling hung on that somehow my life wasn't going to be there when I went back for it. Or maybe I wouldn't be there, maybe I was hollowed out and changed in some horrible way, so that I couldn't find anything anymore.

Why wasn't I crying? Why wasn't I on my way home to mourn my friend and comfort her daughter? Why was I carrying on as if this meant nothing to me, as if Laura's was just another incidental death, no more than a nonsurvival surgery dog, a fact, nothing to be done? Emotion is a waste of energy. Work to do. Cannot read, cannot study with swollen red eyes. Be practical.

Oh, I was practical. It was a habit now, a part of me, deep in the grain. I would mourn when there was time in my schedule to mourn. I would feel when there was time to feel. I didn't allow myself to wonder how long you can keep a life in cold storage and expect it to survive. That would have made me crazy, and being crazy was just another one of the things that I had no time for right now.

CHAPTER 19

The Fifth of the Critters—Bones

THE skeleton of the cat suggests movement. The long column of vertebrae curves and arches to the tip of the tail. You can read in the bones the power of the hind legs that can propel the animal from a sitting position to a height of six feet. The relative size of the cranium suggests intelligence. It is a predator's skull: The capacious brain cavity has evolved to contain the wit and cunning of a hunter. The hinges of the front legs are built for stealth, for crouching, for springing—a mechanical trap. It's all there, in the bones, easier to read than the words on a page.

I could name the bones now, each one, down to the smallest metatarsal, from which emerges the sliver of claw, translucent and pearly. I could assemble a cat from a pile of bones, fitting ball to socket, aligning the long white bones that are connected in life by muscle and tendon and ligament.

But it didn't take much training to recognize the cat skeleton sitting at the foot of the stairs in the snow when I returned to Fort Collins at the end of Christmas break that year, for it was still animated—though barely—and hung with a ratty coat of orange and white and greasy dusky brown. Alive, but a skeleton still.

Its yellow eyes bulged from their sockets, their size exaggerated by the atrophy of facial muscle. The cat crouched, watching, not moving, in the circle of light cast by my headlights. I sat in the darkness of my little car and looked at it. It was a stranger to me; I'd never seen it before. And its shabby, bare existence in the dark, cold January night seemed emblematic of life itself. Though it seemed cursed already, I added my silent curse. Damn it.

It was late and I was tired from the ten-hour drive from Albuquerque. In my Honda, those hours were long, and the winds had picked up north of Denver, so that my arms and shoulders ached from holding the car to the road.

Ten hours alone in a car is a lot of time to think. Radio stations faded in and out as I passed through towns and back out into the great eastern slope of the Rocky Mountains. Laura had been on my mind. Her absence had permeated this vacation. She hadn't been there to put my semester's worth of agonies in perspective, to escape with into hedonism and pleasures of the flesh, to listen to my stories about Ken and his parties and entertain me with fantasies of how she would deal with him. Instead, there had been her empty house and her new friends, sorting her things, readying it for rental. There had been Nicole, superficially warm enough but holding back from grief and anger, our years of closeness canceled by my not being there when she most needed me. I'd had drinks with Laura's new friends; we'd shared our memories. Laura had missed me, April said.

I couldn't quite say that I'd missed her while she was missing me. I'd been too busy for that. But I'd missed her over this break. I missed her now and I would for a long time.

I was tired, both from the drive and from the thought of the semester ahead, end of vacation, accentuated by the weather changes I had driven through that day. I'd left a mild, sunny New Mexico winter day, the temperature in the high fifties, and driven into the bitterness of the mountainous north, where the ground was white, frozen, and inhospitable.

No one was home at Ken and Suzi's. The driveway was empty, the windows dark. I would normally have been glad, but tonight it just seemed dark and lonely. The cooling engine ticked in the silence and the temperature in the car plummeted to meet my mood. I sat behind the steering wheel and contemplated the half-dead animal in front of me.

Home over Christmas, my sister and I had lingered over coffee at her dining room table. The conversation had meandered, and she'd posed a question from some kind of ethics quiz or personality inventory she had come across: Suppose you're in a burning building with barely time to escape. As you run down the hallway, you come across a painting by Rembrandt. Beside it is a kitten. You can save only one. Which?

"Why can't I save both?" I'd asked, being contrary.

"You just can't." There were other rules to the question, too. You can't consider the monetary worth of the painting; you can't say, "I'd save the painting and sell it and give the money to the Humane Society, or rescue ten kittens from the pound." You can have only one standard: Which would you value more—the kitten or the Rembrandt?

"Maybe I'd leave them both and just save myself."

"Come on," she'd chided. Supposedly, there's no right answer. But I knew that to my tenderhearted, romantic sister, there was. So, to satisfy her, I'd said, "The kitten."

It was true, anyway. I could imagine the hallway. The smoke chokes the air; I feel the heat pressing behind me. The kitten cries piteously. The kitten, sure.

Nancy had wanted a discussion, though, and she'd kept pressing. "Maybe you don't like Rembrandt," she'd said. "Maybe it's a Frederic Remington, with a herd of cows and all those horses and Indians. Or, wait, I know—an O'Keeffe. What's your favorite? The cow's skull with the red, white, and blue? Or the skull of the deer with the huge antlers in the sky, with the clouds and a yellow daisy, above the red mesa, out by Ghost Ranch." O'Keeffe's country is our country. You drive through it on your way to our mother's place in Chama. "So which? The O'Keeffe or the kitten?"

"The kitten."

"Maybe it's an ugly little scraggly kitten," she'd goaded, wanting a philosophical argument about the value of life versus art.

"The kitten."

"Maybe it's an ugly, *sick* little kitten."

"The kitten."

"What if it's a mouse?"

If I had answered, "Mouse," she'd have asked, "Cockroach?" So I'd shaken my head to stop the game. I had been annoyed with her, annoyed at the luxury she had to indulge in these hypothetical questions of ethics. If this hypothetical kitten was really sick, maybe I'd take the painting. I'd probably take the painting.

I was not a heartless person, I defended myself. And I could be as irrationally sentimental as anybody. I had saved mice from cats before, interrupting nature's game plan. I hate those nature films where the lions rip apart the gazelles, even knowing there are hungry lion cubs waiting for the meat. But I had killed kittens and cats for lesser reason than saving a Rembrandt. I'd kill more, no doubt, before it was over.

There's just no shortage of cats. The Roman Coliseum is alive with them. They lurk in every city alley, every country barn. There are kids in supermarket parking lots every weekend giving them away. Newspapers advertise them every day in every city. They fill the pounds and animal shelters—more kittens than takers. At the VTH, there are even more: the litters and strays dropped on the doorstep in the middle of the night, the research cats that have finished their "work." Cats aplenty.

The cat still crouched in the beam of my headlights. I don't need this tonight, I thought.

I slipped off my moccasins and pulled on my snow boots, which had remained unused on the floor of the backseat for the last four weeks. I struggled into my down jacket and hoisted my overnight bag over the seat. My books and the rest of my stuff could wait until morning. The cat loomed before me like an obstacle that I had to clear before I could rest.

I shut off the headlights and opened the door. The eerie whiteness of the snow itself lighted my path. The night air was sharp and the wind drove the cold through my jeans. I brushed the four inches of new snow from the rickety wooden banister and knocked it from the unswept step with my boot.

The cat slunk a few feet away, as if it were well acquainted with boots. Then, risking a kick, it darted between my feet and threaded itself up the stairs with my every step. I held to the rail for balance, pushed the cat with my foot, and cursed. At the top, I struggled with my keys. The screen door pushed the snow into a ridge, a natural doorstop that allowed me only a foot or so of clearance, and I wedged my way inside, pulling my bag behind me and closing the inner door.

I was home, such as it was. Two small rooms, cheap, clean, simple, functional, a monk's cell. I flipped the light switch and banished the darkness. I crossed the room and turned up the thermostat from fifty degrees, where I'd set it to keep the plants alive and the water from freezing. The low *whoosh* from the wall heater was comforting, almost warming in itself. I'd keep my jacket on until the room was toasty. I turned on the water to clear the old pipes of rust and sediment. I'd brew a small pot of coffee, sit awhile, let the road vibrations fall away. I filled the pot and looked back at the door. The cat was silent, as though its voice had atrophied with its flesh. It expected nothing of me and my kind.

Or, I rationalized, it had gone away, under the house, or into the garage, out of the wind and the worst of the cold. It had a fur coat, however shabby. It was gone by now . . . probably.

I measured the coffee into the basket, plugged it in. I looked back at the door. It's gone, I said to myself. But I crossed the room again, pulled back the curtain, shielded the glass against the glare of the overhead light, and looked out onto my small landing.

Sunk down and huddled in its misery, it looked back at me, its yellow eyes bulging, unblinking. God, it was ugly and dirty. It had a haunted look, a cat from a horror film, almost evil in its cowering, glaring crouch. A rangy old tom, I thought, judging from its size and the angular shape of its head. I stared into those yellow eyes for a moment before I dropped the curtain.

The small rooms heated up quickly, and I shed my coat, sat down in the old secondhand red upholstered chair I'd hauled up from Albuquerque, propped my feet on a stool, and drank the coffee from a mug I held in both my hands. Out of that life, back in this one, I pushed away thoughts of New Mexico. Tomorrow was Sunday. Monday it would all begin again. I sighed again and again, as though changing the air inside me.

At last, my fatigue won out. I got up, changed into my nightgown, and pulled back the covers of my narrow bed. I looked back across the living room at the door between me and the winter, between me and the cat. I sighed again. Defeated, I crossed the room and peeked out the window. As though frozen, the cat still crouched in front of my door. I pulled the door open and pushed the screen outward. "You win," I said. "Come on in."

Slowly, the cat stood up; slowly, it stepped into the open space between its world and mine. It stopped on the threshold. No doubt it owed its life, however meager and tenuous, to this caution.

"Come on," I said. "Kitty, kitty, kitty. It's cold, come on." In its maddening catly way, it looked and sniffed, turned its head only slightly as it took in the entire room. Finally, it was satisfied and slunk through the door, keeping to the wall.

I opened a can of tuna, and the cat gagged it down with what seemed desperation. In seconds, the can was empty.

"This is just for tonight," I said. "This is not a relationship."

The cat turned at the sound of my voice. It licked its lips and then, with its paw, began to clean its face and whiskers. I sat down on the edge of the red chair and reached to stroke its bony head. The cat stretched up to press into my caress. I ran my hand over the matted, dirty coat. Its spine was a string of stony knots. The cat was a rack of bones. It began to purr as I stroked it, and I closed my hand around its middle, just in front of its hind legs, taking the measure of this sepulchral animal. My thumb and forefinger met. It was on the brink of starvation. I lifted the cat onto my lap and it stretched its front legs along my thigh and began to knead with pleasure. I braced myself for the prick of its claws, but there was no needlelike prick. I lifted one paw and stretched out the toes. No sheaths, no claws. They had been surgically removed, the toes amputated at the first knuckle, a standard barbaric operation for house pets whose owners worry about their furniture or drapes.

No wonder it was starving. Wild cats don't live long lives, anyway. Cars kill them. Dogs kill them. Humanity has eradicated much of their prey—mice and shrews and grasshoppers—and left them slim pickings. But a declawed cat has no chance at all—except the long shot of finding another home, some person to take it in.

"You're just bones," I said, and the cat turned at my voice and blinked. It had probably never been a pretty cat, and it was very dirty, but it didn't look so demonic now.

I carried her to bed—it was a female, I'd discovered—and she lay beside me, warm and full, sheltered and body-to-body with another creature. I stroked her gently and, almost automatically, as I drifted toward sleep, I began to test myself, to name the bones and joints as I felt them, palpating her as if she were a specimen and this was an examination of my knowledge, and not my heart. She leaned into my inspecting caress as I went through the silent litany of bones. We fell into our separate dreams.

It felt good and different to share my bed, to share my breakfast, to speak to some living thing besides my own reflection in the mirror.

I knew just a little bit too much about the diseases of cats by this time, however, and I wondered whether she had feline leukemia, for she looked none too good, and this disease, which is a retrovirus, suppresses the autoimmune system. It is the feline version of the AIDS virus, and is thus able to present in many different ways. It makes the body vulnerable to invasive bacteria, viruses, or fungi, which do the dirty work of death.

I thought about fe-leuk not because she showed any particular signs but just *because*. It would figure. I wasn't seeing a lot of survivors these days. I looked at an animal and saw a fatality coming my way. If this cat had fe-leuk, I knew I could put her down. I knew that it was what I should do, for it's a contagious and fatal disease. But this old girl and I had slept flank-to-flank like buddies, and it would be hard, even harder than it always was.

So I brought home a heparinized blood tube—one treated to

keep the drawn blood from clotting—and a syringe, enlisted Dalton's help to hold her down, and drew up the little bit of blood I needed for the test. I called her Bones, not really that pretty a name, but then, she wasn't that pretty a cat.

The next day, I dropped the blood at the lab window. When it came back negative, I almost thought there'd been a mistake. The poor old cat might have one more life left in her, though, and it now looked as if she'd share it with me. The timing wasn't all that great. I had been thinking that I'd have to move before too long—the downstairs soap opera was getting on my nerves and cutting into my sleep—and it's always easier to find a rental if you don't bring along any animal life. Still, if she wasn't fatally ill—it would have been an exaggeration to say she was actually healthy—I guessed she could throw in with me. I guessed I didn't really have all that much choice, and besides, she and I seemed to have a few things in common.

We'd both had some hard knocks, though I could only guess at hers, and we'd both lived through them. We were both tall, thin, and kind of graceless; both a little bit disheveled, a little scruffy. Neither one of us spent much time in front of the mirror. We didn't fix up much, Bones and I. We could do with a pretty simple life.

Neither one of us was exactly poetry in motion, so I guess I wasn't too surprised the day she fell off the second-story roof. What did surprise me was how much it upset me.

It was spring by the calendar and starting to feel that way by the weather, too. The days were a trifle longer than they had been, and we were both feeling good about being outside in the late afternoon. The Colorado winter had bred a good case of cabin fever, and I had uncoiled the garden hose from its long winter of disuse and was watering the bulbs that were beginning to send up tentative green spikes along the back fence. Bones lay on the porch railing, her eyes shut, her long front legs stretched out before her. I spoke to her from down below, and she opened her eyes, stood up, and sauntered along the rail. At the end, she looked up to the roof, gave a chirpy little meow, and jumped to new heights. She sat there, content, warming in the sun, looking pretty good, considering what a wraith she'd been in January. I spoke to her again, and she spoke back. She seemed to have just awakened from her winter's hibernation and she had a lot to say. She walked along the gutter edge, looking out over the outlying farmland, and then, suddenly, she fell.

If she had had her front claws, she might have had a chance to hold on, but she just tumbled. It seemed slow to me, how she fell and turned over and over in the air.

My heart churned with her. I was halfway across the lawn before she landed, on her feet, though it's a myth that cats always land feet first. This time, though, this cat did, and her joints coiled and recoiled as little shock absorbers. She landed in a crouch, and before I could touch her, she slunk away quickly to the shade of the house and then up the rickety wooden stairs and into the apartment. I followed her up and held her in my arms a long time as she lay there, purrless and stunned. I wondered how many of her nine lives she could have left.

The weather turned back to cold, and Mama came to visit. We were cabin-bound again, at least when I wasn't at school, and it wasn't a very big space. This particular evening, we were working on a crossword puzzle together. Since Mama's eyesight had failed, she liked to have somebody help her with the puzzle, reading the clues and counting the spaces. It was quiet.

Suddenly, there was a great noise from under the kitchen sink, inside the cabinet—scrambling, clamoring, and Bones's agitated voice, a voice I hadn't heard from her before.

"Has she got a mouse?" Mama asked. My first thought was that somehow another cat had gotten in and was trapped under the sink with Bones, beating the tar out of her. It was that kind of sound, the kind you might hear on a cartoon while you watch a blur of two different colors of cat fur going round and round, blending and melting together like Sambo's tigers into butter, with multicolored stars popping out of the ruckus.

I ran across the room and flung open the cupboard door. Just one cat, just Bones, but she *was* going round and round as if she was on spin cycle. Doing flips and circles, all by herself among the dish rack, the cleanser, and the bucket, stirring up the whole mess.

A seizure, I thought, and then I saw she had a cord in her mouth—an electric cord, from the wall to the cat. She seemed unable to free herself of it as she screamed and flipped end over end, peeing all over herself and the inside of the cupboard.

I stared, paralyzed in horror, and then I screamed her name and clapped my hands together. It was enough to jar her, to summon her strength, her tiny remainder of voluntary control, her last bit of fight. The black electric snake didn't have her so packed full of venom that she couldn't break free, and she managed to loosen her hold on the snake's ugly head. The grip of the electricity broke and she literally fell off the wire. When that force field altered and its jaws unlocked, it dropped her to the floor of the cupboard like a stone.

We were both motionless for one long moment, and then she flew past me, her hair wet and sticking up in tiny spikes, straight through my legs, back into the farthest corner of the apartment, to the bedroom.

The twin beds, one against each of the two far walls, abutted end to side, and under both beds were cardboard boxes—the ones I'd moved with, emptied, folded flat and stacked, jammed from the floor to the bottom of the box springs—and other boxes full of stuff and shoe boxes wedged into the smaller spaces.

Behind all this clutter was Bones, though how she found the space and the pathway, I do not know. I started to yank away the flattened cardboard like a crazed woman.

Mama stood behind me in the doorway. "What's wrong?" she cried. "She's okay now, isn't she? Just leave her alone. She'll be okay, won't she?"

"No, she's not all right," I called back, not stopping in my frantic tearing at the stuff under those beds. I feared Bones was drowning, for electric shock initiates a release of fluid into the lungs. I had to get to her.

I saw her dart from one corner to the other. Finally, I had a good-sized area cleared under the beds, and the room behind me was almost filled with the boxes I had flung away. I had her in my sights, a wretched animal in the farthest corner. Her ears were pinned flat to her head, her pupils dilated, so her eyes were solid black. She smelled horrid—of cat pee and burned flesh. I reached my arm in under the bed, up to my shoulder, and grabbed the scruff of her neck. She was quiet, dark, and wet as a storm.

I drew her to me and held her tightly against my chest. "Don't die," I whispered to her. "Don't you die, Bonesy girl. Don't die."

I took her into the kitchen, grabbed my stethoscope, and held it to her chest. I listened, and I could hear my own heart pounding in my ears, and her heart, even faster, but solid and regular. It sounded good. She hadn't been jolted into cardiac arrhythmia. Her lungs sounded clear, no gurgling, no bubbling. She wasn't glowing, smoking, or smoldering. I held her until her heart and mine slowed to normal.

There was blood around her mouth, and I knew there was damage. I pried her jaws open to examine the wounds. She had bitten her tongue, mangled it pretty badly. A half-inch strip across the tongue was denuded; raw, swollen tissue remained where there had been a forest of taste buds. The natural space between her canine and premolar was raised and filled with fluid, a blister about the size of a dime.

Within a couple of days, another problem with electric shock presented itself: The tissues in her mouth had been fried—they were dead meat—and were sloughing off. The tissue beneath was raw, exposed, full of nerve endings not meant to be so exposed. Of course, she wouldn't eat or drink; she kept her poor mouth as still as possible.

I had to force fluids down her through the corner of her mouth with a syringe. I didn't want to have to resort to IV fluid therapy. I didn't want her in the hospital. I wanted her home with me, where I could wake several times each night, just to be sure she was still there and still alive.

She hated this force-feeding, for it hurt. I mixed the fanciest canned cat food with water until it was a thin gruel, heated it a bit, and forced it into her, trying to get it past the tenderest part of her mouth. I got a prescription for antibiotics at the

VTH, because her dead mouth was filthy now, a prime spot for a riproaring infection to set in.

She was for the most part a stoic patient, but she had suddenly developed an overwhelming need to sit on my lap. She would sit facing me, her eyes sealed shut, purring. She wanted to rub her cheek on my cheek. The sloughing tissue caused her to drool, but I couldn't bear to push her away. She seemed to get such comfort from my company, from my being near. And actually, I, too, took some comfort there. I had developed a need to hold her. In truth, I loved her.

CHAPTER 20

Through the Swinging Doors

RON Hadley, the guy with the rough touch in the bovine palpation lab, was no longer with us when we reconvened for second semester, a victim of Langford's stringent standards for Diseases of the Nervous System. Having failed the final, he was allowed to take a makeup exam, but, according to school policy, could then earn no higher grade than *D* for the course. We were allowed to graduate with as many as eighteen credit hours of *D* on our record, but no more. It seemed Ron had already chalked up those eighteen hours, so he didn't bother to retake the test. Except for our run-in in the palpation shed, I had had no relationship with him, but you couldn't watch a classmate fall without some sympathy pains. I hadn't known he was in trouble, but then we all hid our weaknesses from one another. I couldn't help but think that his marriage had been a victim of vet school, which now had proven futile, anyway.

This term would be the end of our systems courses—Diseases of the Digestive System II, Diseases of the Reproductive System, Diseases of the Integumentary System, and The Special Senses (a half-semester course that was followed by The Body as a Whole, or "The Body Asshole," as we came to know it). I also had an elective in Equine Lameness. The shape of our days was the same as last term—mornings in junior practicum, afternoons in lecture. The time we spent in the VTH clinics was becoming more and more relevant, as the cases we saw often illustrated what we were learning in the systems courses. The two were symbiotic, and the total gain often seemed greater than the sum of the two parts.

For example, the cancer lectures in the Diseases of the Integumentary System (skin) fell during my rotation through clinical oncology and gave me a nice overlap in material. Seeing a case in the morning made the afternoon lecture much more vivid, and helped me to sort one condition or disease from another, for in every system there seemed to be dozens of different possible diagnoses for every set of symptoms. The material was never tidy and the exceptions and variations were maddening. Seeing actual cases nailed the information. Again, it was the repetition that Lloyd had promised would be my salvation, and repetition at precisely the right moment was worth a lot. There was no substitute for the actual experience of seeing, diagnosing, and treating a disease or injury; it made it yours forever.

As we studied tumors of the skin, I worked my stint in the Oncology Clinic. A Norwegian elkhound came in with several skin lesions, tumors called ICE—intracutaneous cornifying epithelioma. This condition occurs most often in the so-called Arctic Circle breeds, so the acronym was useful. The lesions occur predominantly on the shoulder, neck, and upper back of young dogs, and the prognosis was excellent in the case of solitary tumors, poorer when there were several. With the elkhound as my living example, this particular tumor was particularized for me. It was mine forever and would be forever associated in my mind with that particular dog.

As we neared the end of our systems courses and the overwhelming bulk of the veterinary core curriculum, our education became more and more dependent upon the swinging doors and what came through them. If twenty-three cases of osteosarcoma and little else came into the clinic while you were on Oncology rotation, you could consider yourself an osteosarcoma specialist and let it go at that.

Or you could keep your ear to the ground and circle back to Oncology after you'd left that service, on independent field trips looking for other cancers. It was common for students to cruise the hospital, looking for the new, the different, the unseen, and a clinician who would let them have a look. Word would get out: "There's a sick sinus syndrome in ICU—check it out," or "A horse just checked into the barn with purpura hemorrhagica." We networked our way into the widest menu of disease we could manage, both on our own and more systematically through rounds, when clinicians made an effort to bring the interesting and relevant cases of the week to our attention.

In the spring of the year, the junior-senior banquet rolled around. This party is given by the junior class for the senior class, and while many of my classmates worked hard to put it on, I had never been the student-council type. When the call went out for juniors to take over clinic and hospital duties that night so that the senior class could be free for the festivities, I volunteered to work in the barn, however.

Jimmy Fulmer and I both ended up on Food Animal Service, the 4:00 to 11:00 P.M. shift, doing treatments, checking on hospitalized cases, and answering any emergency phone calls. We hoped to see some action, and we were pleased when a call came in from a farmer whose small heifer was in trouble calving. We summoned the on-call clinician and made ready for the arrival of the farmer and cow.

The heifer was quite small, a slight representative of the Hereford breed, probably too young and too small to be safely bred. However, the neighbor's hefty Charolais bull had broken through the fence and gotten to her.

The farmer had seen her when he'd thrown the morning hay at about 6:00 A.M., but she wasn't with the herd when he did the evening feeding. He'd found her down in some brush, and apparently she'd been in labor quite awhile. She was spent, and only the calf's two hooves were visible. He'd winched her onto his stock trailer and they arrived at the VTH about 8:00 P.M.

Quickly, we lubricated the heifer's vagina, hooked the calf to obstetrical chains, and tried to pull it free. It didn't budge. We tried again, using the brute strength of three good-sized and good-natured cowboys in our class. We tried again. There were two options—cesarean section and fetotomy. The calf was dead, so the farmer and the clinician chose the latter, which is a safer procedure for the dam.

We got the heifer onto the "fly operating table" and tilted her over to begin the tedious process of sawing the calf into deliverable parts while protecting the uterine walls so as to reduce scar tissue and retain her future worth as a fertile animal. We were giving her IV fluids and antibiotics and working fast, trying to reduce surgery time, and, thus, the risk of her bloating or developing a nerve paralysis secondary to massive weight bearing down on a nerve or nerve branch, or muscles supplied by said nerve. There was plenty to do.

The calf came out piece by grueling piece. This wasn't pretty medicine, but it was real, and the heifer made it through. Though tired and weak, she walked back to her pen afterward, her life saved by our work.

I can't say we had the same elated feeling you have when a live baby is standing on the ground, but we were pleased that the cow was alive, we were proud that we'd been skilled enough to do the job, and positively glad for the experience, that we'd been in the right place at that right time. Of course, we knew that the farmer might likely cull her from the herd and ship her to slaughter, because she was no longer a prime candidate for breeding. Maybe, though, he'd give her the chance to bear again. And at least she was alive and no longer suffering now.

There was still plenty to do afterward—a fetotomy makes a mess, and we were the grunts, after all. We were there late, with an early-morning rounds call the next day. But none of us complained; none of us wished we'd been at the banquet or at home in bed.

Most births are uneventful. There weren't a lot of fetotomies to be done, certainly not enough that everyone who felt a need for the experience got it. That's one reason why we had had mock-up fetotomies in the bovine reproduction lab. But simulations were always only approximations—lacking everything from the bleeding, contracting, hot, wet, and unpredictable nature of the living tissue to the jolt of adrenaline and the urgency of teamwork, the satisfaction of having given it all the skill and knowledge and effort that you had to give.

The routine of the hospital could make you feel as if you were edging toward becoming a veterinarian on little baby feet, but that night each of us there felt as if we had taken a giant step forward. It was one more procedure we could cross off our long scavenger list of experiences we were seeking.

Being on that service when that cow came in was not what your average citizen would have called good luck, but it was what we were there for, and that was what I called it. Very good luck, indeed.

PART 4

Senior Year

CHAPTER 21

■━━━━

All Kinds of Luck

SENIOR year was different from the first three in several ways. We were finished with our core curriculum—our anatomy and physiology, the study of the development, function, and diseases of every system of the body. We would meet no more in large lecture halls; we would not meet again, all of us together, until graduation night.

Of course, we still had lots to learn, just as we would still have lots to learn a year from now when we were finished with our formal training. Then we would go off into *practice*, a perfect word for what we would do—put into practice what we had learned and continue to practice toward elusive perfection of our skills. *This* year, we would practice in preparation for practice, to refine and solidify our knowledge and skills in the safety of school, under the eyes of our teachers.

We would be working now only in small groups in tutorial or clinical settings. We would work exclusively in one block, or unit, before moving on to the next, so the year allowed us to devote ourselves completely to the topic at hand. We would rotate again through the services of the VTH, this time with more responsibility and now assisted by junior vet students. We would be doing actual work for which actual clients would be paying real money, and because of our staffing function, the year would have a shape different from the last three.

Seniors had to work in each of the services at all times for the whole year; we were an integral part of the staff. Without us, the VTH would not and could not offer its services to the public. That meant, naturally, that our vacations and breaks from school would not all fall at the same time. We would not all have the summer off, or Christmas.

Our rotations would last from one to four weeks. Some were required of everyone—Small Animal Medicine, for instance. Some rotations, such as Ophthalmology, were elective but would be taken by almost everyone because they were basic to clinical practice. Some electives, such as Small Animal Surgery and Radiology, duplicated required rotations and allowed us to get more experience in a particular area. Some, such as Llama Medicine, were almost esoteric, electives pure and simple.

There was a master schedule that guaranteed all the services of the VTH were covered for the year. It offered electives when the pertinent faculty were free of their responsibilities in freshman, sophomore, and junior courses; the schedule also respected the laws of nature (Calving Management was offered in the spring, when most calves are born). This master schedule broke down into twelve different individual schedules representing different packages of requirements, electives, and vacation times. We were asked to choose our first, second, and third choices from among the twelve. Getting a certain elective was the deciding factor for some. Others, who had lined up internships in other institutions in various parts of the country, needed a particular block of time off. All else being equal (which I don't suppose it ever is), you and your buddies would like the same schedule so you could pass the year in congenial company.

High on my list were the Llama Medicine elective and ending the year with a five-week block of vacation so I could prepare single-mindedly for state and national boards.

If only nine others wanted what you wanted, there was no problem, but if there was competition for a particular schedule, names were drawn from a hat to fill the slots. So luck counted.

I had learned to improve my luck in these three-plus years. I'd learned to get some of what Ralph Waldo Emerson called "the luck that the good players have." But the CSU lottery required the other kind—blind luck, the kind that just might respond to a magic charm. So I loaded mine on—my Apache teardrop earrings, the silver horseshoe necklace Sam had given me, all my lucky clothes, right down to my lucky socks.

The magic worked. I was to have one of the few spaces in the highly sought-after Llama Medicine rotation (offered only three times that year) and my block of study time in April and May. What I was not to have was my running buddies, and I'd miss them.

Friday afternoon after the last of junior finals, Dalton, Eric, Mae, and I sat on the back lawn of the VTH and drank a couple of beers to mark the occasion. I imagined that the freshmen just finishing their first year were raising hell just about then in the anatomy building on the main campus. But this small party would do for now.

It hardly seemed a great moment. The next night at 9:30, Dalton and Mae would begin senior year with a twelve-hour night shift in the Intensive Care Unit. My own vacation would be somewhat longer—officially, until Monday morning when I started my Small Animal Surgery elective, but in reality, only until Sunday afternoon when I would arrive at the hospital to prep my dog for the next day's work.

Senior year had a lot to recommend it, not least of which was that we would do far less killing than we had as juniors. One exception was the Small Animal Surgery elective (another was Ophthalmology, which has a surgery lab). Again, our surgical patients were throwaways from the pound.

We worked in surgery teams of two; Elaine Davis and I paired up. The day started early, and we were officially done at 1:00 P.M. because the clinicians had clinic responsibilities and other obligations in the afternoons. In fact, though, the rest of the day was full—we prepared our patients and ourselves for the next day's surgeries.

We did several procedures each day, a wide range of operations—circumcostal gastroplexy (securing a dog's stomach to a rib to prevent a torsion from recurring), enlargement of the pyloric diameter (the opening from the stomach into the small intestine), cruciate ligament repair and patella stabilization (knee repair), onychectomy (declawing a cat), and others.

Thus, each afternoon we reviewed the upcoming anatomy, anatomical maps that guided us through layers of tissue to the pertinent structure below, the procedure itself, pinning techniques, and proper suture patterns. In addition to our texts and notes from different courses over our three years of study, there were videotapes to watch of each procedure and literature to review from current medical research in the area. We were responsible for any and all questions the clinicians might pose about a particular surgery.

Everyone in the lab gathered upstairs in the video library to watch the relevant tapes, and there was a good deal of joking around, chatting, and fast-forwarding through routine parts of the operation.

Every day, Elaine and I stayed behind after the crowd cleared and watched the tapes for the next day's surgeries over again in their entirety, even the repetitive and boring parts, as if we felt we'd deal ourselves some bad luck if we didn't watch each one of Dr. Creed's ten simple interrupted skin sutures.

I hadn't realized until then to what extent Elaine shared my insecurity and fears. I was reminded again that many, if not most, of my classmates were probably hiding some anxiety behind poise and bravado. All week long, Elaine worried aloud that we would flunk this rotation (she included me in her fears, though worrying was something I needed no help with). If two of the clinicians were standing aside talking quietly, she imagined they were discussing our miserable skills and lousy performance.

There were several orthopedic surgeries on "harvested" bone; that is, bone removed from an animal earlier and stripped of muscle. These seemed somewhat pointless, because they little resembled surgery on a living animal. It reminded me of carpentry, as if we were fixing broken table legs.

One of our "surgical" tasks was to collect two femurs, a humerus, and the radius and ulna bones from the cadaver of a recent surgical patient and "debulk" them, remove the muscle.

It was somewhat like being in the kitchen, except it didn't seem at all wholesome.

Wednesday was both the best and worst day of the week. We performed a perineal urethrostomy on a cat (amputating the penis and securing the cut-back urethra to the outside of the abdomen). I loved the procedure, and it was one that worked miracles, relieving a cat of the pain and threat of trapped particles in the very narrow urethral opening of the penis and restoring the animal to absolute health. It was a surgery I expected to perform quite often in practice, and I was glad for this chance to do it.

The downside, of course, was that the procedure did not restore this particular cat to health, for we euthanized him when we finished for the day. He was an affectionate cat, purring and rubbing against us as we prepared to anesthetize him, giving us no trouble at all until we inserted the IV catheter in his foreleg. He fought us then, and Elaine was gruff with him. She wasn't a cat person, and I was. We were beginning to get on one another's nerves.

She began to point out to me places where I could improve my technique. I began to snap back at her. We finished the urethrostomy and moved on to the procedure of stabilizing a broken jaw (known as high rise kitty syndrome, since cats that fall from windows often sustain this injury) with circumferential wire. We finished with our poor patient by removing his claws, actually amputating his toes at the first knuckle, a procedure I find morally offensive.

Educational as it was, when the week ended, I was ready to move on.

Llama Medicine, my next rotation, was the perfect antidote to the stressful week before. It was late spring, the weather was warm and clear, and we did most of our work in the mountains near Fort Collins.

Llamas are gaining popularity as pack animals and pets. Their soft, padded hooves are less destructive to terrain than the hooves of horses and mules. They are surefooted. And they are still somewhat exotic.

There wasn't a good, practical reason for me to take this elective, however. I didn't know whether I would ever see a llama in practice. But I just liked these animals. They were just plain pretty, with their serene faces and large doe eyes. I liked what I knew of their temperament; they are generally gentle creatures.

I already knew their one infamous bad trait—spitting. They are accurate marksmen, and their spittum is foul, without question. The putrid stuff seems to come from the depths of hell, but actually it is regurgitated from the rumen. There's no reason, though, to be a victim, especially if you're a veterinarian. We are supposed to be good at reading animal body language; it is one of our best diagnostic tools. And the body language of an about-to-spit llama is not subtle. They begin to work their lower jaw and neck muscles, pumping up the fluid. They are likely to pin their ears back and assume an erect, aggressive posture. They will move between the perceived threat and whatever they are protecting—their mate, their offspring.

The llama perceives a returned stare as an act of aggression, so the best course of action is to avert your eyes while you go about whatever it is that needs to be done.

They also have a reputation for being stubborn. By nature, they are quiet and submissive, and their stubbornness takes a docile form, as well. When they've had enough of whatever they're having, they typically take a "llama time out"—they simply lie down. They curl their front legs and tuck their hind legs under them; they look like a woolly, dreadlocked cross between a deer and a camel. Fighting is counterproductive; you'll get tired of tugging before they get tired of lying down. It's a frustrating piece of work. The easiest solution is simply to get behind the animal, find its hind legs, and reposition them directly behind its body. Since this is a fairly uncomfortable position, the llama will most likely rise and bend to your will.

If the llama takes time out when you're trying to palpate her reproductive tract, it's a good idea to go with the flow, lie down beside her, flat as a lizard, and simply palpate her where she lies. Likewise, if you're trimming hooves when the llama goes down, the easiest thing to do is pull out one leg at a time, trim it, and then replace it under the Rastafarian puffball.

These two negative traits are more than counterbalanced by their good ones. Their dung piles are odorless and communal. And, most endearing, they hum. Dr. Anderson says they hum because they don't know the words, but, in fact, there are several reasons. They hum when they are happy and content. They hum when they are agitated, when they are processed through a chute for worming or vaccination, or when a stranger passes among them. They seem to take comfort in the sound. And it's a nice sound, a herd of llamas humming.

We began the week at the "llama research facility," which had no office or laboratory that I ever saw. This was the home of some of Marvin Anderson's llamas. The llama business was booming, and the animals, especially reproductively sound females, commanded a rather fetching price. Dr. Anderson is a recognized expert in the field; as such, he received llamas with reproductive problems from all over the country. His deal with some owners of compromised females was this: If he could diagnose and resolve the problem and the animal bore a live young, called a cria, the female would be returned to the owner for subsequent breedings and Dr. Anderson would keep the cria as payment; if he could not fix the problem and the animal remained barren, Dr. Anderson would keep her in his herd in settlement of the bill. Consequently, he had a pretty good-sized herd, which also included some males who suffered from "berserk male syndrome."

I thought I'd known some humans who suffered from this very thing, but it turns out that the term describes what typically happens to a bottle-fed male llama when he reaches sexual maturity. The very word *puberty* strikes fear into the heart of any parent, and when the child in question is a llama, he has no social conventions to contain and mediate his hormonally driven desire to establish dominance over other members of his "herd," which in this case includes unsuspecting and often terrorized humans. These rogues in Dr. Anderson's herd, though, were never truly threatening, perhaps because they'd had the chance to become acclimated to their own kind and were living in harmony among them.

During our turn out at the llama ranch, we practiced leading the animals into the chute; we trimmed their hooves, which are really more like toenails; we gave them injections; we palpated them; we assessed their body conditions; and we drew their blood, a rather difficult proposition because, for aesthetic reasons, their thick fleece is generally not clipped; their hide is extremely thick; and the jugular vein courses under the protection of the cervical vertebral processes.

At the Great Divide Llama Ranch, we castrated several young males. We drugged them with an intramuscular ketamine/xylazine injection and stayed beside them as they went down, first on their knees and then on their woolly rumps, folding their legs under them in the tall grass. Then one person tied up one hind leg and the surgeon did the castration. When we finished, we released the leg. The llamas lay as if merely napping in the Colorado sun, towels across their eyes so the sun didn't bother them or arouse them prematurely.

We got our sack lunches from the truck and sat among the woolly lumps to watch over them as they revived and to revive ourselves and meditate over what we'd done that morning, what we'd learned, how far we'd come.

Slowly, one by one, the llamas shook off their towels, rolled up into a sternal position, and lay there among us. They were calm, as if they, too, were meditating upon the morning's activity. Unlike the horse, which thrashes about and can seriously injure itself when recovering from anesthetic, the llama remains tranquil and serene, and thus safe from falling.

Dr. Anderson was as tranquil as his subjects, and we'd take a break after lunch, perhaps nodding off ourselves into a most civilized siesta.

This didn't seem like vet school. It seemed like heaven.

While most of our work was in the field, we were in the VTH late one afternoon, almost ready to call it a day. We were restocking the truck, swapping jokes with Dr. Anderson, talking about the next day's work, and just getting ready to head out the door when a message came over the intercom for Dr. Anderson or one of his Llama Medicine students to report to the large-animal desk.

One of my classmates who was something of a case hog, enhancing her "good player" luck, I guess, immediately said she'd go, and she did. By the time she got to the desk, however, the client had come back to the barn, a dying black cria in her arms. The woman was distraught, and when she stepped into the barn from the bright sunlight of the afternoon, her eyes roved anxiously over our small group, searching for Dr. Anderson.

He stepped forward and took her burden. Apparently, the cria had been born that morning, probably shortly after the owner left for work. Her small llama farm had had problems with bacterial infection before. Ideally, the dam should have been vaccinated twice at two-week intervals about a month before she delivered. But for one reason or another—this delivery was quite a bit earlier than the owner had anticipated—the vaccinating hadn't been done. And also ideally, there should have been somebody attending the birth who could have painted the cria's naval with 7 percent iodine. As it was, the unprotected umbilicus was an open door for the unfriendly bacteria.

A different Dr. Anderson from the laid-back ranchhand he'd been all week long, he began asking her pointed questions and giving us short, clear orders: To one, "Get his vitals." To another, "Prep him for a jugular cath." To still another, "Get the crash cart." And to a fourth, "Get the donor." The donor was one of Dr. Anderson's own llamas, which stood by waiting to give blood. All the while, he nodded to the owner's answers and calmed her with his own quiet, efficient manner. He told her she'd done all she could, and he kindly dismissed her so we could do our work.

The cria seemed already gone, his eyes half open and unseeing.

Dr. Anderson drew a pint of blood from the donor with little apparent effort, but it was not so easy to find a place to put that pint. The blood pressure of the little black cria was so low that we couldn't get a vein to show itself.

"He's going to table top," someone called out, meaning that his temperature was falling, approaching that of the table top. He was cooling out, dying.

"Get some hot water bottles on him," Dr. Anderson said, "and shine that lamp on him." He turned his attention to the cria's abdomen, which he swiftly clipped and scrubbed, then transfused the blood directly into the little guy's belly. Before he was half-done, the cria moved its head, lifting it off the table an inch or so. It was as if he'd been resurrected.

Crias resemble serpents as they are being born, all long snakelike neck, finally followed by small body, to which are attached long, long legs. And this guy hadn't been in this world more than a few hours; there was not much to him except neck and legs.

We finished the transfusion of blood and loaded him up with antibiotics, steroids, and antitoxins. He shut his eyes, lowered his head, and began to shiver a little, which was more life than he'd shown an hour before. Dr. Anderson stood back and looked at him, nodded, then told us he was going to go call the owner and that we should hustle our patient over to ICU and let them look after him for the night.

We got milk and a bottle for him, in case he should improve enough to want to eat, and we left these with the ICU students. We made a plan to meet back there to check on him at 7:00 A.M. before we headed out into the field. It was late by now and we were tired.

At 7:00 A.M., the cria was lying up on his chest, his long legs tucked away just like a great big llama. He blinked his long-lashed eyes as he sat in what appeared to be a very contented daydream. The on-duty student said that he'd just had his breakfast bottle about fifteen minutes before. I was more than a little impressed with Marvin Anderson, the miracle worker. Maybe he could turn me into a miracle worker, too.

"Thanks for your hospitality," Dr. Anderson said. "We're checking him out now. He's going home." It seemed too sudden a change from near-dead to going back to the ranch, but Dr. Anderson said that the cria's mama would give him better care than we could. And animals are remarkable in their ability to heal and bounce back. They don't tend to be invalids. They die or they get well. So we bundled him up in his "crib" blanket and he rode home, his head upright and alert, on Liz Murdoch's lap in the front seat of the truck.

I think I would have called him Lazarus, but his owner named him Lucky.

CHAPTER 22

The Summer of Horses

MY left arm was deep inside the rectum of a horse, a tall, sturdy bay mare. Her anus was tight, like a rubber band around my bicep, and my arm was beginning to ache. I was doing everything very slowly and carefully on this, my first palpation in the Equine Reproduction rotation. Slowly, I opened my fist, my fingers unfolding like the petals of a flower. It was a strange sensation. My arm was beginning to sweat in its latex sleeve within the hot, secret entrails of the horse. I felt a trickle down my ribs, under my cotton T-shirt and lab coat. The heat, the nerves.

"Easy, girl," I said softly, not quite sure whether I was talking to the mare or to myself. *She* was easy, anyway, standing quietly in the palpation chute, as if her two ends were not connected. This was just a routine physical for her. I suspected that she was a pro, though we knew nothing about many of these mystery horses, bought at auction and brought here by the truckload to train us. Of the six mares locked into the chutes this morning, two were visibly upset, trying to kick and twist their heads around to bite. They were teaching us not only about their reproductive systems but also about their body language, how to handle them, and how to protect ourselves.

"That's a good girl," I said, and patted the sturdy rump of the quiet bay mare with my free hand.

I had palpated cows in the Bovine Reproduction lab, but this felt completely different. I was looking for the sleeker uterus of the horse, with its two "horns" and elongated body, and the ovaries. And I wasn't finding them. I was to determine everything I could about this horse's current reproductive state—whether she had just ovulated or whether she was about to; whether there was a developing foal inside her; whether the tone of the uterus was firm or sloppy; whether there were any pathological structures, tumors, cysts, or fluid in the uterus.

I had studied this anatomy, of course. As a freshman, I had dissected a mare and examined closely these organs for which I was now groping. Just the night before, I had reviewed my notes from that Gross Anatomy lab and had looked again at the diagrams of the reproductive systems of the male and female horse. I had palpated a few mares before, too—one long ago when I was Jill Henderson's technician, and then a couple of times during sophomore and junior years. So it was all inside my head. I could even see the diagram with its sharp lines and labels. But the problem was that my head was just not talking to my fingertips and vice versa. The insides of this mare felt like hot mush to me.

"What you need to locate first is the ovary—either one. But which one is more caudal, Loretta?" asked John Parrish, one of the Equine Reproduction professors.

"The left" was my automatic reply.

This was a constant game with our instructors senior year: The questions rolled off their tongues readily and we were like voice-activated answer mills. Usually, the exchanges were relaxed, casual, and nonthreatening, but they could get downright ugly, given the right clinician, the right student, and the wrong answer. It could feel as if you'd been called on the carpet in front of clients, classmates, and God Himself. It could feel as if the clinician had decided that the price of a wrong answer was sweat and humiliation, and once your brain had short-circuited, it rarely re-engaged until it had had time to cool down. The questions would keep coming, sounding like a foreign language, and the synapses kept misfiring. It was as if you went out of body—at least that's the way it felt to me. The body was standing there, but the spirit had bolted and run. I'd seen some of my classmates cry, sputter, and drool a little until finally the clinician had collected enough of their soul to satisfy his appetite. Then he could end the grilling by saying something such as, "Well, it's pretty obvious you have some reviewing to do."

John didn't badger, though. "That's right," he said, "the left. So go for the left initially, mate." He was a handsome reproduction specialist from down under, and a favorite with students. He wasn't opposed to having rounds at Potts, a popular local pub. "It's going to feel like an ovoid structure lying along the body wall. Backhand it, mate. Come on now, move those hands. Get 'em working." He moved along the row of chutes, coaching and encouraging the six of us who were inside the mares.

He stopped and spoke to a student who was just gloving up. "What's the bloody point here?" No response. "Look, mate, you've got to use your head. If someone was going to have his arm up you, you wouldn't be too keen on all the rings and watches and bracelets, now would you?"

The student peeled off his glove and quickly undressed his fingers and arm of their rings and watch. A smile whipped across John's face. "Okay, this is reproduction, so let's get naked."

I took a deep breath. Easygoing and chummy as John was, he was still the clinician in charge, and I was a little in awe of him, too. He was a true leader in the field and had contributed a great deal to ultrasound use in the mare, determining when the fetus first enters the uterus (five to six days), how long it traverses the horns until finally implanting (sixteen to seventeen days), when the fetal heartbeat is first detectable (twenty-two days).

I pushed against the smooth muscular wall of the rectum. Under gentle but steady pressure, I searched that wall, running the back of my hand along its left side, wanting and willing that firm ovoid structure to be in the neighborhood soon.

It was like being blind. I closed my eyes to help my concentration and to block the comic sight of my arm disappearing inside the horse. I didn't want to laugh. In fact, I didn't really feel amused, but my nerves were tight, clamped down like the mare's anus. I heard an occasional burst of laughter from my classmates. I was trying to use my eyes to see where I was inside the horse, but it wasn't working.

Maybe the horse had been spayed—no ovaries left—and John was just having a bit of fun with us. He had been known to do that, to run a gelding in with the mares and see how long it took a student to discover that not only did the horse lack ovaries but a vulva, vagina, and uterus, as well.

Or maybe I just hadn't yet learned to "see" with my hand.

My Uncle Deemer had suffered a stroke but had recovered most of his abilities. His left side dragged a bit when he walked, as though it was moving just a fraction more slowly than the right. The left side of his face looked more fatigued than the right. But he could speak, drive a car, read, and do most anything that anyone else could do—except for two things. He couldn't distinguish gender-linked pronouns, so he would say things like, "My daughter and his kids are coming over." And he couldn't recognize names that were *spoken* to him. His hearing was fine, but there was some neural pathway that just didn't work anymore. You could say to him, "Have you heard from Uncle Clark?" He would puzzle, knit his brow, even repeat, "Clark?" Then he would shake his head, his frustration starting to show, as he realized that his abilities were damaged. "I'm sorry," he'd say. "This damned stroke. I don't know who you mean." But if you took a slip of paper and wrote *Clark* on it, he'd nod, embarrassed to realize that you'd been asking about his older brother. "Ah," he'd say, "Clark! I saw him Monday when I was up in Montrose." The information just didn't pass through the aural pathways.

Information wasn't passing through my fingertips, either. They moved up and down the same few inches of bowel for what seemed a long, long time, feeling the tubular bowel and nothing more. And then suddenly, there, under my hand, was the left ovary, as though it had miraculously emerged, as though a magician had conjured it up. But it wasn't that I'd suddenly felt it. Rather, I had suddenly *recognized* it. I had passed over it just moments before but thought it was a road apple in another fold of the intestine. I had been feeling it all along, like looking at a deer on a hillside among winter-brown foliage. "Right there!" your friend will say, pointing. "Right *there*, by the little piñon." And you'll look and look, right at it, and then, suddenly, you, too, see. And once you do see the shape of that deer, its edges outlined against the vegetation, it is impossible not to see it.

I cupped the ovary in my left palm and ran my thumb over its contours. It had multiple small bumps protruding from its surface. They were small, 5 to 10 mm., and I closed my eyes to visualize them as my thumb described them—their size, their firmness. No one follicle stood out; these would probably regress, reform, until finally one follicle was ready to release its egg. By then, it would be much larger, 30 to 40 mm., and it would be painful to the touch. I followed the left uterine horn down from the ovary to the body of the uterus, turned to the right, and up the right horn to the other ovary. Everything was right where it was supposed to be. All I had had to do was find that first ovary and follow the yellow brick road.

My arm no longer felt numb. It had become a perfect instrument, a good tool.

"Eureka." John Parrish's voice was quiet and near. I opened my eyes, to see him standing at the mare's flank, smiling at me.

"What?"

"I said, 'Eureka.' You should see your face."

"I think she has multiple small follicles."

"How large? Which ovary? How many?"

"Umm . . ." I measured with my fingertip. "Left ovary, five or six of them, about five to ten millimeters."

He nodded. "Close enough for government work. I'd say ten to twelve millimeters, but you're in the ballpark." John had palpated and written down the inside scoop on each mare we would examine that day. "Go on to the next one."

I hesitated for a moment, none too eager to let go of this ovary, these follicles, this small victory.

"You've got it," he said. "The next one will be easy."

He'd turned around now and moved on to the next student. Another test was behind me. I was another step closer.

The experience, which I would have again and again in my senior rotations, was one of exponential gain, as the moment, the technique, the understanding suddenly and miraculously doubled with—or tripled, quadrupled—the charts, diagrams, laws, and principles I had learned in isolation during freshman and sophomore years. A dim memory from Anatomy lab or from a book read in the wee hours of the morning suddenly connected to real life and was back, strong, alive, and kicking, in my mind. Things started to make sense. It was a feeling of competence and power. I was standing in the palpation shed, alone with my work while my classmates worked alongside me, my arm covered with horse shit. It was the beginning of a long day, and I felt, as my cousin Ernie always said, as if I owned the place and had come to collect the rent.

I gave the bay mare another pat. "Thanks, girl," I said aloud. Her ears rotated back to catch my voice. "I'll be the best I can be. That's a promise." Her ears flicked. She would spend her time here teaching vet students how to see in the dark, or maybe she'd spend a day, when she was in heat, being the "tease mare," arousing stallions so that their semen could be collected. Perhaps she would be artificially inseminated by vet students, who were again learning a technique. Maybe the embryo of her foal would be flushed from her and implanted in another mare who would carry it to term, or maybe she would be implanted with another mare's foal through an incision in her flank, a surrogate mother. Her unborn foal might be taken from her and used as a teaching specimen, or perhaps it would be born and then used in some research project or other. Perhaps the mare would be used eventually for teaching surgical techniques—or sacrificed for an "anthill" surgery, in which, for practice, students swarmed over the anesthetized horse like ants, doing whatever procedures they chose. Pieces of her might end up in the gross anatomy lab, teaching another class of freshmen. Then again, she might be resold at auction. "Good luck," I said to her.

"Are you finished here, Retta?" Another student had come up, ready to palpate.

"Yeah, go ahead. I'm done with her."

I moved down the row to the next mare. I watched her head as I lubed up my sleeve. I stroked her hip with my ungloved right hand. She was frightened and fought her cross-tying. "Easy, girl," I said. "I'll be quick." I moved her tail aside and got to work.

The day wore on. Mares were moved in and out of the chutes. I palpated them all, feeling the differences in size and tone of uterus, in size of follicles. My arm began to ache for real now, from the heat and sweat, from the constant position of the arm, held up unnaturally until the shoulder throbbed. Down to the bone, it felt like—a deep, steady pain. Over and over again, I practiced, hand in and out, until that interior landscape made perfect sense, until I could see as well with my fingertips as I could with my eyes. Repetition was the key to understanding and truly knowing. I repeated and repeated and repeated until my hand knew its own way, until my fingers took on their own understanding, until it became second nature and I knew just how hard to prod, how deeply to push, until I no longer consciously and slowly directed every movement, until comprehension resided in the hand as well as in the brain.

Ideally, you palpate with your "off" hand, which would be my left, in order to leave the right free for writing notes. A vet moving through a herd of horses or cattle carries a clipboard and jots down each finding. The right hand is then free for other procedures, as well, particularly artificial insemination.

During artificial insemination, your left hand enters the vagina, carrying in it an infusion pipette. The fingers or thumb cover its tip so you don't jam the hard plastic into, or through, the vaginal wall. When you reach the tip of the cervix, you must dilate it if it is closed. Slowly, a finger presses and the sphincter is opened enough to begin passing the pipette. Slowly, you feed the plastic tubing in through the cervix and into the uterus, thus creating a tunnel for the passage of the semen from a 55 cc. syringe attached to the pipette outside the mare and being stabilized by your right hand, which then pushes the plunger.

Late in the day, a sorrel mare heavy with foal was run into the shed and locked into a chute. John said we should get a feel of her and see whether we could say the baby was viable. I pulled on a fresh sleeve and approached the mare, talking to both of us. My hand went smoothly inside her, a small fist that flowered inside, though the uterus was huge with the foal it carried and pressed solidly against the bowel.

I was probing harder and harder, trying to figure out just what it was I was touching—not feeling for organs now but for discernible parts of the foal, for legs, hooves, spine, or head—when suddenly something grabbed my finger, clamped on it tightly, and wouldn't let go.

I gasped and jerked back a little.

John turned at the sound and then started to laugh. "Did something bite you?"

"Yeah." I was laughing now, too. It was the foal, I realized now, sucking through the uterine wall, through the rectal wall. He'd been feeling me as I'd been feeling him, and he responded the only way he knew how. I pulled my hand free of the little horse's strong, hungry mouth and reported that we had a viable foal.

"You've got that look on your face again, Loretta," said John.

I felt a blush creep up my neck. "I do not!"

"Eureka!" was all he said.

Equine Reproduction was held at the Stallion Lab, a busy facility where various research projects were going on, where clients brought stallions that had reproductive problems of one sort or other. It was about five miles from the VTH, near the rodeo grounds, and was a great collection of pens, pastures, chutes, and barns.

Our week there was long and physically arduous—seven days, from 7:00 A.M. until 5:00 or 6:00 P.M., running horses up from one pasture or other to the palpation shed (either for our own work or for one of the graduate students collecting data for a research project), handling the stallions or tease mares during semen collection, and even scrubbing the walls of the palpation shed.

Horses are predictably unpredictable. They are said to be rather stupid, but, in fact, they are, like most animals, quite intelligent in the ways that they need to be intelligent. Part of their function in the natural world is to be dinner for wolves and big cats, so, like other animals that are preyed upon, they are reactive. Their instinct is to startle and run. They're big, and they can hurt you a lot without intending to. (They also seem to have long memories, and sometimes, if they've been badly treated in the past, they *do* intend to maim or kill.)

The horses at the reproduction center were generally more dangerous than your average ranch pony. Their hormones tended to be raging. The majority of the mares had been bought at auction and thus were unknown quantities. They'd probably all seen a bit or more of misuse in their lives, and many had developed the habit of biting or kicking people and one another. They learned after a time or two through the palpation shed that something unpleasant was going to happen to them there. So rounding them up and driving them through the various gates and chutes that led from the lower pastures to the shed was a lot of work and a little danger besides.

You tried to examine as many mares as possible during that week, for the more you palpated, the more learned your hand became. There was no substitute for experience. So you palpated until your shoulder muscles ached and your arm was sore from the constriction of the mares' rectal muscles. And then you palpated some more.

There was a multitude of other procedures to learn, as well. We did standing castrations of stallions that were not valuable for breeding. We artificially inseminated mares. We did embryo transplants, flushing the uterus of an impregnated mare, examining the filtered flush for a microscopic embryo, and inserting that embryo into the uterus of another mare through an incision in her flank. This procedure allows a particularly valuable mare to produce more offspring, since her reproductive system is not tied up for 340 days carrying each foal to term.

The center does reproduction work for clients, trying to resolve physical and psychological breeding problems in both stallions and mares, but it is primarily a teaching and research facility. So the transplanted embryos might, for instance, be part of an ultrasound project on fetal development. They might be part of a study of the influence of one drug or other on the viability of the embryo. The pregnancies might be terminated or carried to term as part of another study, after which the foals themselves might become subjects in a neonatal project.

It was a busy place, and one of the basic activities that went on was stallion collection—or, more accurately, semen collection—again, for a variety of reasons.

Many of the stallions at the lab had IV catheters in their necks, taped in placed, and small pumps that released lutenizing hormone (LH) into the bloodstream. This hormone is naturally produced in the pituitary gland of both mares and stallions, and in the stallion, it stimulates LH receptors in the testicles and causes the release of testosterone and the production of sperm. The semen of these stallions was collected regularly and examined for sperm count, morphology (form and structure), and motility (spontaneous movement). Did the sperm look normal? Did they have one head or two? Did they have forked tails? How were they behaving?

The semen of some stallions was harvested because it was valuable (a son of Seattle Slew was there at the time). It can then be divided, for it's not good economics to allow a valuable stallion to ejaculate 500,000 sperm into one mare when the same ejaculation could impregnate many. The semen can be frozen and stored indefinitely for later sale and use. The sperm of a valuable animal often appreciates with time. The late, great holstein bull Valiant is still producing offspring, and as the finite supply of his sperm is used, the price goes up accordingly (and it is a carefully guarded secret how much is left for the future).

Stallion collection is a basic skill of the equine practitioner, and we each practiced the four different jobs involved:

1. Handling the "tease" mare (a mare in heat used to arouse the stallion, although he will actually mount a dummy mare).
2. Handling the stallion.
3. Collecting the semen into an artificial vagina (AV).
4. Conducting the laboratory procedures necessary to determine the horse's reproductive soundness.

The object is to control this natural process, but, we were cautioned, too much control can scuttle the mission. Stallions are temperamental creatures, particularly when they are sexually aroused. The first concern of everybody involved is safety, making sure the animal doesn't hurt anyone or himself. Ideally, the stallion handler should be experienced with horses, someone who can read the animal's signs and respond to them, someone who can balance control and license.

Too much discipline can make some stallions lose interest in breeding. Many of the horses at the lab were there specifically because they had behavioral problems in connection with breeding. Some of them "savaged" mares; that is, they bit them so viciously that the resulting injuries were serious. Some were too difficult for the owners to handle safely. And some would become aroused but, for some unknown reason—some past trauma perhaps—were unable to complete the act.

Some horses thus need encouragement; some need sternness. Handling stallions is an art in which experience plays no small role.

There was a wide range of experience among us students at the lab, and on the day that I was to collect, the woman handling the stallion, Mona Vaughn, had very little. The horse, a big chestnut thoroughbred called the Dragon, had quite a bit more. He was a veteran of the stallion lab, well acquainted with Sally, the vinyl padded dummy, or phantom, mare he was to mount.

I had assembled and lubricated the artificial vagina, a rubber-lined cylinder, and filled the outer chamber with warm water. Filled, the AV weighs about fifty pounds, and I held on to it with both hands while I waited for my part in the program. I was nervous.

Dragon came into the shed snorting and prancing, head high, neck arched, ears pitched forward, nostrils distended. The tease mare called to him in her high, squealing whinny, and he answered, his voice deep and guttural. I could see the tension in Mona's arms as she held tightly to the leather end of the stud chain.

Dragon had a reputation for a certain impatience with the process. He was easily frustrated, and if he got upset or angry, there was no calming him down. He would have to be returned to his pen until he had time to forget, and then he could try again.

He had more sexual experience with the pole-mounted phantom mare, Sally, than with the real thing, and the sight of Sally's padded vinyl body seemed to excite him more than the sound and smell of the tease mare. He approached on his hind legs, ready to mount, while he was still several yards away. Mona brought him down, talking to him steadily, and led him closer to Sally. He rose up again, as though oblivious to Mona; he lunged forward, successfully mounting the phantom. He wrapped his forelegs around what would be Sally's shoulders and gathered his power, beginning to thrust, though his penis hung in midair.

As I had watched and studied, I did my job. I crossed quickly to the stallion, my shoulder to his flank, and guided his penis into the artificial vagina, which I braced on my hip against the power of his thrusting. His neck was arched, a humped extension of his back.

Ideally, as the stud finishes and reaches ejaculation, the handler—who is looking for the "flagging" or pumping of his tail—will tell you, and you can be ready to drop the AV down so that it is vertical, then with your free hand you can drain all of the semen from the penis, squeezing gently and pumping him out. And then you have seconds, or less, to get out from under the animal before he comes down.

This day was not ideal. For some reason known only to Dragon, he changed his mind and came down off the phantom without warning, apparently angry, frustrated, or somehow disappointed with the whole experience. His hoof grazed my bare head and I went to ground.

Dragon was in one place but in full motion, all the tension in his body now in his four dancing legs. They blurred in my sight like a stampede of horses and I rolled away from under him.

My heart rattled in my chest and I said over and over again that I was all right, as much to reassure myself as the clinician and my classmates, who hovered around me. I stood up and laughed, clearing the tension from my body. I brushed the sawdust from my butt and legs.

The code of the West meant that you couldn't cry, couldn't whine, admit to a headache, or do any sissy thing that a cowboy wouldn't do. The code of the West was why I hadn't been wearing the football helmet that the official rules require the collector to wear. The code of the West was why the rule was often not enforced.

When Dalton rotated through Equine Reproduction, she would get her nose broken by a little bay Arabian stallion, not because the animal was vicious but because he was oblivious to her and highly agitated by everything else in the vicinity. As she was leading him up the aisle between two rows of mares, the horse whipped around and popped her head with his much larger one. I doubt that he even noticed.

It was a good rotation, in spite of the wall scrubbing, the danger, and the physical exhaustion. I lived through it; that counted for a lot.

While the reproduction unit was constructed to teach us specific skills, the content of the remainder of my horse courses—Equine Medicine, Large Animal Surgery, and Equine Ambulatory—depended in large part on what came through the swinging doors and what cases we were assigned to care for.

My medical case was also a surgery one, for animals in the VTH often have multiple problems, or at least problems that require the services of more than one department. This particular horse, a two-year-old thoroughbred called Steeler, had fractured a cannon bone while racing in California and on the trip to Colorado had developed pleural pneumonia. So after the orthopedic surgery, he was mine to care for. He was sick and gaunt, and we were treating his pneumonia with twice-daily doses of penicillin, injected intramuscularly. Horses require high doses of penicillin, too much to inject into any one site. The gluteal muscles on the top side of a horse's rump are considered unsuitable (by the VTH) for these injections, for, should an abscess result, it is difficult to get the proper drainage needed to manage the wound. Large quantities also cannot be given in the neck muscles, so I was left basically with the two sides of his buttocks. It was a challenge to keep finding sites that were not sore or bruised from earlier shots.

Poor Steeler had been working for almost his entire short life, most of which had been spent in a stall or on the track. His diet had consisted of rationed grain, hay, or alfalfa pellets. One day, I took him outside for some sunshine and air therapy. I wondered whether he knew what green grass was and what it was for, for some of the racehorses that came to the VTH led such artificial lives that they didn't know enough to eat it. Steeler stepped out into the world, alert and interested, head high, ears pricked forward, nostrils distended as he read the scents in the air. After a moment, satisfied that he was safe, he dropped his head and began to graze with a vigor that made me think this one was going to be okay.

Equine Surgery was a two-week unit. It was busy, and we students were charged primarily with day-to-day care of patients (bandaging, grooming, administering medication) and assisting in surgery (passing instruments and observing). A lot of our time was spent conducting lameness exams and radiographing horses, and many of these cases did not end up under the knife.

The rotation was not particularly pleasant, partly because equine surgeons are often arrogant and self-important. An exception was Paul Warner, another Australian, who seemed to relish teaching as much as performing surgery. He'd rotated through our freshman Perspectives in Veterinary Medicine course, showing films of lame horses, which he would stop in the middle to fire questions at us eager freshmen, asking us to characterize the lameness, identify which leg was affected, and tell what we knew about the condition and the prognosis. I'd liked him then and I liked him now. When our work was caught up, he would review with us slides of musculoskeletal injuries in the horse. He seemed committed to our taking something useful with us from these two weeks with him.

We students wielded scapels only once during the rotation, in an "anthill" surgery. There were four students and the surgical resident. Someone opened the mare's abdomen and did a colic surgery, "running" the bowel for torsions or foreign bodies. Someone else opened the throat. Yet another "nerved" the hind legs, cutting the nerves to the hoof, a last-resort procedure to reduce pain and restore a lame horse to some degree of usefulness.

I had hoped to do surgery on the check ligaments. These ligaments are part of the stay apparatus of the horse, which allows it to sleep standing up. The superior and inferior check ligaments are located above and below the knees; the horse can "lock" these ligaments, which keep the legs extended. Occasionally, horses are too upright in the fetlock (the joint just above the hoof), and some horses become broken down in the fetlock, from a combination of poor conformation and hard use. Cutting the ligaments can help correct both the hyperextended and hypoextended fetlocks, and I wanted to try my hand.

The resident, Cory Smith, staked out both forelegs for himself, however, and he had seniority and priority over us. So I observed his surgery in lieu of practicing my own. I was angry. This was my last opportunity before I was out in practice, and although I would learn much of what I needed from the veterinarians whose practice I joined, I still felt somehow cheated.

That bad feeling had something to do with the horse on the table, never to wake up. She (for it was a bay quarterhorse mare) was being sacrificed, and I was getting very little good from her death. I knew my anger was not quite rational (there was, after all, a lot of learning and practicing happening on her inert body, even if little of it was mine). And I knew, too, that my feelings had to do with my being the technician who had prepped her for the surgery/sacrifice. It is not so bad when you come into the operating room to find the anesthetized horse on the table, for the animal is almost a cadaver, is certainly devoid of personality. And it's a little easier emotionally to prep an animal that tries to bite or kick. But I had had the luck of the draw; I was the one who the night before had clipped and washed this mare's belly, legs, neck—all the likely surgical sites. It had taken quite a while, and she had stood gentle and still, kind-eyed and trusting for me, her grim reaper.

I wanted something from it, some particular, identifiable bit of skill that I could use to justify the taking of her one and only life, as I had justified now for more than three years the taking of this life and that one. Always with a promise, unspoken but to myself and to the spirit of whatever cat or dog or horse lay before me, that for this life, I would save many. It was an ideal devoutly to be wished.

Life was not always ideal, of course, and promises not always kept. I was old enough, I thought, that I shouldn't have to learn that lesson again and again. But again and again, I would learn it and hope that it was for the last time.

CHAPTER 23

Internship

THE summer of horses was followed in the fall by still more horses.

My old friend and boss, Jill Henderson, had her own mobile equine practice now in New York, and the bulk of her work was at Belmont and Aqueduct racetracks. She had called at the end of junior year to ask whether I would like to do an internship with her during my senior break, from late August through September.

While veterinary medicine has not yet instituted a required internship, as human medicine has, veterinary colleges encourage their students to serve some kind of apprenticeship before they launch into practice. In reality, the first job as a new D.V.M. is often a de facto internship—low pay (usually less than twenty thousand dollars), long hours, and close work with a practitioner who ideally provides supervision, instruction, and wisdom to the recent grad. There are also more formal practica, however, and I had applied to the famous and prestigious Animal Medical Center in New York City that spring and been denied. I was still resisting making the choice between large and small animals. Jimmy Fulmer had said at one time that he welcomed the large number of women in vet medicine because, his logic went, fewer men in the profession meant fewer large-animal practitioners, or potential large-animal practitioners, and thus, less competition for him. I resented the assumption; it didn't seem accurate to me, anyway. Jill wasn't the only woman I knew who was an equine vet—not by a long shot. It wasn't at all a ridiculous ambition, but was it what I wanted? It was time to find out.

Jill lived in South Huntington, in Long Island's Suffolk County, and my plane landed at Islip, a small, downright homey little airport. I had kept my face to the window, searching for the famous skyline, the Statue of Liberty, the Empire State Building—but there was none of that, just highways and cars and nondescript urban sprawl. Jill was waiting at the gate. We climbed into her station wagon and pulled onto the parkway, though I could see no logic in the name. The air was brown, the traffic thick, though no worse than I'd seen in Denver. Along the highway were abandoned and stripped cars. I was in New York at last.

At first light, we headed to Belmont. I sprinted along behind Jill, trying to keep up as she made her rounds and trying to pick up racetrack etiquette as I went—the unwritten rules of right-of-way, the hierarchy that was as rigid as that of a medieval fiefdom.

The horses had worn a trench, or moat, around every barn, where they were led counterclockwise to cool them out after they'd worked. Most of them were youngsters, full of adolescent energy and the spirit of their breed. They pranced, sidestepped, kicked, snorted, and bucked as they were led around. From the stall doors darted the heads of stabled horses, ears pinned, teeth flashing as they reached for a piece of flesh. Pedestrian traffic moved against the stream of horses and their "hotwalkers," clockwise between the row of stalls and the parade of horses.

The air was filled with the squealing and neighing of horses and the constant stream of human voices. It felt like a carnival, people yelling at each other, every fifth word a *fuck* or *fuckin'*.

Jill moved fast, slipping in and out of conversation with this groom or that walker, darting under the webbed nylon stall gate to check on a bowed tendon or hot knee and then out again.

I seemed to duck under that stall door just as she had finished her business. I was going to have to move a little faster if I wanted to learn anything at all.

In each stall grouping, there was a trainer's office. I followed Jill into the small, crowded, and cluttered office of Paul Brousseau, one of the top trainers in New York. "Hey, Doc," he called as we came through the door. Then he picked up the ringing phone, slid into his high-backed imitation-leather office chair and barked staccato orders to someone on the other end.

His desk was fair-sized and filled most of the room. It was cluttered with dirty foam coffee cups, ashtrays, racing forms, a pile of rubber snaffle training bits, *Playboy* magazines, and a sleeping cat. The rest of the room was filled with a small refrigerator, a coffeepot, and two straight-backed kitchen chairs. Sitting in one of them was a fat Italian guy. The sleeves of his white shirt were rolled up to the elbow, his bifocals rode low on his nose, a cigar hung from his lip, and papers and ashes littered his lap. He didn't look up from the paper he was reading, just chewed his cigar and ignored the activity in the room.

Brousseau hung up the phone and shoved the cat from the desk. "Go kill a rat, you fuckin' cat!" he said. The cat hit the floor and slunk to the door, waited a moment, then darted out between horses. Brousseau plucked a manila radiograph envelope from his desk and tossed it to Jill. "Look at these. It's the chestnut colt I just got in from Florida." As if rocket-launched, he sprang from the chair and out the door. "Get your ass on the end of a lead rope!" he yelled at somebody I couldn't see.

"I just got back from the doctor . . ." a voice answered.

"Shut the fuck up! You don't know a goddamned thing about a horse. You're a fuckin' idiot, and all you wanna do is lay around your mama's house, suckin' her tit."

"Ah, shit, I got the flu!"

"Get the fuck outta here. You got the fuckin' flu? Get the fuck outta my face. Come back in two weeks if you figure out you wanna work." Brousseau came back into the office. "Fuckin' little bastard," he muttered as he crossed to his chair. "That's Tony Franchini's boy. What a prick. You can't get fuckin' nothin' outta these bastards, not one lick of honest work. So whatta ya do, Pete?" he asked the fat man. Apparently the question was rhetorical. Pete didn't answer.

A skinny young man popped his head in the door. "You want him galloped hard this morning?"

"Oh, yeah, yeah, let him out a little bit. He went okay yesterday?"

"Yeah, he fuckin' sails," the exercise rider answered.

"Once around hard, then lighten up. Keep him out there awhile. I want to watch him go."

The boy nodded and disappeared.

"And get a clean shirt by tomorrow," Brousseau yelled after him. The phone rang again, and Brousseau reamed somebody else a new asshole. A young rider came in and got twenty dollars from him. And then Jill gave him a ten-second assessment of the new colt's X rays. Then, business apparently over, Brousseau was out the door to watch his horse work, and we were out the door and on to our next trainer.

"Don't pay any attention to him," Jill said. "It's just the way he is. He doesn't mean anything by it. He's okay." But Brousseau hadn't offended me. I thought he was a pretty colorful guy. He sure wasn't boring.

The veterinary vans and station wagons cruised the barns like hungry cats. Vets paused here and there to walk through a barn, take an X ray, draw blood, assess some damage, drum up business. Being Johnny-on-the-spot is the name of the game, because there doesn't seem to be much loyalty to veterinarians. The vet who's standing there is the vet who gets the job. In this fast-moving world, there's rapid turnover in almost all the jobs. Even—or especially—the horses changed hands quickly and often.

The hotwalkers were the lowest rung on the social ladder. They worked long enough to get whatever money it was they needed, then they'd be gone for a day or two, but there was always another waiting to make the meager wage for walking the horses around and around the barns until they cooled out from their workouts. They spoke a dozen different languages, it seemed, and none of them English.

Trainers were on top in this ecosystem, since the owners

weren't often around, but there was a great range of status within that group, as well. Brousseau was at the top, but there were many who had to hustle to get a horse—any horse—to train, who hadn't won many races, who drank too much or had a drug problem. And the physical layout of the track reflected rank. The more marginal trainers had stalls on the backside, the farthest from the track itself. There were no flashy stable-color banners flying in front of their stalls, no carpet runners in front of the barn, no stable-color uniforms for the workers. These lower-echelon trainers were the dreamers, waiting for the unknown filly from Buttfuck, Florida, to cross the line ahead of the big boys and make them rich and sought-after.

Mad Dog Monty was somewhere in the middle. He had eight to ten horses. He always had a pot of coffee on in his office and a sack of doughnuts. I liked him. He moved more slowly than most of the folks I'd met at the track, maybe because he weighed three hundred pounds or more. He called me Doc. Maybe that was why I liked him. "Come on, Doc," he'd say, "let me make you deliriously happy." He liked to grab his horses' faces and give them a good shake, so that their lips flapped loosely. "You're a dog," he'd say, shaking some horse's head. "You're a no-good dawg."

Most of Jill's work was treating leg problems, muscle soreness, or the running of "jugs" to the horses. A jug is a 500 cc. bottle of saline or lactated ringers or another benign fluid vehicle used to get large doses of vitamins into a horse's vein. Each vet has a private recipe for his own jug, a more carefully guarded secret than Colonel Sanders' eleven herbs and spices. And when a vet consistently has horses in the winner's circle, people—from other trainers to the New York Racing Association (NYRA) officials—will start paying attention to find out what his concoction is. There's always an assortment of vitamins in some secret ratio, but there was also sometimes something more. Racehorses are given drugs, make no mistake. The trick is in the timing, in knowing the half-life of each drug for varying doses, the route of administration, the combinations, and how to factor in an individual animal's metabolic rate so that you can gauge almost to the minute when any given substance will be out of the animal's system.

It's a harsh life for a thoroughbred racehorse—no room for sentiment. A horse finishes out of the money enough times and he's sold down, smaller races, smaller tracks, smaller owners, until there's no place down to go. It's a short career at best, and one misstep and the game's over.

We saw them in the predawn hours, at post time, and after the race, to assess the damage. They're all young animals and are taken out of their small box stalls twice a day—for early morning workout and for the race. Like Blacknose, the greyhound, they are bred to run, and they have far more energy than they can use. They tend to be fractious and unruly, looking to bite or kick their keepers. They aren't lovable, but they are beautiful. And you worry.

They break from the gate, a crowd of 1,200-pound animals at a peak of excitement and agitation. They launch into a stride that puts the weight of the animal on the diagonally opposed hind and forelegs, most particularly upon the leading foreleg, and this is at a time when the ligaments, bones, and tendons are still immature and growing, not yet at their peak of strength. On their back is a man they may never have seen before, and he whips the animal's neck and butt from start to finish. The industry is stacked incredibly in favor of misfortune, as these horses are pushed to—and past—the breaking point. I was glad that our work kept us in the barns and away from the track itself.

That afternoon, Jill and I took a break to go up into the grandstands so I could buy a souvenir T-shirt. Paul Brousseau was standing under a TV monitor with a small group of people and he hailed us down. "Willie's getting ready to go off," he said, and motioned us to stop and watch. We'd seen Willie Rock It that morning, the new chestnut colt from Florida that Brousseau had high hopes for. I looked at the monitor; the horses were still in the paddock area. Willie was getting tacked up and was giving his groom a hard time, prancing sideways. He was a shiny red thing, bright as a penny, with a big white face, full of himself and showing it. Brousseau never took his eyes from his colt, watching the monitor, absently tapping himself with his rolled-up program, like a jockey encouraging his mount. He was into the race already.

Willie went off well. Brousseau urged the colt on with the movement of his own body, building in intensity as his horse gained ground. But just as the red colt edged up on the leader of the herd of thundering horses, he faltered. A low moan issued from the group at the monitor as if from a single body. Willie didn't go down, didn't cause a pileup of bodies, but he faded quickly to the back of the pack and then straggled to the finish line at about half speed.

"Let's go," Jill said. Brousseau was nowhere in sight. By the time we got down to the track, it was all over. One of Brousseau's assistants was standing there, shaking his head.

"He's in the pit already," he said to Jill. "It's all over."

The pit was on the far back side of the racetrack where they stacked the fatalities for the rendering truck to cart away. We drove over to have a last look at Willie Rock It.

He lay in a tangled heap, his right foreleg bent at an unnatural angle, white glistening bone sticking out the back. The cannon bone was dislocated from its articulation with the phalanges, the seasamoid bones, paired on each side of this joint—the fetlock, which had been shattered, the ligaments torn, the skin given way to the force of the bone's splintering under the weight of the big red colt. That he didn't go down, taking his jockey and several of the field with him, attested to his heart, which was stronger than his fine, white bones.

There was another horse in the pit, a gray filly. Her body wasn't misaligned; its angles were still natural and lovely. But her side was flecked with dark red blotches, a spray of blood that had blown from her nostrils as she ran. Her nose rested in a pool of foam and blood that continued to ooze from her mouth and nostrils. She was still wet with sweat and blood, which flecked her entire body, except where the saddle had been. She must have ruptured some pretty big vessels to have blown this much blood. She was what is known on the track as a "bleeder," a victim of exercise-induced pulmonary hemorrhage. It's not uncommon.

Jill and I didn't say anything as we drove away from the pit. It was a gruesome place. I glanced over at her; her face was a mask, expressionless. Her emotions showed only in her uncharacteristic silence.

The track was there seven days a week, and Jill was there, too, hustling business in the early, early dawn and taking care of business with those trainers for whom she usually worked. Every day, she dropped in on her trainers, keeping herself available and fresh in their minds.

There was another trainer on her daily route, as well. If Paul Brousseau was diamonds, Merle Rozzell was rust. He was tall and skinny with dirty, thinning hair that fell across his forehead in greasy ropes. When it fell below his eyebrows, he'd toss his head like a horse. A cigarette dangled constantly from his lip. Merle had two horses in training, to Paul's fifteen to twenty, and he didn't have a hotwalker or a groom. Except for the riding, he did everything himself—hotwalking, feeding, mucking stalls, and wrapping legs with any one of an assortment of magic leg paints, muds, or poultices made of ashes, duck bills, mustard, cat fur, and other mystery ingredients to strengthen, tighten, relieve inflammation, draw off fluid—to cure, mend, and salvage. Merle's two horses were "cheap claimers"; that is, their owners had bought them relatively cheaply when they'd run in a claiming race.

Merle—and the owners of his horses—reminded me of the uranium miners back in Grants, New Mexico, of the poor blue-collar dreamer, waiting for the gold mine to come in, waiting to get lucky on a broken-down racehorse, to get that kazillion-dollar lottery ticket; of the gamblers in Las Vegas, the ones with nothing extra to lose, looking to parlay a few hundred dollars into a stake on better days; of my dad.

Merle's luck was none too steady, but he had a chestnut colt that was coming along nicely, his times improving with every trip around the track. The colt's owner, a Chinese-American, was happy, coming around more often, smiling and joking with us when we stopped in. Jill needed to talk to Merle about the colt's pre-race jug and whether he needed his "points" done; that is, the injection of a benign solution into the acupressure points to decrease musculoskeletal pain. The race was to be on Friday, and we stopped in on Monday to find the horse three-legged lame, cross-tied in the stall door, one leg in a white plastic bucket full of ice water. Merle squatted beside the horse, heaping more ice into the bucket.

"Fix this one, Doc," he said without getting up. His voice was flat, without much hope. Jill questioned him about tendons, swelling, heat, medications, and Merle answered dully. She said she needed to X-ray the leg, but Merle said neither he nor the owner could afford it. There was nothing to be done, and we left, cursing Merle's black luck.

The next day, the colt was the same, no improvement. He stood hangdog in his stall, that leg cocked and supporting no weight. "Get the X-ray machine, Retta," Jill said with a sigh. She couldn't stand seeing Merle this way, not knowing what was going on with the colt, so she'd give him this one. We took the film over to the vet clinic on the grounds, and Jill sprang for the use of their radiograph developer. The colt had a slab fracture, and it was a long drive back to Merle's barn.

It was a repairable break—just two pieces that would probably go back together nicely with a screw or two—if the colt was worth the cost of the surgery. Merle shook his head. If the horse had been worth even that much, he probably would have been in Paul Brousseau's barn and not Merle's. Jill tried to offer some cheaper alternatives—maybe he'd mend with simple casting and strict stall rest for nine months to a year. Merle shook his head again. He knew bad luck close up and personal, and this colt had luck just as bad as Merle's own.

The track was a sad place. An ambulance hauled off a dead hotwalker one afternoon, and Jill said it was a crack overdose. Nobody paid too much mind. Death was a commonplace, no great novelty.

This was a hard world—and a man's world, too, mostly, from what I could see. There were a couple of other women vets working the tracks, and a trainer or two, a few jockeys, but

258

most of the women I saw were really just girls, young but aging quickly, hangers-on who did some hotwalking and stall mucking. A woman could make a life at the track if she wanted to; I just couldn't see why she would want to.

I hadn't ruled out equine medicine altogether, but I knew by the end of my stay that I wouldn't be joining Jill in her practice. I had learned some things about equine medicine. I had practiced some skills. But mostly, I had learned what a racetrack practice was like and that it wasn't for me.

CHAPTER 24

Critical Care

THE year marched on and we solidified our knowledge through repetition and new examples of disease and injury. I constantly referred back to my bookcaseful of textbooks and black binders filled with notes of each course I'd taken in the last three and a half years. This took no small skill, and it was important—finding my way quickly and efficiently to the information I needed. I learned the layout of the bookcase and structure of each notebook and text just as I had learned anatomy and physiology.

The end of school was bearing down upon us, both longed for and dreaded. We checked off each rotation from our individual schedules, which meant the last time in school that we would do a particular procedure or see a particular disease or syndrome. The repetition that Lloyd had assured me would be my salvation was coming to an end. As he had promised, it had worked, had served me well, and I now knew quite literally volumes more than I had a scant four years before, and some of it I knew as well as I knew my multiplication tables and quite a bit better than I knew my state capitals.

I knew I could do this. I'd come far enough, anyway, to know for sure—or almost sure—that I could finish vet school and pass all my courses. My rational mind even knew that I was going to pass my national and state boards. Still, I worried and feared, at least in my weaker moments, that I would be unsure in practice, occasionally incompetent, bumbling, just plain *wrong* when I got on the other side of the doors of the VTH, when there was no experienced and able clinician free and ready to redress that wrong and save whatever poor animal I might be killing.

How I would miss that clinician—whoever he or she happened to be on any particular day or rotation—the clinician who was always there to put things to rights if we got in past our skill and knowledge, if we just plain made a mistake.

They didn't let us do permanent damage. If we should nick an artery during surgery, the clinician on duty let us feel the fear, the sheer terror of being inside a creature while its heart was pumping out its lifeblood in a chaos of destruction. He let us grope through the slick, hot, and terrifyingly abundant blood for the break and try to patch it back together with a few sutures from our baby-surgeon hands.

Usually, we did just that. We managed to come through. When it seemed that we would not, however, the clinician did not let the animal die, though he let us think he might, and he let us feel the frustration and embarrassment of our slow, panicked, and graceless fingers, so that we could learn to conquer that panic and find the speed and dexterity we needed. And when we didn't find it soon enough, he was there, finally, with his own experience and skill to save the patient.

Yes, I would miss that clinician, although in practice, of course, most of us would work for and with practitioners who had some years and experience beyond ours. We would often be alone, though, and the thought of that sometimes unnerved me.

I knew a lot, of course. They wouldn't set us free in the world if they hadn't given us what we needed to do the work. But like all good educations, this one had taught me most of all how much there still was to know.

Our instructors were bucking us up now, giving us their calm assurance that we were almost ready and would do fine. Over and over again, I heard it said that, anyway, 80 percent of our patients would get better no matter what we did or did not do for them.

So much for our godlike power. I supposed we had gone through all of this for the 20 percent that really would need us. I didn't believe it about the 80 percent, anyway. Of course, it would make a difference what procedures we practiced, what drugs we administered, what treatments we prescribed.

The fear that had driven me so hard the first two years had abated a bit when we got to the hospital as juniors, but now, as the real world knocked on the doors of our safe haven, our ivory tower of medicine, the fear came back. It had been only dormant. There was so much to learn, and so much of it seemed miscellaneous.

Necropsy was a required rotation and a busy one. Every animal that died in the VTH was given a postmortem exam unless the owner objected. A plaque hung on the wall—THE HALLS OF TRUTH—for here, dead bodies yielded the last of their secrets.

The external surfaces of each body were examined for signs of trauma and dermatologic disease. The skin was split from jaw to anus. The tongue, esophagus, and trachea were pulled free. The ribs were cracked and the lungs and heart lifted out. The abdomen was systematically examined, each organ and gland. Fluids and tissue samples were collected for microscopic study. For each necropsy conducted, a student filed a written report, which included a presumptive cause of death and a listing and analysis of every lesion in the animal. At the end of each day, the Necropsy crew rounded on that day's cases; interesting cases were saved and presented in the weekly rounds to which the entire hospital was invited.

It was a fascinating rotation, for there was a lot to learn from almost every case. The room stank, yes, and it was hard, messy physical work. The floors were kept rinsed by constantly running hoses to keep the very slippery blood from collecting. From time to time, a stray piece of tissue clogged the floor drain, and the bloody water could fill the room to a depth of several inches as the crew worked on in tall rubber boots, oblivious to the flood.

The Intensive Care Unit was another high-learning rotation, also required. There was more life-and-death drama per square inch in ICU than anywhere else in the hospital, and each rotation included a week-long daytime assignment, a week of night duty, and several 4:30 to 11:00 P.M. shifts after those two weeks were up and you'd moved along to the next block, from which you often had to take an early out in order to get back to the ICU in time to go on duty at 4:30.

ICU was one of the best rotations, filled with intensive learning cases and a good chance to hone skill. However, the day shift was where most of the real learning took place. Nights were disagreeable, of course, simply because they were nights and your whole routine was turned upside down. Nobody quite made the transition to daytime sleeping in time for it to do much good. But beyond that, the night shift was generally maintenance—high-level maintenance, to be sure—but generally doing the technician-type duties of carrying out somebody else's treatment plan. There was little diagnostic work, except for emergencies. In fact, there wasn't even a clinician working the night shift, although there was always one—or more, actually—on call.

It was rather like the work I had done as a technician at the Emergency Animal Clinic in Albuquerque back before I got through the guarded gates of CSU. After the evening hospital staff went off duty at 11:30, the work included answering the phone and fielding emergency-type questions, questions that I'd found tended to increase in number and incoherence about 2:30 or 3:00 A.M., right after the bars closed and people got home without all of their critical faculties fully operative.

I remembered—in fact, would probably never forget—a woman who had called in the dead of night all those years ago to say how worried she was because her dog's penis was swollen and erect, extruding from its sheath and just *would not go down*. Even then, I thought I knew the answer, but I truly *knew* nothing, and I knew I knew nothing, so to be safe, I'd awakened the veterinarian on duty to ask his opinion. He had looked at me from the thicket of sleep as if he thought he must be dreaming, as if he could not believe he was hearing me correctly. I had grown increasingly embarrassed. Finally, sure he knew what I was asking, he'd growled, "What in the hell is she doing up at three in the morning examining her dog's dick? Tell her to leave it alone and it'll go down." Which it must have, for she didn't call back.

Then there was the woman who'd called to say she'd just gotten home and noticed that her dog was "lethargic." Devoutly to be wished of a dog at 2:30 A.M., I thought.

Occasionally, though, an emergency was truly an emergency. Duke was such a one, a sable sheltie that interrupted the tedium of one of my nights in ICU.

The receiving student for surgery walked through the open ICU doors with the limp, unconscious dog in his arms. He set him on the treatment table and said, "Big dog, little dog," by way of explaining what had happened to this guy—a dogfight.

Like a several-armed machine, we swung into action. We clamped an oxygen mask over the dog's nose, took his temperature, got an electric water blanket for him, set up for catheterizing his cephalic vein—ripping pieces of tape, getting the scrub, clipping his hair—then readied the bag of IV fluids.

The on-duty resident bustled in to tell us that the on-duty small-animal surgeon, Gordon Powell, was on his way.

Duke reminded me of the see-through plastic anatomy model, the Visible Man, that had been a popular toy when I was a kid, for there was a five-by-eight-inch flap of skin stripped from the dog's belly, and we could look inside this window and see Duke's inner workings.

With every breath Duke took, the peritoneum, the serous membrane that lines the abdomen, caught the reflection of the overhead lamps; it shone like Saran wrap. The fat-streaked and lacy greater omentum was visible; it was turned back half through its typical traverse from stomach to urinary bladder, revealing the loops of small intestine. There was bruising. The peritoneum was torn, the belly entered. If a loop of bowel had been punctured, the threat of peritonitis was severe.

The fluids we pumped into him revived him somewhat, and when Dr. Powell showed up, the little dog greeted him with a feeble two-beat wag of his tail. Powell conducted a quick examination, nodded, and said that we were right to have called him in; the dog definitely needed surgery. Then he said, "Wake me when he's ready for the OR," and he pulled a fleece cage liner from a clean cage, rolled it up into a pillow, hopped up onto the study island at the far end of the room, and curled up for a nap.

The anesthesia technician went to work, and in about fifteen minutes she roused Dr. Powell to the OR. He woke as quickly as he'd gone to sleep, as if a hypnotist had snapped his fingers and brought him out of a trance. His hands fairly flew as he put Duke back together again, important because anesthesia is particularly dangerous to an animal that has had a trauma and is in shock. He stretched and slid the pieces of Duke's chewed-up hide, tacking here and then there, never wasting a motion, basting the little guy back into one continuous piece of dog with more than sixty sutures. The little sheltie had been lucky—his intestines were intact, no tears. He'd been lucky, too, to fall into these particular hands.

I was impressed. Maybe I was beginning to get a definition that would fit the laws of surgery we had studied the year before, the laws that were so confounding in their philosophical bent. But Gordon Powell *did* seem to represent that ideal—integration as doctor, surgeon, veterinarian in the true sense of the word.

And then he was out the door and Duke was left to our care.

The little dog was restless as he surfaced from the anesthetic, but his respiratory function and heart rate and rhythm were normal, so he was cleared for pain medication. I drew up 1 cc. of oxymorphone, rechecked his temperature, which was climbing toward 100, nearing normal—he was finally warming up—wiped the injection port of his IV with alcohol, and slipped the needle through the rubber. I crimped the IV line upstream to stop the flow and allow me to deliver slowly just the painkiller. He quieted, and I adjusted the flow of the drip line and left him to sleep away the trauma of the night.

By very early morning, Duke was standing in his cage, full of the 1,000 ml. of fluids we had run into him throughout the night. I capped off his IV, flushed it with heparinized saline, and wrapped his leg in a bright blue Vetrap bandage while he waited uncomfortably to go outside. He walked gamely to the concrete slab just outside the hospital door—step, gimp, hesitate, step, gimp, hesitate—the pain of his wounds competing with the urgency of his full bladder.

It was still dark and very cold, only a light grayness beginning on the eastern horizon. Duke managed to lift his leg against the chain-link fence. He sniffed around a bit, registering the scents of the dogs who had been there before him, interested in the world and forgetting the hurts of his body. He wagged his tail when I spoke to him, a good little trooper, somehow knowing to trust, or trusting to trust. He was doing so well, I doubted he would need our services past the 11:00 A.M. checkout time.

It was cold out there on the concrete pad. There were patches of old snow scattered across the field beyond. To the south, a car approached on Drake, signaling the turn into the VTH gate. Some student was arriving, getting started on his day. It was too slow for an emergency, too early for regular clients. The headlights shone across the snow as the car pulled around the side of the hospital, making its way to the student/faculty parking lot in the rear. In a moment or two, it would pass by me and Duke, and suddenly I felt a wave of fear at the unknown, the irrational, crazy, silly kind of fear that can come over you like a shadow when it's dark and you're all alone. I could almost laugh at myself, so ridiculous to be afraid of nothing but a car bringing one of my classmates to work.

The ICU could do that to you, though. My partner and I were the only ones in the hospital the whole night long, after the emergency-surgery personnel had decamped—the only humans, anyway, alone in the bright ICU filled with equipment and monitors beeping and blinking like the controls of a spaceship. The hospital was full of animals, of course, the "others" that were not sick enough for the ICU, or those whose owners couldn't afford intensive care, or those in research wards and the wards beyond those, at the very rear of the hospital, that housed the animals slated for junior surgery. From the center of the ICU, we could see almost every critter under our care, except for those that had come from Oncology. These animals were housed in a special wing where a water spray constantly cleansed the floor and where we had to wear special gloves because the animals had been treated with chemotherapeutic drugs that could be toxic to other cells and not just to the cancer cells that were their target.

At 11:30 P.M. and again at 4:30 A.M., one of the two students on duty had to take a turn through the building, doing treatments when they were ordered and merely checking the status of the rest of the occupants. It was a scary walk, or it could be, if you let your imagination run away. It was scary, too, to stay behind in ICU, though we could page one another via the intercom or our beepers. The night before, I had been surprised on my rounds by a campus cop strolling through the building on a routine check. My heart had pounded, it seemed, for the rest of my shift. This place just seemed a perfect setting for a horror movie, and I could almost write the script.

So I was happy to be back inside, away from whoever was driving up before daylight, and Duke was happy, too, for the warmth, I imagine. I took him back to his cage and settled him down for another curative nap, then turned to the rest of the critically ill charges of the ICU. It was time to get them "up and dressed," their treatments done, their medications administered, and their cages cleaned before the change of shift. At shift change, this place would come back to life, beginning with morning rounds, when we would be responsible for passing the torch and bringing the day team up-to-date on the various patients.

I stole a few minutes to prepare my notes on Duke, for no doubt I'd be grilled by the clinician. Every choice of therapy would be challenged, for even if everything you'd done was textbook perfect, you still had to defend it.

I was beat and ready to go home and cross one more night off the calendar, one more shift down, one less to go on this scary and sleepless service. Even when it was good, it wasn't any fun.

Winston was a German shepherd, and he had been hospitalized in the Small Animal Medicine Service a couple of weeks before I rotated through. The woman who had had his charge the week before told me to make myself as inconspicuous as possible when Dr. Glaser was handing out cases and came to poor old Winston. This dog was a lot of work and wasn't particularly interesting. I made up my mind to avoid him if I could.

I couldn't. Dr. Glaser came to my name and, with a little smile, gave me Winston, almost as if he knew I was in the corner of the room trying to be invisible.

The poor dog was old and chronically ill, which made him seem that much older. He was fat, mostly due to the redistribution of tissue caused by his Cushing's disease (a.k.a. hyperadrenocorticism, or cortisol excess), an endocrine disorder. This endocrinopathy wreaked havoc with more systems than seemed possible. The syndrome, or group of symptoms, is insidious in onset and slowly progresses to include a spectrum of dramatic clinical signs and lesions on many organ systems. Winston seemed to have them all.

These included a wasting of skeletal muscle due to the catabolic effect on protein metabolism; a pendulous abdomen; long, clicking toenails, simply because he didn't move around enough to wear them down naturally and nobody had gotten around to clipping them for him. Centripetal redistribution of fat left him with prominent fat pads on his neck, and the abdominal fat gave him a potbellied appearance. His hair coat was thin, rough, and dry; he was balding down each side of his trunk. He had bedsores on points of pressure, since he just lay like a lump in his cage. He had an increased susceptibility to bacterial infections of the skin, urinary tract, and lungs, because cortisol stomped out his body's inflammatory defense system to halt bacteria establishment. He had a ravenous appetite because of his metabolic imbalance, and therefore had a tremendous output of feces, as well. He was polydipsic; that is, he had increased thirst, because cortisol antagonizes the action of antidiuretic hormone on the kidneys. Cushnoid dogs are usually polyuric as well—have increased urination because of the diuresis that is taking place. Winston did produce a lot of urine, but he had lost all tone and control of his bladder, so the urine just sat in his huge abdomen until it would simply overflow in a trickle from his low-slung penis.

His hyperadrenocorticism was being treated with a drug that kills off the cells overactively secreting cortisol, and it's a tricky dosage to figure. Kill off too many of these cells and you have a dog with *hypo*adrenocorticism (a.k.a. Addison's disease). It's a difficult line to maintain, especially since dogs are quite individually sensitive to the drug. He was also on two different drugs to help his bladder tone and antibiotics to combat his urinary-tract infection. That infection was resistant to treatment because the urine just sat there like a stagnant pond without the benefit of the normal flushing mechanism that helps keep bacteria from setting up housekeeping. His skin lesions required twice-daily bandage changes. He was on orders to be taken out every four hours to have his bladder manually expressed, and because of his abundant stool, his cage (and he) needed frequent cleaning. If I found his bladder to be quite full and turgid, then he automatically went to a two-hour bladder expression, because the longer and bigger the bladder was stretched, the poorer the prognosis for its return to normal functioning.

Taking Winston out to empty his bladder was no easy job, either, for the old guy had no energy. He weighed more than seventy pounds, and his breathing was labored because the normal diaphragmatic excursion into the abdomen with each breath was hindered by an enlarged liver and fat deposits in the belly itself.

In short, Winston was a mess.

He was hard to get out the door. He was constantly panting, stopping, refusing to take another step as he clicked down the hall, a big-necked, big-bladdered big dog on his big trip outside. Once outside, he wanted only to lie down. I would hoist him up, supporting him under his hips as I tried to get his front legs upright as well. This position often expressed his bladder prematurely, before he was in a good position.

Winston didn't care for that and would whirl around and growl, curling his lip back from his yellow tartar-covered fangs. I didn't care for it, either, for I often got a pant leg soaked and was left without the numbers that Dr. Glaser liked to have—

accurate measurement of how much liquid the old dog took in and expelled.

I took good care of Winston. Dr. Glaser noted it on my evaluation, and that was my reward, I thought, for the old dog was less of a learning experience than pure and simple grunt work. No sense in whining. There was plenty of grunt work mixed in with the valuable learning cases; we all had our share. You did it, moved on, and hoped for better next time.

I moved on to the next service and then the next. It was several weeks later when I crossed the wide expanse of the VTH waiting room/reception area one afternoon and heard someone call my name. There were several small groups of people and pets in the room, as always, students and clinicians scattered among them. I looked around and saw that it was Dr. Glaser who had hailed me. He was standing with a man, a woman, and a dog, so I crossed to them. He introduced me as someone who had taken care of Winston. It was only then that I realized that this German shepherd was the very same.

"What do you think?" Dr. Glaser asked, smiling. "He's just in for a checkup today."

What I thought was, You surely must be joking.

Winston looked like a new dog. He had a waistline. He was bright-eyed. His tail was wagging. His coat was full and shiny. He was impatient with standing there and moved from one foot to the other, looking around at the other critters in the room, looking for action. I reached out to pet him, to feel his good, thick coat. He seemed to know that he was beautiful.

I wouldn't have given much for his chances just two months before. I would have put my money on his continuing decline until his suffering had gotten greater than his owners' faith. I would have given good odds that they would have had him euthanized by now.

I had considered his care something of a waste of my time, a chore, an annoyance and distraction, a pointless exercise in shitwork, a hoop to jump through to please Dr. Glaser. It was an attitude that everyone who had had a turn with Winston shared. A dying dog, and a waste of our good energies and training.

I wondered whether Dr. Glaser was aware of that attitude. I thought that he probably was, for he had called me over to this little group for no apparent reason. We were generally too busy for social introductions such as this seemed to be.

Dr. Glaser turned his attention back to Winston's owners, and I stood there for a moment, petting the dog, feeling a bit out of place, without a function. And yet I knew my function. I was standing there as a student, learning what this dog had to teach me: a lesson not in endocrinology but in faith and humility; a lesson in not giving up too soon; a lesson in not burying my patients before they were dead.

Dr. Glaser had called me over so I could learn what Winston had to teach me. I learned it and took it to my heart. Then I excused myself and went on about my work.

CHAPTER 25

The Sixth of the Critters—Tasha

LLAMAS are exotic and pricey animals, the females particularly so. Sometimes, however, one is valued for herself, plus or minus her reproductive tract, and not because of what she can do, make, or deliver. Tasha was such a llama. She was beautiful, carmel-colored, with black points on her legs and face. Gentle and patient, she was also three-legged, the result of an accident.

The Llama Medicine elective, and thus the Llama Medicine Service, operated only three weeks of the year, and it wasn't one of them when Tasha came to the VTH. So she was taken in by the Food Animal Service, the rotation I was on at the time. She was no stranger to the hospital, for it was there that she had had her right foot and lower leg amputated some weeks before and become something of a pioneer.

Because llamas have quiet and tranquil natures, Dr. Mark Cherrod had decided to try fitting Tasha with an artificial leg. You wouldn't try this on a horse without learning new lessons in disaster (in fact, because of its size and weight, a horse would not survive three-legged long enough for its stump to heal). If you tried it on a dog, you'd likely get the leg chewed up and off for your trouble. Try it on a cow, and you'd probably find you'd invested your time, trouble, and money in something that you couldn't even locate, likely flung across two or three pastures and washed away in an arroyo. Try it on a cat, and you'd probably have an animal that simply goes to ground or turns into an acrobat. In its efforts to shake itself free of the appendage, it would invent gyrations never before seen by humans. A llama has an accepting outlook on life, however, suggesting to Dr. Cherrod that a prosthesis just might work.

He called a prosthesist in Denver and she agreed to accept the challenge and try to craft a fourth leg for Tasha. In fact, she was delighted to be of service, driving the more than 120-mile round-trip numerous times and donating her expertise and energy in order to work with this beautiful and exotic creature.

Everything had gone well, for Tasha had had the best of care, her own cheering squad of vet students, her loving owners, and a lot of luck. She'd had her surgery, she had had time for her stump to heal, she had been fitted with her artificial limb, she had been declared a success story, and she'd gone home.

Now she was back. Gradually, her owners said, she'd been using the new leg less and less adroitly. She was lying down more than she was up. She was not her old self.

She looked good, a little on the lean side, bright-eyed and alert. She was wearing her leg, and it looked good, too. Even the color was right. The size, shape, and angle were all normal. You had to look twice to notice that it wasn't her natural leg. That is, until she moved, and she moved with a definite gimp.

When we removed the prosthesis, it was obvious an adjustment was needed. The fleshy end of her leg was very pink and it jiggled too much, like a hot-pink piece of Jell-O. The muscle and skin of an amputated limb are typically left much longer than the bone so that there will be plenty of healthy, good, blood-supplied tissue to provide a buffer for the severed bone. A stump can be very sensitive; the periosteum, or bone covering, is what makes a fractured bone so painful. The break of that membranous cover disrupts the nerve endings contained therein and accounts for most of the pain of a broken leg. So the bone is the shortest part of an amputation, with muscle to tuck around and pad it, and the skin left longer still to wrap down and cover the package. Thus, an amputated leg is quite a bit fleshier and less firm than the real thing. Therefore, it wiggles and jiggles quite a bit more.

Tasha's stump was swollen, filled with fluid, and bright pink because it moved too much inside the prosthesis and thus was irritated with her every step. She needed a snugger fit, even though the prosthesis had a formfitting and somewhat forgiving liner that ideally conformed to the stump's every bend, curve, dip, and angle.

First, she needed an X ray, however, for the health of the bone had to be determined. The possibility of bone infection loomed as a real threat. This would have resulted in some dead bone tissue and necessitated more amputation; and the shorter the stump (and the nearer to the knee joint), the less likely it was that fitting with a prosthesis would be successful.

Tasha's luck held. The radiograph showed healthy bone. She needed only to have the anger taken out of the surrounding tissue, to get that tissue back down to a normal size and condition, and an adjustment made in her fake leg. Some anti-inflammatories, some measurement, a few visits from the prosthesist, and she'd have her fourth leg back and a new lease on life.

She was going to have to spend some time with her leg absolutely naked, and she'd gotten used to the prosthesis in just the few weeks that she'd had it. She could get around without it, but she preferred not to, thank you very much. After we removed her leg, she lay in her pen like a woolly toadstool. She tucked away her perfect left foreleg back up underneath her, but she extended her stump, as if to say, See here, see what you've forgotten.

The prosthesis required many fittings, and each time we came with the artificial leg, she got up and stood still as a summer night while we made our way around her, taking measurements, making adjustments, and assessing the fit. She had her leg on and off many times that week, and always we took it away with us. Although a docile creature, she was getting visibly frustrated by the apparent teasing she was forced to endure.

Her confusion was visible. She was clearly excited when we strapped on the leg, upright, interested, her ears pricked forward. But she was beginning to learn that we were going to take the leg away again, and she vacillated between excitement and anger during our visits. She never offered to spit, but she often pinned her ears back against her head and gave us dirty looks.

I so wanted to be able to tell her that everything was going to be all right, to communicate to her somehow that she'd have her leg back, and permanently, by the end of the week, that we were on her side and trying to help—if she'd only bear with us and be patient a little longer. But for all our advances, we cannot communicate anything nearly this specific and abstract to the other beasts that share the planet. We can speak with some of the specially trained apes that we've taught to sign. We can communicate love and praise and pleasure in a general way. We can give commands that are understood by dogs, cats, horses, pigs, even birds, but we could not tell Tasha that her leg would be ready next Tuesday. For all our training, all our knowledge, all our sophistication, only Dr. Doolittle can talk to the animals.

However, Tasha could communicate to us that she was upset, unhappy, and frustrated.

The appointed day came. Her tissue had healed and her artificial leg remade to fit snugly. A fair-sized party made its way to her pen in the barn. There was a TV news crew from Denver, a big support group from within the VTH, the Food Animal rotation students, Dr. Cherrod, and the prosthesist.

Jeanette Hay held the lead rope attached to Tasha's nylon web halter, and Tasha stood still, only occasionally glancing down at Dr. Cherrod and the prosthesist as they adjusted and fitted the leg to her. She seemed for a moment overcome by the lights, the camera, the crowd around her pen, and she pinned her doelike ears flat and shook her head in a violent half-circle, as if to shake off the commotion and confusion. But the camera kept rolling, the voices kept humming in the background, the excitement kept building, and Tasha regained her good, if bewildered, manners.

Finally, the device was buckled on to the satisfaction of Dr. Cherrod and the fitter. Tasha's short leg once more touched the ground. Jeanette led her from the pen. The crowd followed down the aisle to the door that opened onto a half-acre field. Jeanette led her outside, unhooked the rope from her halter, and stepped back.

Tasha looked at the crowd watching her. She took three slow, long, deliberate steps away. A sideways glance back at humanity, and then she twisted her long neck askew, dropping it down between her knees like a rodeo bronc, and let go a beautiful buck. A shivering, twisting jolt of joy, the pure gladness of being whole, ran through her. Freedom worked its way down her neck to her back, where it kinked in the middle and shot out through her hind legs. It wasn't a star-aiming kick, but it was more than a crow's hop, and then she wheeled, farted, and gathered ground, sprinting across the pasture to the dirt pile at the far end. She paused at the top of this mound to glance back at the humans standing in the doorway of the barn, as if to say, Thanks. Or maybe, You'll never catch me now. And then she tore off in another burst of joyous movement. Even though one part was not her own, she owned it now. Her grace was not diminished. She was fluid across the expanse of the field.

CHAPTER 26

———

Big Girls *Do* Cry

RAIN is a blessing in the arid Rocky Mountain West, and the blessing came on graduation day, May 13. It rained off and on all that day, all that weekend. A light and nourishing drizzle fell past the open windows of my apartment. Wild cloudbursts sealed us cozily inside. A break in the storm, as if ordered, occurred around 6:30 while we assembled at Moby Gym. A steady, hard rain then settled in for the night.

We cried, my family and I, like the rain, off and on all weekend long.

People cry at happy moments, but not from happiness. I'm certain of that, though I'm not sure why it happens. Perhaps it is that at those moments, when we are feeling truly blessed, we are also deeply struck by the fleeting nature of our lives, that we feel our mortality with a stab that is true pain. Or perhaps when we are feeling so safe or cherished or lucky, we are able to release our deep and buried anguish, whose source we may not even know, an accumulation of disappointments, failures, losses. We cry not because something wonderful has happened but because we so feared that it would not. It's an intensity of feeling that, for that moment, undoes us completely. We call it weeping for joy.

We wept for joy all that weekend, and especially that night in Moby Gym.

I cried not only with relief that the four hard years were over but also because they were. I cried not only because my family was with me and so proud but also because my father was dead. I did so not only because I had achieved this long-sought goal but also because of everyone who had ever said I couldn't do it, and because part of me still believed that I couldn't, in spite of the fact that I *had*. I cried for everything it had cost—a good bit of innocence, the insults of Dr. Howard, the depression and anxiety of my small failures along the way, the occasional poor grade, the one C evaluation during senior blocks. I cried because Laura was dead and Nicole lost to me, at least for now. I cried because every beginning is an ending, too, and because life is short and joy fleeting. I cried because I had always believed that someone such as I couldn't be a doctor.

The sporadic rainfall of that Saturday settled into a steady, relentless downpour by evening. I dressed in the crowded apartment, put on a slim black skirt, the red silk shirt I had bought for the junior-senior banquet that year, and black pumps with one-inch heels. I slipped on the black gown and bobby-pinned the mortarboard to my head, carried over my arm the green and gold doctoral hood that Dean Osbourne would put on me when my turn came.

I had been to Lloyd's graduation two years before, and it had been a high-toned affair, held in one of the medium-sized theaters on the main campus. For some reason, we were graduating in the basketball arena. Our class sat in folding chairs facing the small temporary stage. The basketball hoops were folded up and away toward the high ceiling. Our guests sat in the bleachers. That didn't matter. The rain didn't matter. None of it mattered.

I settled my folks in the bleachers and joined my class in the auxiliary gym, where we were to line up. Flasks came out of boots and hip pockets for impromptu toasts. Warren Giese popped the cork on the champagne we had bought as freshmen for this moment. We squished together for a class portrait. The powers that be wrangled us into alphabetical order. A five-piece band struck up "Pomp and Circumstance." I began to cry.

We filed out into the main gym, to the great and sustained

cheering of our fans. We walked at different speeds, we bumped into one another, and we looked up into the stands and waved to our families. A smile locked on my face, I followed the black robe in front of me. It was only a blur. We filed into row after row of folding chairs and, finally, sat down. Dean Osbourne rose and opened the ceremony. My heart was pounding.

My friend Jimmy Fulmer invoked the presence of God, which was just a formality, for the life-force and spirit had long been moving among us. Professor Glaser retired that night and we honored him. Professor Howard retired, as well. He had graduated at the top of his class from this college forty years before and had taught here for the past twenty-seven years. In my own happiness and safe now from his harm's way, I applauded his career.

Jake Wilder was awarded the 1989 College Special Service Award. He had been a major feature of our freshman year, and we had seen him only off and on since then. But we rocked the gym as we clapped and shouted our respect, affection, and gratitude.

En masse, we received our degrees of doctor of veterinary medicine. En masse, we took the Veterinarian's Oath:

> Being admitted to the profession of veterinary medicine, I solemnly swear to use my scientific knowledge and skills for the benefit of society through the protection of animal health, the relief of animal suffering, the conservation of livestock resources, the promotion of public health and the advancement of medical knowledge. I will practice my profession conscientiously, with dignity, and in keeping with the principles of veterinary medical ethics. I accept as a lifelong obligation the continual improvement of my professional knowledge and competence.

And then we were hooded. One at a time, we crossed the platform to shake the hands of the university's president and the dean and to have the ceremonial doctoral hood draped over our shoulders.

I remember that my eyes were veiled with tears; that my

heart beat against its bony cage; that I trembled; that Dalton turned in her seat to wink at me; that Jimmy, just ahead of me in the order, squeezed my hand; that the whole gym was like a carnival seen from the careening roller coaster, a blur—but with moments of absolute clarity, like snapshots, of first this face, then that, my dear and sustaining friends. Too much emotion, too many moments to capture forever in memory, too much ceremony. I felt as if I were having an out-of-body experience, floating above the assembled class, above the bleachers where my family sat, above the dignitaries, as if in some crazy way this had nothing at all to do with me.

It had been eleven years since I had made the decision to become a vet, sitting beside the cold gray Pacific in Sitka, Alaska, with my good dog—my husband's dog—Coyote.

If it wasn't for the videotape of the graduation ceremony that someone made and sold to us, I could never have remembered—nor could I have invented—the details.

As Dr. Osbourne hooded us, we stood in rows for this honor. I waited and watched, applauded my classmates. The D's began to be hooded. I shouted for Josh Dabney, "Strange Eagle." Several others followed, and then would come my running buddies, Dalton and then Mae.

My good friend Mae Daniels was a Blackfoot Indian from Montana, a quiet woman with a ready smile and a certain shyness. She had gone to Dr. Osbourne, the dean of the veterinary school, a couple of weeks before and asked to be allowed to graduate in her native ceremonial dress. He had turned down her request. No, she had to wear cap and gown, just like everyone else. There would be no hood over buckskins. She accepted his decision, and on this night she was dressed as the other 119 of us were, capped and gowned in black. Her braids were, to be sure, a bit exotic, each swathed in the skin of a mink, but a traditional mortarboard topped that head of shining black hair.

When Dalton was called and Mae was next, I saw that Mae was unzipping her gown, splitting out of her white man's shell. As they called her name, she shrugged away the robe and it slid from her shoulders, the satiny fabric falling across the white buckskin to the floor like a bride's nightgown.

She was a hero. She was a princess. She was simply splendid.

Her ceremonial dress was white leather, with turquoise beadwork covering the bodice and long fringe swinging from the sleeves. The gym was filled with cheers for her and her spunk. I could see her trembling and knew she was afraid, but she walked bravely across the floor, stepped onto the platform, shook Dean Osbourne's hand, and turned her back to him so he could confer the hood. She had defied him, and there was no choice but for him to lift the ceremonial hood of this august ritual and place it over the ceremonial gown of this Blackfoot Indian.

The smile on his face said that perhaps he didn't mind. No one looking at her that night could have wished her to be in the white man's black robe at this moment of triumph. Dean Osbourne turned and watched her walk off the stage, as he had for none of the other new doctors.

They cheered for Mae, and they cheered for me. Or perhaps it only seems that way because it is *my* memory. But from the tape, I can clearly hear my classmates—colleagues now—and their cheers are loud and mixed with laughter. Or perhaps there really was more laughter than cheers, for I was completely unhinged. I guess I was pretty funny.

I was crying so hard, I could barely see to get to the platform. A photo my sister took shows me standing, my back to Dean Osbourne, receiving my hood, my face contorted in what could almost be anguish, my hands clenched together in front of me.

Dean Osbourne leaned close to my ear and said, "Easy, Dr. Gage, or you won't make it through this night." I do remember that. He patted me on the back, a little extra encouragement.

I stumbled back to my seat, and my classmates laughed at the spectacle that I was. This was not a fine misting of tears over the eye, or even one or two rolling prettily down my cheek, but all-out sobbing, as if my heart would break from the emotional wallop of this night.

Their laughter was friendly, though, and kind. They were happy for me. Some of them had affectionately called me

"Mom" from time to time. I hadn't much appreciated it at the time, but I *was* the old lady of the class. I'd always worn my terror on my sleeve for everybody to see, and I'd fretted overmuch most of the four years, and now they laughed, as if to say, See, Mom, you made it, just like we said you would.

We were the first class in the history of the school to graduate over 50 percent women. I was proud to be part of that statistic, proud to be one of these dedicated women, proud to be a friend of Mae's, and proud, too, to be a colleague of Emma Piper, who had had a baby a short twenty hours before the graduation ceremony and was there with us, receiving her hood and her D.V.M.

I sat there and drew myself back together, fingering the precious doctoral hood that I had tried on again and again, as I had once tried on my new green lab coat, shyly and with disbelief. Now, though, it was different, for the dean had placed it on my shoulders and called me Dr. Gage.

Warren Giese, speaking for the class, thanked our families and friends, our Creator, the faculty, each other. And then Paula Russell rose to speak and amended Warren's acknowledgments to include the animals that had borne our probing, poking, cutting, jabbing, experimenting, and especially those who had borne killing at our hands that we might be here this night, veterinarians at long last. She thanked them for us. Their nameless faces rose in my memory—a particular bay mare, a yellow Lab, a gray tabby cat, and so many others. I said, "Amen."

There was a celebratory dance that night in Lory Student Center.

Mae danced with her huge family, a long string of good-looking Indians stomping a wild Cotton-Eyed Joe around that ballroom. I danced with Jay, with Nancy and Dalton, with Jill Henderson, who had come from New York to see me graduate, and with my high school girlfriend Chris. I danced alone. Nobody was crying now. We all danced.

It was a hard and happy weekend. Everyone was busy with family and packing. By Sunday, everyone was looking ahead to the new job in the new town. I didn't see Dalton after graduation night, nor Mae. They vaporized—Dalton to a job in California, Mae back to Montana. Eric Ferguson's wife had taken a job in Alamosa, Colorado, some months before; he was gone in a heartbeat to his new home. Elaine Davis had taken a job in the Oncology unit at CSU, so she would be there for another round of good-byes. Jimmy Fulmer was as gone as he could be. David Parks, who had shared my senior schedule, left for Connecticut. By Monday, I, too, would be just a memory in Fort Collins.

On Sunday afternoon, I took a break from packing and went to the VTH. It was also alive with activity. The new senior class was already in place, staffing the clinic, working the barn, doing treatments, taking care of the business of their educations and this institution.

I walked through the barn to the pasture beyond and called to my good-luck friends, Milo and Kris Kringle. They came running, as always. I scratched behind their ears. I lifted their faces and looked into their beautiful eyes. I gave them each a last hug. I shed a few more tears as I pressed my lips to the hard forehead of first the steer and then the little goat.

Then I, too, was gone.

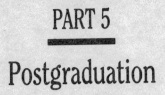

PART 5

Postgraduation

CHAPTER 27

Real Life

I WENT to work in June, in the practice of my former boss, Tom Tromboldt. It was a mixed practice, and my time was split between the small-animal clinic and the mobile equine unit.

Gradually, I relaxed into the work, knowing that Tom and the other equine vet in the practice, Jackie Overman, were there to back me up, only a phone call away, if I was called out on a case that was beyond my experience or expertise. At night I boned up on the procedures that were scheduled for the next day's clinic or read the current research reports in the professional journals that already seemed to be piling up. I would be a student forever, but now the tests and the standards were in large part those I set for myself.

There were no big surprises. I'd known what I was in for. I was prepared for the suffering and death that are inescapable in medicine. I don't think I'll ever get used to that part of the profession, thought it may get easier to accept as I get more experience in accepting. But somehow I don't really think it will.

In the battle for an animal's life, it is hard to lose to a disease, to the tenacity of cancer cells, to the imbalance of the endocrine system, or to the damage of trauma. Then you wish that you were better than you are, that vet medicine was more advanced and better than it is. But when you lose because you aren't allowed to fight, that's harder still.

Animal life has little value (indeed, the precedent for malpractice insurance gives an animal only the status and value of property, and malpractice awards are typically only for "replacement value") and animals have no rights. So the worth of any animal is determined by its owner. This is probably the single hardest thing about being a doctor of animals—when treatment isn't limited by my skill, education, or experience, or even by the state of veterinary medicine itself, but by the depth of the client's wallet.

The worst moment in any day is when I must rein in my impulse to do everything I can for an injured or diseased creature, table everything I've learned in my years of schooling, and curb my ability back to the too-simple procedure of finding a vein and injecting the euthanasia solution.

It is horrible to kill when you've been trained to save. It's a heartbreaker when the question is medical and the answer is economic. It hurts, of course, for the sake of the animal, and it hurts, too, for the owner who truly cannot afford (as opposed to *choosing* not to afford) the treatment. It hurts for the children of the owner, who are often standing there crying, as helpless as I am. (And when a veterinarian works for someone else, she is helpless—unable to offer credit or bargain rates or to recommend another clinic where the prices may be lower. In truth, even if she was in practice for herself, the realities of the business—the rent, equipment payments, staff salaries, malpractice insurance, outstanding student loans—make her rather helpless, too.)

It hurts in yet another way. It hurts your sense of yourself as a professional. Those moments make you feel that all your work and effort and struggle have been pointless. At the VTH, client animals have access to the most sophisticated diagnostic techniques and equipment, the most complex and innovative surgeries and treatments, the newest and best drugs. Those animals are there because their owners are committed to providing the best. And if the client cannot afford the treatment and then donates the animal, the treatment is often carried out because of its teaching value.

In the real world, however, the owner's pocketbook often cuts off before care is much more than routine; therefore, you are rarely challenged to the depth of your knowledge and ability.

And so, because you got into this business in the first place for the sake of the animals, you do what you can to compensate for those bad times. You try to make as many happy endings as you can. There are lots of things you can do, and most vets do as many of those things as they can.

You volunteer to spay and neuter the homeless dogs and cats waiting for adoption at the Animal Humane Society. You give of your limited time to educate people about preventative medicine, about vaccinations, and the necessity of spaying and neutering their pets. You try to absorb as much of the animal surplus as you can, to treat the injured stray that somebody picks up off the street and brings to the clinic, and then to find it a home.

Every vet remembers ones he's saved.

I worked for Dr. Jerry Steiner years before I made it into vet school. One day, a woman brought in a German shepherd crossbreed; she wanted it "put to sleep" because it played too roughly with her children. Jerry offered to try to place the dog somewhere, and the woman gratefully said yes and made a quick exit, her day brightened and her conscience lightened. It would not be easy to find a home for a rowdy full-grown dog, but Jerry had another idea—to enlist Penny, for that was her name, in the Air Force.

It took awhile for Penny and her paperwork to be processed; she needed to be spayed, vaccinated, X-rayed, and photographed. We did all that, sent the application, and waited. Several weeks later, we were notified: Penny had passed initial muster. The Air Force would take her on a trial basis for training as a drug- or bomb-sniffing dog.

We'd grown fond of her, and it was with some pain that we delivered her to the airport, where she was put into a crate and then into the belly of a plane and shipped away to Texas. The Air Force doesn't entertain inquiries about canine inductees. Once a dog is gone, it's gone—with one exception. The application form gives one choice: If the dog washes out, do you want it returned to you or do you want the Air Force to dispose of it? We had marked the first option, and Penny never came back, so we assumed she had made a career of some sort in the military.

I think of her from time to time, and I think of what Jerry said: "You try to help more than you've hurt on your way to becoming a vet."

Generally, people are not cruel, merely ignorant. If Penny's first owner had known how to handle her and train her as a pup, the dog would have been a good and gentle companion. If people routinely had their pets spayed and neutered, there would be no heartbreaking animal surplus.

No small part of what veterinarians do on behalf of animals is fight that ignorance. We preach vaccination and preventative medicine. We remind owners of how early their kitten or puppy will become a fertile adult. Sometimes we can help an owner correct his pet's bad habit (a cat can learn not to pee in the laundry basket, a dog not to dig in the garden) rather than have the offending animal put down.

These efforts probably help prevent untold suffering, but we usually don't know about it or see the results of our effort. It's the memories of those like Penny that we hold on to; those memories of particular critters keep us healthy. We keep coming back to them, as if to a fountain, for nourishment.

One day right before Christmas, Tom Tromboldt shoved through the swinging door into the small-animal treatment area, carrying a small kitten. He handed it to me.

"Is this my Christmas bonus?"

"A gas company meter reader just brought her in. He saved her from a bunch of kids who were using her for a football. Looks like she's been out for a few long passes, a couple of fumbles, maybe a field goal or two."

"You're kidding."

No, he wasn't. He gave her to me to do with as I wanted—fix her up, put her down, whatever I thought best. The first step was to assess the damage. I set her down on the stainless-steel table and she just folded up in the hind end. I slipped my hand under her belly, then she stood, but with her left hind paw turned wrong side down, seemingly unaware that the furry top of her foot was to the tabletop. I turned her right paw over to the incorrect position, too. "Don't you know where the top of your foot is, sweetheart?" I asked.

She seemed content for a few moments to leave it as I had placed it, but after a bit, she righted it. I turned the right foot over again, and again it took her a long time to perceive the malposition. But after a delay, she righted it. The left paw remained upside down, as if it didn't belong to her at all.

I set her on the floor and went off to fetch her some food to encourage her to show me her walk. She began mewing when I came back into the room with a small dish of cat food. She was one hungry little football, and there was nothing wrong with her sense of smell. I set the dish down about five feet from her, and she cleared the distance quickly, though her left leg hung useless behind her like so much freight and her right foot randomly landed right side up or upside down.

As she wolfed down her dinner, I pinched the toes of her left foot. She turned around and gave me a dirty look. Yes, she felt that. At least there was something to work with in the extremity of her nervous system, and that was very good news. Traumatic compromises are usually nonprogressive; that is, the initial damage is generally as bad as it's going to get.

I decided to try twice-daily injections of steroids to reduce inflammation and see what the tincture of time could accomplish. I hoped that whatever it did, it did it in time for me to find her a home for the holidays.

I thought that if she got control of her hind end, she'd be a pretty good-looking kitten. A Siamese-cross, she was creamy white and tawny brown; her eyes were bright blue and enormous. I could imagine her peering from a Christmas stocking, a regular calendar picture.

Each day, I saw a bit of progress as she began to carry her left leg a little closer to her body. A good bit of the time, she carried it pad to the floor, but she was far from a normal kitten. I couldn't guarantee that she would fully recover. My guess was that she'd always be a bit lame, with an unnatural swivel in her hips and somewhat withered hind legs.

And I could find no one among the clinic staff and clients who wanted this little cripple.

Christmas fell on Monday that year, and the clinic was closing at noon on Saturday, to open again on Tuesday. I was on call for the weekend, so I was responsible for any in-house patients. But luck was with me, and the kitten was the only one. Since she belonged to no one and there was no potential liability, I decided she could spend the holiday with me and my family.

Mama had come for Christmas. She was sitting on the couch when I walked in on Saturday afternoon. She seemed small to me, and unhappy. Her life had shrunk quite a bit in the last few years. She'd lost most of her vision to macular degeneration, and a good part of her physical freedom to emphysema.

She looked up and asked what I had in my hand, for she could see the general shape of the cat carrier, but nothing more. I put the cage next to her on the couch and told her the kitten's story. Mama peered closely at the wire-mesh door. "Take her out," she said. "She doesn't want to be in there."

The chaos of Christmas began in earnest that afternoon with the arrival of Jay's family. There was a constant shuffling of dogs in, dogs out, Nancy's three cats, people, too, and through it all, Mama sheltered the kitten, fending off the exuberant advances of the household dogs and the curious sniffing of the bigger cats. The kitten stayed quietly in Mama's lap like a lost child, found at last.

Mama had fallen in love, and the kitten's future was settled without a word. She named the kitten Baby. She thinks she's the best cat in the world. No doubt she is, at least in Mama's world.

I meet lots of people in my work. The vast majority love animals, and a fair number are just plain dopey about their pets, as Mama is about Baby. They are the ones who make my job a great one. They share their homes, their lives, their beds with their pets. They—we—are a little bit crazy, I guess. (For not only was Bones still with me and much adored but I had a fabulous dog now, too, a bulldog-pointer cross named Skinner, who was to me the crown of creation.)

Some people might tell me straight out how they dote on their dog or their cat; they might say out loud just how terrific their pet is, how special, how perfect, without peer or rival. Or they might express their pride and affection in other ways that I can also hear. I recognize those people easily, heart-to-heart, for we are kindred souls.

One such soul brought her Australian shepherd, Shannon, to the clinic one day for annual shots. I was done in just a couple of minutes, but the woman didn't seem to want to leave so quickly. I could tell that she wanted me to know and appreciate just how great this pretty dog really was.

I wanted to hear it, too. That's one of the things I've learned that wasn't in the books—to let people talk, to take the time to connect with them. It helps you do your work; it helps make you a good vet. And, as the owner of an equally wonderful dog, I understood perfectly.

"I never miss her shots, not anymore. I almost lost her," the woman said. "When she was a pup, she had parvo virus."

A very bad virus, I allowed.

"The vet"—she mentioned a local vet who had recently retired—"he knew I didn't have much money and couldn't afford to keep her in the hospital, so he showed me how to take care of her at home. He showed me how to take care of an IV, because she had to have IV fluids. She was so sick, so very sick."

I nodded. It's a bad disease, parvo is.

"He came out to the house to check on her and told me I ought to start thinking about putting her to sleep. He said I ought to prepare myself for her death. He just didn't see much hope. I didn't want her to suffer, but I couldn't make the decision to let her go." She stroked the dog's mostly white coat.

"And then he pulled her through after all," I offered.

"No," she said. And then she corrected herself. "Well, yes, of course he did. But one night, she actually died. It was the middle of the night and he wasn't there. She was gasping for breath, but she wasn't really conscious, either. She was almost comatose, I guess you'd say. And then she just quit breathing. She *died*." The woman watched my face to see whether I was going to laugh or correct her. I nodded for her to continue.

"She really did die. She was dead, and she came back. And do you know why?"

I shook my head.

"Shannon is alive today because she is so loyal to me. I held her in my lap and I stroked her, and I told her I loved her and I knew she was going over that line, dying, walking off into the light, however they say it is, and I literally called her back to me. 'Shannon,' I said, 'come, girl. Shannon, come. Shannon, stay. Stay with me. Come here, girl, come to me.'"

Shannon looked up from the exam table, wagging her tail, trying to understand this command when she was right there under her mistress's hand.

"She's alive because she wouldn't leave me when I commanded her to stay." The woman's voice was intense, and then she sort of laughed and said, "It was that, plus the good treatment, the IV fluids, of course. I don't mean to belittle the treatment."

She was embarrassed, I guess, because I was a vet. Perhaps she thought she had offended me. She hadn't. I liked the story. I believed it; I'd already seen enough in my short career not to dismiss it out of hand.

I would continue my studies, to be sure. I would keep up with innovations, follow the treatments and procedures I'd learned. I would devote my life to veterinary science, to understanding the anatomy and physiology and pathology of animals. I would apply all my intelligence and everything I learned to the battle against disease and injury. I believed with all my heart in the truth of what I'd learned, the tools of knowledge and skill I'd been given.

In my mind, there was no inconsistency in adding the laying on of hands to the application of veterinary science. I would soon find myself planting kisses on the forehead of a very sick horse. And against the odds, she would rally and recover, perhaps another tiny bit of evidence for the power of touch. Animals understand kindness. They are comforted and encouraged by it; it seems to give them strength. The innate life force within each of them—each of *us*—is strong, as least as strong as our medicine. Miracles come when we combine the two—everything we've learned and the wisdom of their good bodies.

James Herriot

Join the world's favorite veterinarian, master storyteller
James Herriot, as he takes us into his wonderful, unique
world, for irrestible, heartwarming tales of animals and
people you will want to read over and over again.

EVERY LIVING THING
_____ 95058-6 $5.99 U.S.

JAMES HERRIOT'S DOG STORIES
_____ 92558-1 $5.99 U.S.